To Jaymann

Getting Along
with Almost
Anybody

Florence Littauer

Other Books by Florence and Fred Littauer

Personality Plus (also available in French, German, Spanish, Polish, Dutch, Indonesian, and seven other languages)

Personality Puzzle with Marita Littauer (also in Indonesian)

Put Power in Your Personality!

Personality Plus—audio

Daily Marriage Builders

Beat the Blahs (also in Afrikaans)

Blow Away the Black Clouds

After Every Wedding Comes a Marriage

It Takes So Little to Be Above Average

How to Get Along with Difficult People (also in Korean)

Out of the Cabbage Patch

Freeing Your Mind from Memories That Bind (also in Spanish)

The Promise of Healing

I've Found My Keys, Now Where's My Car?

Silver Boxes (also in Spanish)

Dare to Dream (also in Spanish, French)

Raising Christians, Not Just Children

Your Personality Tree (also in Spanish and as video album)

Hope for Hurting Women

Looking for God in All the Right Places

Touched by the Master

The Gift of Encouraging Words

CLASS (Christian Leaders, Authors, and Speakers Seminar tape, album, and manual)

The Best of Florence Littauer

For information on seminars and workshops conducted by Fred and Florence Littauer or by Marita Littauer, please call 1-800-433-6633 or see the CLASS web site:

www.classervices.com

Getting Along with Almost Anybody

Anybody

The Complete Personality Book

Florence & Marita
LITTAUER

Fleming H. Revell
A Division of Baker Book House
Grand Rapids, Michigan 49516

© 1998 by Florence Littauer and Marita Littauer

Published by Fleming H. Revell
a division of Baker Book House Company
P.O. Box 6287, Grand Rapids, MI 49516-6287

Fourth printing, October 2001

Printed in the United States of America

Library of Congress Cataloging-in-Publication Data

Littauer, Florence, 1928–
    Getting along with almost anybody : the complete personality book / Florence Littauer and Marita Littauer.
        p.   cm.
    ISBN 0-8007-5659-2 (pbk.)
    1. Christian life. 2. Personality—Religious aspects—Christianity. 3. Temperament—Religious aspects—Christianity. 4. Success—Religious aspects—Christianity. 5. Littauer, Florence, 1928– Personality plus. I. Littauer, Marita. II. Title.
BV4501.2.F552   1998
155.2'6—dc21   98-5014

Scripture marked KJV is taken from the King James Version of the Bible.

Scripture marked NASB is taken from the NEW AMERICAN STANDARD BIBLE®, copyright © The Lockman Foundation 1960, 1962, 1963, 1968, 1971, 1972, 1973, 1975, 1977, 1995. Used by permission.

Scripture marked NIV is taken from the HOLY BIBLE, NEW INTERNATIONAL VERSION®. NIV®. Copyright © 1973, 1978, 1984 by International Bible Society. Used by permission of Zondervan Publishing House. All rights reserved.

For current information about all releases from Baker Book House, visit our web site:
http://www.bakerbooks.com

Contents

Acknowledgments   9
Prologue   10

1   Understanding Yourself: Do I Have a Personality?
     Marita Littauer   11

Part 1   Family and Home Life

2   Marriage: What Personality Is Best to Marry?
     Marita Littauer and Chuck Noon   25

3   Single Again: What Makes Us Attractive to Others?
     Grace "Rocky" Graziano   39

4   Divorce and Remarriage: Why Couldn't He Be More
     like Me?
     Rose Sweet   48

5   Parenting: Understanding Your Children's Personalities
     Cheryl Kirking   59

6   Home Schooling: What a Difference a Personality
     Makes
     Sheryl Arthur-Haney   70

7   Attention Deficit Disorder: Disability
     or Misunderstanding?
     JoAnn Hawthorn   80

Part 2   In the Workplace

8   Job Preparation: Finding the Right Job for Your
     Personality
     Mae Harbor   95

 9   Education: Managing the Personalities
     in the Classroom
        Arlene Hendriks   110
10   Law Enforcement: Making Order out of Law
     and Disorder
        Kurt Hardy   123
11   Medicine: Patients and Patience
        Joyce Wesseler   134
12   Network Marketing: Can It Work for All Personalities?
        Steven and Teri Olson   143

Part 3   Spiritual Life and Worship
13   Your Church: Pastor's Personality Profile
        Florence Littauer   157
14   Clergy: Pastoring with Different Leadership Styles
        Chuck Alt   174
15   Spiritual Life: How the Personalities Respond to God
        Rosa Maria Faulkner   183
16   The Personality of Jesus: What Personality Is Jesus?
        Evelyn Davison   193
17   Women's Ministry: Reaching All the Personalities
        Shirley Lindsay   205
18   Youth Ministry: From Stumbling Blocks to Stepping
     Stones
        Carol Miller   217

Part 4   Life Issues
19   Money: Financial Challenges for Different Personalities
        Vivian Baniak   227
20   Organization: Making Time Work for You
        Sandi Lucas   237
21   Trouble: How the Personalities Cope
        Georgia Shaffer   248
22   Humor: Our Funny Bones Are Different Too
        Patsy Dooley   260

Part 5   Women's Matters

23   Fitness: Change Your Body, Not Your Personality
          Danna Demetre   273

24   Shopping: What Kind of Shopper Are You?
          Venna Bishop   285

25   Friends: The Care and Feeding of All Kinds
          of Personalities
          Pam Stephens   296

26   Home and Hospitality: Martha Stewart, Martha
          Washington, or Just Plain Martha
          Susan Ponville   313

Epilogue   323
Appendix A: Your Personality Profile   325
Appendix B: Personality Test Word Definitions   328
Appendix C: An Overview of the Personalities   336
Appendix D: Recommended Resources   340

Acknowledgments

We offer special thanks to each of the contributors whose expertise and experience have truly made this book "the Complete Personality Book." Thank you for taking our teaching and training and applying it to your areas of specialty. By doing so, you have taken the concepts of the Personalities further than either of us could have done on our own. Your contributions will enrich the lives of our readers.

If you, as a reader, would like to contact any of the contributors (including us) with questions, comments, or an invitation to speak, we would love to hear from you. Because people's lives change and they move from one location to another, you can reach any of the contributors through CLASS. Please call 800-433-6633 or write to: CLASS, P.O. Box 66810, Albuquerque, NM 87193.

We wish you God's best for your life as you learn to get along with almost anybody!

Florence Littauer and Marita Littauer

Prologue

Oh, Lord, I don't know what to do.
I don't like anyone, it's very true.
Isn't there someone who thinks like me?
Please, dear Father, hear my plea.
I just can't seem to get along,
Or is it me who's always wrong?

Listen, my child, and you will see
That I have come to set you free
From your own narrow view of life,
Your frenzied world, your grief and strife.
No one's perfect, no not one.
All is vanity under the sun.

Popular people want your ear,
Powerful ones will make it clear,
Perfectionists always do it right,
And Peaceful ones just will not fight.
I've made them different, not the same,
Unique players in life's game.

So get your focus off of you
And look at others' points of view.
Know they too have a narrow range
And some of them may never change.
Be at peace with others along life's way
And you'll get along better today and always.

Understanding Yourself

Do I Have a Personality?

Marita Littauer

ave you ever noticed that there are people out there who are different from you? Perhaps you live with them. Maybe you work with them. But chances are you have noticed differences and you have wished you could change those people. You may have even gone so far as to attempt to "fix" them by suggesting that their thinking, attitudes, and approaches to life be more like your own. These attempts are usually an exercise in futility and frustration.

Our job is not to try to change others, but to follow the wisdom of Romans 12:18 by doing what we can to change our approach to them, so that we can "be at peace with all men." The concepts presented in this book are a proven and effective tool that will allow you to make those changes. As you understand the principles of the basic personalities, you can identify the personality types of the people with whom you live and work, you can adjust your expectations of them as you understand their strengths and weaknesses, and, most important, you can begin to communicate more effectively with them as you meet their emotional needs. The end result: You can "be at peace with all men"— at least "as far as it depends on you"!

Each of us has a basic personality type. It is something that came prepackaged within our genetic makeup. Modern science has spent countless hours and dollars trying to understand where our personality comes from. Yet any teacher or parent will tell you that each child is born with his or her own identity. Scientists are just now beginning

11

to get a grasp on this. Recent research indicates that a person's personality is determined before birth in the individual genetic makeup. Environment does play a role in how that personality is shaped, but the basics are predetermined.

I once had the opportunity to speak to a group of preschool directors while doing my own little research project. I asked them if they had had siblings go through their schools. Of course, the answer was yes. These children had the same parents, grew up in the same house, went to the same church, and attended the same preschool. Often they wore the same clothes and slept in the same room. I asked if these siblings were the same type of children. No! Despite having virtually the same environment, these siblings each had their own distinctive personalities. Some were incessant talkers who liked to be the focal point and whom others wanted to emulate. Others were "born leaders." They told the other children what to do and when to do it. They would take over the class if the teachers would let them. Some were quieter children who were afraid to get messy and avoided projects like finger painting in favor of tidy methodical activities like building with blocks or looking at books. Other quiet children were content with any activity and easily went along with the program, although they rarely initiated any ideas of their own. These same types of patterns follow us throughout our lives—they are inborn personality traits.

Over two thousand years ago, in about 400 B.C., during the golden age of the great Greek thinkers, scholarly men sat and philosophized about much of life. Like us today, one of the areas that aroused their curiosity was the differing nature of people. Just like the preschool teachers of today, they noticed that people were different. Without the benefit of modern science, Hippocrates, now called the father of medicine, theorized that what made people so different were the chemicals in their bodies. Only recently have we come to see that he and the other Greek scholars may have been right on more counts than we have historically given them credit for. They believed that people could be categorized into four basic groupings, based on the chemicals or "fluids" in their bodies. These fluids supposedly gave rise to the behaviors that identified the four personalities. The original terms they used sound foreign to our ears today because they are—they're Greek! They are Sanguine, Choleric, Melancholy, and Phlegmatic.

Sanguines are high-energy, fun-loving, outgoing people. They are the people with the bumper stickers on their cars asking, "Are we having fun yet?" Hippocrates believed that these people were this way because they had red-hot blood coursing through their veins. If you have any background in medicine, you know that the word *sanguine* relates to the blood. In modern vocabulary Sanguine is used synonymously with optimism. In a recent interview regarding China's takeover of Hong Kong, I heard something said about why some people were "sanguine" about the outcome. Because this use of Sanguine is foreign to most of us, we have chosen to add a modern-day adjective to it when using it to represent a personality type. Throughout this book, you will see Sanguine coupled with the word Popular—a Popular Sanguine. If you are familiar with this teaching from another source and are accustomed to just the word Sanguine, feel free to use it. Likewise, if you have trouble pronouncing the Greek word or can't remember it, simply use the word Popular. These ideas are not about labels, they are designed to help us understand ourselves and improve our relationships with others.

The Choleric person is the one who is naturally goal oriented, who lives to achieve, and who organizes quickly. Cholerics are very task focused, yet outgoing like the Popular Sanguine. Their motto would echo the Nike advertising slogan "Just do it." With these positive traits, they tend to be short-tempered and bossy, which earned them the name Choleric. Hippocrates thought that these people had yellow bile in their bodies, giving them these specific traits similar to a baby with colic or a person with cholera. To make it easier to remember and understand, we have added the adjective Powerful to the Greek word Choleric to represent this strong personality type—the Powerful Choleric.

The Melancholy person is quieter, deeper, and more thoughtful. Melancholies strive for perfection in everything that is important to them. Their motto would be, "If it is worth doing, it is worth doing right!" With perfection as a goal, these people are disappointed and even depressed more than others. How often have you had a perfect hour, let alone a day, week, month, or year? Hippocrates believed that these people's tendency toward depression was due to the black bile that was in their bodies, giving them the term Melancholy. The word Melancholy is often used in modern-day media to represent a mood of depression or negativity. To focus on the positive aspects of this personality, we have added the word Perfect to the Greek word Melancholy, creating the personality type Perfect Melancholy.

The fourth personality type is the Phlegmatic. Phlegmatics are listed last because they are less obvious to identify. The other three personalities live life in the extreme. The Popular Sanguine is extremely fun-loving, extremely loud, extremely energetic. The Powerful Choleric is extremely driven, extremely focused, and extremely goal oriented. The Perfect Melancholy is extremely neat, extremely quiet, and extremely organized. But the Phlegmatics are the more balanced, contented people. As such, they do not stand out like the others. They do not feel compelled to change the world or to upset the status quo. The original conservationists, the Phlegmatics view all of life through the filter of conserving their energy. Their motto might be, "Why stand when you can sit? Why sit when you can lie down?" To the more driven personalities, the Phlegmatics appear to be slower than the rest, which caused Hippocrates to think that they had phlegm in their bodies, thereby giving them the name Phlegmatic. As this word is also foreign to most of us, we have added the positive adjective Peaceful to the Greek word Phlegmatic. Throughout the book you will see this balanced, steady, easygoing person described as the Peaceful Phlegmatic.

These terms provide us with a vocabulary by which we can discuss our personalities. You have probably already labeled people in your life without using these specific terms. Of the Popular Sanguine you would make comments such as, "She talks all the time" or "He never met a stranger." You may call this person a "talker." Of the Powerful Choleric you might say, "He sure gets in your face" or "If you want to get something done, ask a busy person." You would call this person the "doer" or the "worker." On behalf of the Perfect Melancholy, you might say, "She is so together" or "He is such a perfectionist." You might call this person a "thinker." When referring to the Peaceful Phlegmatic you would say things like, "She is so sweet" or "He is such a nice guy." You would view this person as a "watcher."

Today there is a great variety of teachings available on this general topic, but all come back to these four personality types first described thousands of years ago. Some of the other systems will refer to what we call the Popular Sanguine as Emotional, Influencing, Socializer, Expressive, or the Otter; the Powerful Choleric as Volitional, Dominant, Director, Driving, or the Lion; the Perfect Melancholy as Rational, Cautious, Thinker, Analytical, or the Beaver; and the Peaceful Phlegmatic as Personal, Steady, Relater,

Personality Comparison Chart

Littauer Personalities	Popular Sanguine	Powerful Choleric	Perfect Melancholy	Peaceful Phlegmatic
Larry Crabb	Emotional	Volitional	Rational	Personal
Gary Smalley & John Trent	Otter	Lion	Beaver	Golden Retriever
Personal Profile System	Influencing	Dominance	Cautious	Steadiness
Alessandra & Cathcart	Socializer	Director	Thinker	Relater
Merrill-Reid Social Styles	Expressive	Driving	Analytical	Amiable

Sources:
Lawrence J. Crabb, Jr. Ph.D., *The Training Manual*, (Institute of Biblical Counseling, 1978).
Gary Smalley and John Trent, *The Two Sides of Love* (Focus on the Family Publishers, 1990), 34–36.
Carlson Learning Company
Anthony Alessandra and Jim Cathcart, *Relationship Strategies* (Nightingale-Conant, 1990).
Merrill-Reid, Social Styles, "How Do They Manage?" by Susan Fletcher (*American Way Magazine*, October 1982), 192–94.

Amiable, or the Golden Retriever. If you are familiar with one of these other systems, realize that we are all talking the same language, just using slightly different terms to mean the same thing.

Most people who are familiar with these other approaches find that our personality program, which we refer to as The Personalities, focuses more on the positives and is more helpful in solving relationship problems, not just labeling them. If you are not familiar with our approach, you may want to go back and read some of our basic books on this topic, specifically, *Personality Plus, Personality Tree, Personality Puzzle*, and for those who enjoy history and politics and the study of leadership, *Put Power in Your Personality* (available in your local bookstore or through the order form in the back of the book). If you do not know your own personality type, please take a few minutes now to complete the simple Personality Profile in Appendix A. Once you know your own personality type and are able to identify the personality of the people you live and work with, you will find innumerable applications for improving your relationships.

Personality Combinations

While we all have a basic personality type, virtually none of us are 100 percent any one type. Most of us have one dominant and one secondary personality type, with a smattering of traits in the other two categories. We are all unique individuals. Sometimes our two primary personality types are closer to fifty-fifty, making it harder to determine which is the dominant and which is the secondary. Getting it down to such specifics is not necessary, but understanding the basic personality or personalities is helpful as they are the filters through which we view life.

Throughout this book you will see a chart, or the "squares" as we call them, in each chapter. The top two squares are the Popular Sanguine and the Powerful Choleric. Both of these personalities share several qualities that make them a natural combination in one person. They are both outgoing, optimistic, and energized by people. If you have a teenager who is either the Popular Sanguine, the Powerful Choleric, or a combination of both, you may have noticed that he or she may be dead tired—until a friend calls and invites him or her to do something. The idea of the activity and being with people will miraculously restore their energy. Someone with the Popular Sanguine and the Powerful Choleric personalities combined is someone who is supercharged, super wound-up, and super high-strung, someone who accomplishes a lot and wears out other people. The Popular Sanguine/Powerful Choleric needs to be careful not to dominate conversation and run over others. Someone who is mostly Popular Sanguine will be more people oriented. Someone who is mostly Powerful Choleric will focus more on accomplishment.

The bottom two squares are the Peaceful Phlegmatic and the Perfect Melancholy. Both of these personalities are introverted, pessimistic (or "realistic," as my Perfect Melancholy husband says), and drained by people. These common factors make the Perfect Melancholy/Peaceful Phlegmatic a natural blend. This combination makes for a very likeable person who also accomplishes what needs to be done. The danger, however, is that unchecked, their weaknesses can overcome their strengths; Peaceful Phlegmatic/Perfect Melancholy people can become so withdrawn and introverted that they turn into a couch potato who is hard to get blasted out of the house. Someone who is mostly Perfect Melancholy will be more task focused, and someone who is mostly Peaceful Phlegmatic will be more relationship focused.

The two squares on the right side, the Powerful Choleric and the Perfect Melancholy, are another natural combination as they are both task focused. This combination makes the best worker of all and therefore is the favorite of most employers. However, if they are not careful, people with this combination can put so much into their work

How to Understand Others
By Understanding Yourself

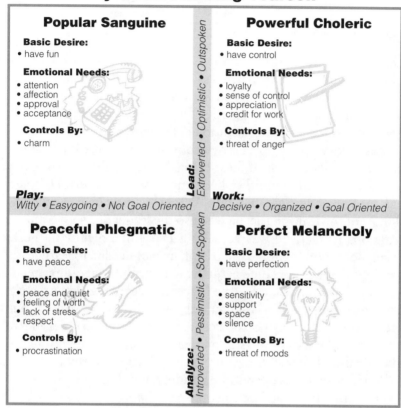

Popular Sanguine	Extroverted • Optimistic • Outspoken	Powerful Choleric
Basic Desire: • have fun		**Basic Desire:** • have control
Emotional Needs: • attention • affection • approval • acceptance		**Emotional Needs:** • loyalty • sense of control • appreciation • credit for work
Controls By: • charm		**Controls By:** • threat of anger
Play: *Witty • Easygoing • Not Goal Oriented*	**Lead:**	*Work:* *Decisive • Organized • Goal Oriented*
Peaceful Phlegmatic	Introverted • Pessimistic • Soft-Spoken	Perfect Melancholy
Basic Desire: • have peace		**Basic Desire:** • have perfection
Emotional Needs: • peace and quiet • feeling of worth • lack of stress • respect		**Emotional Needs:** • sensitivity • support • space • silence
Controls By: • procrastination	**Analyze:**	**Controls By:** • threat of moods

that all of their personal relationships suffer. If you have this combination and are more optimistic and people oriented, the Powerful Choleric is probably your dominant personality. If you are more withdrawn and prefer to be alone, you are probably mostly the Perfect Melancholy.

The two squares on the left side are the Popular Sanguine and the Peaceful Phlegmatic. Since both of these personalities are very relationship oriented, they combine naturally together. This combination makes everyone's favorite people. Their Popular Sanguine makes them fun, and their Peaceful Phlegmatic makes them agreeable and easygoing. If you are a parent of this type of child, you may be very frustrated trying to get them focused. Don't worry. While this personality combination seldom makes it to the presidency of anything, they don't care. Their charm will pull them through most situations, and people will want to help them. If *you* are this combination, realize that focus and finances are going to be areas on which you need to work.

Common Misunderstandings

Sometimes after reading a book, hearing a speaker, or taking the Personality Profile a person believes that he or she is a combination of either the Popular Sanguine and Perfect Melancholy or the Powerful Choleric and Peaceful Phlegmatic. This is confusing because the two personality types involved seem to be diametrically opposed. One of the most frequent types of calls that come into our office is from people who believe they are one of these opposing personality combinations.

A pastor wrote to our office believing he was a Powerful Choleric/Peaceful Phlegmatic combination. While he knew he had the Peaceful traits of the Phlegmatic, he was also the leader of a successful congregation. In fact, he was actually a Peaceful Phlegmatic/Perfect Melancholy combination. As a pastor, he had needed to learn leadership skills that did not come naturally to him. But that didn't mean he became a Powerful Choleric. As a Peaceful Phlegmatic/Perfect Melancholy, leadership is always something he will have to work at, but it *can* be learned. Reading books, attending seminars, and observing role models are all effective ways of picking up skills that are not natural. Additionally, of course, the Holy Spirit will help a person mature and develop if he or she is open to His leading and direction.

While it is true that many people *function* in what I call opposite personality types, the Perfect Melancholy/Popular Sanguine or the Powerful Choleric/Peaceful Phlegmatic, we have not found anyone who truly *is* a natural combination of the opposites. More often than not, I believe that someone who tests out to be one of these combinations either doesn't understand the words on the Personality Profile or misses the concept of the testing. At least, this is where I start with someone who is confused about his or her personality combination.

Often the character traits representing a personality type are misunderstood. For example, both the Powerful Choleric and the Perfect Melancholy are organized. The difference is in the type of organization. Once you understand the subtle difference, you can more accurately assess your own personality type. I am a Popular Sanguine/Powerful Choleric combination. By nature I am not organized. However, I run a business. For survival, I have had to learn to get organized and make the best use of my time. Many people who watch me in action perceive me to be very organized. If I did not understand that both the Powerful Choleric and the Perfect Melancholy are organized, I might decide that I must have some Perfect Melancholy in me because I am organized. However, my Powerful Choleric organization is different from the Perfect Melancholy. Perfect Melancholies organize for the pure joy of knowing that their shirts are all facing the same way in the closet (or whatever is important to the individual). They sleep better knowing their life is in order. Perfect Melancholies tend to organize obsessively, while Powerful Cholerics organize quickly, without much thought, and only those things that are needed to function efficiently. Things that don't matter (like shirts that face different ways in a closet) are not worthy of the time needed to organize them. Popular Sanguine/Powerful Cholerics might easily check off traits in the Perfect Melancholy column if they don't understand that subtle difference or if they don't understand the concept of looking at their natural self rather than their trained self. For me, organization is mostly a learned behavior.

Another example comes in the area of emotions and art. Both Popular Sanguines and Perfect Melancholies are creative and emotional. However, both of these traits are generally attributed only to the Perfect Melancholies. Popular Sanguines cry easily too, though. The difference is what moves them to tears. Popular Sanguines will cry if someone hurts them by saying mean and spiteful things. Popular Sanguines want everyone to love them. Since their emotions are very near the surface, they also cry at "touchy-feely" things such as Hallmark commercials and even some McDonald's ads. Popular Sanguines cry at things that are close to them or "fluffy" things. Perfect Melancholies, on the other hand, are moved by the deeper injustices in life. If a Popular Sanguine and a Perfect Melancholy are watching TV together, and they flip to a documentary on the starving people in Somalia, the Popular Sanguine will respond with, "Oh, yuck. Change the channel. I don't want to watch that!" But the Perfect Melancholy will be touched, almost gripped, by the drama on the screen and may be moved to tears over the tragedy of human life.

Another difference is creativity. Popular Sanguines are bursting with creative ideas, most of which they never act upon. However, should they get their act together and actually acquire the needed supplies to do a project, the Popular Sanguines will put it together quickly and lose interest if it takes too long. Most Popular Sanguine women have closets or garages full of partially completed craft projects in which they have lost interest. They may have gone through a macrame phase, a decoupage phase, a needlepoint phase, and a stenciling phase, but will still never settle on anything in particular. In comparison, the creative/artistic side of the Perfect Melancholies tends to gravitate toward one skill and work to master it. They, too, may have uncompleted projects—unfinished not from lack of interest but from lack of the time to do them perfectly.

One of the benefits of understanding your personality type is that you are aware of your natural area of gifting, and you also see those areas onto which you will need to add some "learned" behaviors. For myself, I have had to learn to get organized. Yet that organization doesn't make me into a Perfect Melancholy. I am merely a Popular Sanguine/Powerful Choleric who has learned to overcome some of my weaknesses and has worked to obtain skills in areas that are not natural to me.

One result of applying the Personality Profile to learned traits rather than natural tendencies can be an apparent combination of the Powerful Choleric and the Peaceful Phlegmatic. I find this showing up most frequently in men. Usually I am not talking to these men, but to their wives who have just heard me speak on the subject. They come up to me confused because they believe their husband is a Powerful Choleric/Peaceful Phlegmatic. He is the "boss" at work, but once he gets home, he won't do a thing. He appears to be that combination, but discussing it with his wife, what we usually find is that he is truly a Peaceful Phlegmatic, perhaps with some Perfect Melancholy. I have never actually found a Powerful Choleric/Peaceful Phlegmatic man!

Since our society doesn't typically honor gentle men, men learn to put on a tough, macho, Powerful Choleric image. That alone can be confusing. To make matters worse, most of these men have been in the work force for many years. As is typical for Peaceful Phlegmatics, they are well liked, faithful, and dependable. Over the years they have been pushed up the corporate ladder. Notice the word choice here, "pushed." They weren't chomping at the bit to be promoted, but due to their steady nature and ability, they kept getting promoted, often out of their comfort zone. Along the line, they were sent to sales training courses, Dale Carnegie courses, and management seminars. They learned to be the managers they have become. They learned to discipline employees and fire them if necessary. However, these activities are totally out of their natural comfort level. They can do them. They can run an entire company. But since this is not natural or easy for them, they come home exhausted from struggling all day to be someone they are not.

Once they are home, they fold up in the La-Z-Boy, turn on the TV, and don't want to be bothered. Like the Peaceful Phlegmatic/Perfect Melancholy they truly are, they need solitude to recharge their batteries. The wife looks on, wondering how this man who runs a multimillion-dollar company all day can be such a couch potato at home. But he's not a Powerful Choleric/Peaceful Phlegmatic combination. He's a Peaceful Phlegmatic who has worn himself out. He has learned to be tough and strong. It doesn't necessarily mean he wears a mask or has any deep problems—he has just learned to function in a personality type not natural to him.

Occasionally the situation may be reversed. The husband really is a Powerful Choleric, but he has learned to adopt Peaceful Phlegmatic behaviors in the home to survive. This often happens when both husband and wife are at least half Powerful Choleric. The symptoms will be the same as the previous scenario; he is in charge at work but does nothing at home.

When both the husband and wife have a strong percentage of the Powerful Choleric, they have two choices. They can fight for control, or one of them can agree to be the dominant person in certain settings. Most marriages don't start out with a clear understanding of these concepts. The partners don't sit down and say, "Look, we both like to be in charge. Why don't you do this . . . and I'll do this." They just fall into a pattern to avoid constant conflict. Since the woman is traditionally the homemaker, she naturally falls into being in charge of the home. The man is traditionally the worker, so he runs the business while she runs the family. As a Powerful Choleric, he has an unwritten rule: "If I can't win, I don't want to play the game." When he comes home from work, his natural tendency is to shape everyone up. But he learned long ago that she has a firm hand on the family. So rather than fight, he simply gives up, retreats into his own world, and appears to be a Peaceful Phlegmatic at home.

In discussing these combination misunderstandings with people after my conferences, I find most of the problems are cleared up by thinking through the scenarios I have just presented. However, if they don't seem to ring true in your case, I encourage you to look deeper into what we call a mask. Sometimes the presence of these contradicting personality combinations can be an indicator of some unresolved issues from your past. Such issues can cause you to wear a mask. A mask represents behaviors that you unconsciously adopted, usually in childhood and often to make a parent happy or to attempt to make him or her like you better. Many men and women try to gain a parent's approval by adopting a Powerful Choleric mode of accomplishment. Some continue to do so for their entire lives, even long after the parent has died. To investigate this option further, please read *Your Personality Tree* and *Freeing Your Mind.* These books are specifically written to help you assess and recover from damage that was intentionally or unintentionally done to you by a parent or other relative, a teacher, or even a spouse.

In the rest of this book, many of our Certified Personality Trainers have contributed on their areas of expertise. They attended one of our special Personality Training Workshops and became certified as Personality Trainers because they found the value of applying the personalities in their specific arenas. As we learned what they were doing, we were fascinated by the enhanced insight they brought to our teachings on the Personalities. We invited them to participate in this book to share with you their specialized knowledge. While you may not dwell on every chapter, I do hope that you will read them all. You will find valuable information in each and every chapter as you learn to put the pieces in place in your personality puzzle.

Part 1

Family
and Home Life

Marriage

What Personality Is Best to Marry?

Marita Littauer and Chuck Noon

As a popular speaker for women's conferences throughout the country, Marita Littauer's goal for speaking and writing is to assist people in putting together the pieces of their lives. The author of Personality Puzzle *and other books, Marita is the president of CLASServices, Inc., an organization providing resources, training, and promotion for speakers and authors. Marita and her husband, Chuck Noon, have been married since 1983 and live in Albuquerque, New Mexico, where Chuck is a licensed, professional clinical counselor. He specializes in marriage counseling and has seen changes almost overnight in response to application of personality principles. Chuck served as the marriage specialist at the Minirth Meier Clinic in Albuquerque, and is currently working in private practice.*

Every relationship takes work. Two best friends from high school, an employer and a longtime employee, and a husband and wife all have to invest in their relationship to make it last over the years. Nearly everyone who has been involved in any type of long-term relationship can cite numerous rough spots where either party could have walked away or quit but instead chose to work through the differences. Yet most of us expect the blush of love to cover over the differences in a marriage, whereas we'd accept and expect these same differences in any other relationship.

While every relationship *takes* work, every relationship *can* work, especially when both parties are willing to put in the effort it takes to make that happen. Even if only one party is willing to make changes, remarkable improvement can be made.

Much of the "work" involved in making a relationship work results from the fact that most of us are attracted to someone who is opposite from us. When we look at marriage, we believe this is how God intended it to be. When a husband and wife function in their strengths, varied skills, emotions, and viewpoints, they bring into a marriage balance and perspective, and the two truly do "become one," a whole with a complement of abilities. Where the wife may be strong or gifted, the husband is weak or less gifted; where he excels, she needs help. When we understand each other, our varied abilities, and our opposite strengths and weaknesses, we can take advantage of those differences. Together we bring about personal growth and balance in one another. Without an understanding of our personalities and how we can complement each other, those opposites that attracted us turn from attraction to attack!

Since I had an understanding of the Personalities from childhood, I fully understood the idea that opposites attract. As I attended seminars and conferences where my mother was teaching the concepts of the Personalities, I often heard people ask her, "What personality type should I marry if I want to be happy?" Her tongue-in-cheek reply was, "If you want to be happy, don't marry anybody!" Having seen the struggles in my own parents' marriage of opposites, and having heard years of distressful comments and questions from people attending their seminars who were in similar situations, I decided to date men who were like me. I dated men who were strong, self-starters, outgoing salesmen, driven entrepreneurs, usually older, usually financially solid (or at least apparently so), almost always Powerful Cholerics, some of whom were also a bit Popular Sanguine or Perfect Melancholy. While my dating life netted me many good times and some nice jewelry, I never fell in love . . . until I met Chuck.

Chuck did not fit my profile. He was so opposite from me, and from my usual date, that when I went out with him the third time, my friends knew this must be it. Chuck was only three years older than I. I was twenty-four and he was twenty-seven when we met. He was in the air force. With a degree in art, specifically motion picture production, he was making movies for the air force. With no business background and no entrepreneurial drive, Chuck was an artist

The Marital Balance Sheet

Most marriages are made up of opposite personalities. However, as shared in this chapter, the marriages that work the most easily are those in which both partners share a common square as either their primary or secondary personality. Here you can see the areas of strengths and cautions for the marriages in which each personality is shared.

Popular Sanguine
The "Fun" Marriage

Assets
- spontaneous
- exciting
- enthusiastic
- keep marriage fresh
- flexible
- compromising
- forgiving
- play with children
- creative sex

Liabilities
- lack of plans and goals
- unstable
- flirtatious
- messy
- no one listens
- relationship remains superficial
- fail to put down roots
- blurred generational boundaries
- financial matters lack budgeting, accounting, and retirement planning

Powerful Choleric
The "Active" Marriage

Assets
- goal oriented
- clear boundaries
- high accomplishment
- respect each other
- high energy
- championing causes
- firm parents
- quick sex

Liabilities
- struggle for control
- overcommitted and late
- no time for relationship
- two careers pulling on marriage
- marriage is a low priority
- blurring of personal and professional boundaries
- shouting contests
- fear of sharing

Peaceful Phlegmatic
The "Relaxed" Marriage

Assets
- stable
- agreeable
- content
- low pressure
- satisfied
- modest
- lack of distraction
- patient with children
- special event sex

Liabilities
- low accomplishment
- lack of planning
- kids can take over
- dull
- control is passive-aggressive
- lack of communication
- loss of individual identity
- blurred generational boundaries
- fear of conflict

Perfect Melancholy
The "Organized" Marriage

Assets
- neat home
- long-range plans
- financial order
- punctual
- considerate
- value education
- remember important dates
- committed to each other
- loving and protective with children
- romantic sex

Liabilities
- critical
- danger of mid-life crisis
- depressed
- brooding
- keep a record of wrongs
- reinforce each other's negativity
- stuck in routines
- may be unfaithful
- repeat maladaptive behaviors
- high expectations place heavy burden on relationship

at heart. We got married five months after we met. So much for try-ing to disprove that opposites attract!

In looking at the fourteen years of our marriage, I am so grateful that I understood our personalities. Chuck is mostly Perfect Melan-choly, with some of the Powerful Choleric in him. I am about fifty-fifty Popular Sanguine and Powerful Choleric. My Popular Sanguine part and his Perfect Melancholy part are often at odds, while our mutual Powerful Choleric parts battle for control.

Our differing personalities give us a different framework from which we view life, even a different vocabulary. We had been mar-ried about three years when our different approaches to life became really clear. One weekend morning I cooked a special breakfast for Chuck. This was not just Pop-Tarts and Tang. I went all out. I made homemade buttermilk pancakes—not from a mix—freshly ground coffee, bacon, and freshly squeezed orange juice. I served it in the dining room on a nice plate with coordinating linens. I set the extra-ordinary breakfast in front of him, and he began to eat it. I asked him how his breakfast was, and he said it was . . . fine. FINE! I thought to myself, *I make this great meal and all it is is FINE!*

Chuck was communicating to me out of his personality, and I was hearing him from mine. Our personality impacts even our commu-nication style. As I survey audiences when I speak, I find that the Popular Sanguines universally view the word *fine* as a negative. I ask them, "On a scale of one to ten, with ten being the best, where is the word *fine?*" In unison they shout out answers ranging from one to three. One person in a hotel management group in Australia said minus two! To those of us who are Popular Sanguines, "fine" is not a compliment. However, the Perfect Melancholy sees things differently.

On one of my frequent speaking trips I called home, as I always do. I asked Chuck how his day was, and he responded with a predictable "fine." Without thinking I said, "What was wrong?" "Nothing," he replied, "I said it was fine. You need to learn that for me, fine is as good as it ever gets." I believe that if I had to face a life of "fine," I'd com-mit suicide—a life of "fine" is not worth living. But to a Perfect Melan-choly, "fine" *is* as good as it ever gets. Like fine china, fine sterling, fine crystal . . . fine is as good as it gets!

For the two of us opposite personalities to communicate and ulti-mately stay married, we needed to learn to communicate in new ways for each other. Chuck has learned superlatives—terrific, fabulous, wonderful, amazing. If I have a new dress and I ask him how I look, he has learned that "fine" is not an acceptable answer! When I ask Chuck about something in his life and he says it is fine, I have learned to say "great" and move on to the next subject.

On that day when I served Chuck the lavish breakfast and he said it was fine, I said "wrong answer" as I took his plate back to the kitchen. I turned around and brought it back, placed it in front of him, and asked again, "Chuck, how's your breakfast?" With a big smile on his face, he said, "This is the best breakfast I have ever had in my entire life!" "Good," I said, "now you can have breakfast tomorrow."

We could regale you with numerous similar stories about our differences. But we imagine they are very much like what happens in your home. The difference may be that we understand and use the benefit of our knowledge of personalities. Without an understanding of personalities, we are confident we would not still be married today.

Emotional Needs

Many chapters in this book and our previous books on the Personalities address the emotional needs of each personality. While they are important to any understanding of personalities, I believe they are essential in a marriage relationship. However, most couples do not even know about the personalities, let alone how to appropriate their value. With so much misunderstanding about how to meet an opposite spouse's emotional needs, it is no wonder that so many marriages fail. Without even thinking about it, most of us tend to apply the ingrained "Golden Rule" to our relationships, giving others what we want. As a result, we inherently withhold from our opposite spouse the exact thing he or she needs.

Popular Sanguines need attention and approval. But they are usually married to Perfect Melancholies. Since the goal of Perfect Melancholies is perfection, what do Popular Sanguines need to do or be in order to get the attention and approval they desire from their spouse? They will need to be perfect, and they will never be perfect enough for their Perfect Melancholy spouse to praise them. The Perfect Melancholies feel that they cannot offer Popular Sanguines the praise they need because then the Sanguines will think that what they did was good enough when it could have been better.

With their emotional needs unmet, the Popular Sanguines are set up to get their needs met somewhere else. They may be louder or even more outgoing in their search to be noticed. Since this is the behavior Perfect Melancholies dislike, the gap widens. The Perfect Melancholy withholds approval, and the Popular Sanguine needs it even more. Some Popular Sanguines may go to further extremes, changing jobs or even having an affair. In this type of relationship, the Popular Sanguine is starved for attention. The first person of the opposite sex who offers him or her any type of approval—"You look nice today" or "You are lots of fun"—begins filling a big void that should be filled by the spouse. Before long the Popular Sanguine is in an affair he or she never intended to enter.

To prevent this, the spouse of the Popular Sanguine, usually a Perfect Melancholy, must realize that much of the undesirable behavior of the Popular Sanguine would be minimized by healthy, frequent doses of praise. Rather than the praise causing the Popular Sanguine to believe that their behavior is acceptable, it spurs them on. They bask in the praise, trying even harder. The natural pattern of this pair is the withholding of what the Popular Sanguine needs so badly, which causes an ever widening gap in the marriage. However, when the Perfect Melancholy gives the Popular Sanguine what they need, both parties win. The Popular Sanguine's needs are met and their offensive behavior is reduced, replaced by increasingly improved performance. Everyone wins with an understanding of personalities.

Similar things happen to the reverse combination in the Popular Sanguine/Perfect Melancholy marriage. The most important needs for the Perfect Melancholy in this marriage are sensitivity and space. The Perfect Melancholy needs their Popular Sanguine spouse to hurt when they hurt, to cry when they cry. They also need time to themselves. Perfect Melancholies recharge their batteries with solitude. People drain them, just as leaving the lights on in your car will drain its battery.

Without understanding personalities and their companion emotional needs, Popular Sanguines will never give Perfect Melancholies what they need. Again, we naturally give what we want. To a Popular Sanguine silence is "dead air," and as in radio and television, dead air is bad. It makes us think that we are in trouble or that no one likes us. We feel compelled to fill the silence with chatter. When Chuck and I are driving, I realize that I want to keep up a lively banter. When I think about why I have to do this, I discover a typical Popular Sanguine surface reason, one with which many Popular Sanguines agree. I do not want the strangers driving by to look in our car and see both of us just staring out the window with a blank or disgruntled look on our faces, as do so many of the passengers in cars we pass. When I pass those cars, I look in and satirically say, "Boy, they look like they are having fun." I wouldn't want anyone to look into our car and say that about us—so I talk.

I have had to learn that Chuck does not share my need for constant activity and noise. As a Perfect Melancholy, he actually likes the quiet. He taught me what he teaches his Popular Sanguine clients. As a marriage therapist, he has seen this same scenario played out over and over—the talkative Popular Sanguine is married to the quiet, reclusive Perfect Melancholy. He instructs the Popular Sanguines to learn to "play the silence." When he first taught me this term, my response was "Play the silence?" "Yes, like you play the radio," he said. While I am still not sure what that means, I have worked at playing the silence. Chuck tells me that this means that the Popular Sanguine needs to listen to more of the classical stations. Just as Beethoven placed moments of silence in his works, we need to learn that what we have to say has more impact when we also know when to remain silent. When we go somewhere in the car, I bring books and mail-order catalogs, I look out the windows, and I sleep. All are activities that "play the silence." If I have something we need to discuss, something I need an opinion on, or something I just want to share with him, I ask if this is a good time. Usually he says yes, occasionally he says no. In either case I abide by his wishes. When I have been "good" and quiet, I often point out, with a big smile, that I have been playing the silence and ask if he noticed. Because he understands me, he knows my Popular Sanguine need for approval and gives me the appropriate praise for my silence.

Perfect Melancholies also need sensitivity. Remember, much like the military, they operate on a need-to-know basis. Unlike their Popular Sanguine spouses who constantly spew out whatever thought enters their heads, Perfect Melancholies are private people. They tend to hold their thoughts inside and do not disclose intimate information about themselves unless they sense that they will receive a favorable hearing. While their thoughts are inside, they believe a sensitive and caring partner will intuitively know what they are thinking and feeling, and will act accordingly. Married to the surface-level Popular Sanguine, there is little hope for them of this ever happening. Both parties must be aware of this potential problem. The Popular Sanguine does know something is wrong; a large black cloud seems to fill the room when the Perfect Melancholy is having a tough time. The

Perfect Melancholy hopes for compassion and comfort sending out nonverbal clues of distress. Reading these clues, the Popular Sanguine spouse quips, "What's wrong?" Their tone clearly tells the Perfect Melancholy that they don't have much time and they don't really care, and produces the typical response, "Nothing."

As I share this scenario at my seminars, I ask the Popular Sanguines in the room if they can tell when their Perfect Melancholy spouse is having a bad day. Universally they reply affirmatively. Next I ask how they respond, what they try to do for their spouse? I always get one of two answers: "try to fix it" or "try to cheer them up." To which I ask, "How often does it work?" As if they'd been rehearsing for a choral speaking part, they shout in unison, "NEVER!" Yet every Popular Sanguine who does not already understand these concepts or who does not care enough to put forth the extra effort to make a difference in their marriage continues to give their opposite spouse exactly what they do not want and what their history together has already proven does not work. As I run through these basic questions with my audiences and get predictable responses, I can see the lights go on in their eyes. It is as if for the first time they see what they have been doing and see why it has never worked.

Without having their emotional needs met, the Perfect Melancholy subconsciously looks elsewhere. We have all seen cases where a quiet, brooding, attractive Perfect Melancholy male is married to a cute, bouncy, cheerleader-type Popular Sanguine woman. On the outside observers think it is good that he has someone to pick him up—they make such a handsome couple. Then one day he leaves her, along with all the social standing or prestige they may have acquired in the church or community, for another woman—a woman who has none of his wife's physical attributes. People wonder why, how, and what he sees in the other woman? Usually it boils down to finding in her what his personality type needs—she has time for him and she listens. His wife long ago gave up trying to cheer him up, and set herself up in a variety of activities that brought her the praise she needed, leaving little time to make him a priority.

If you are a Popular Sanguine married to a Perfect Melancholy, you need to realize that their needs are very different from yours. As a Popular Sanguine, you need to tone down your voice and your activities and focus on the Perfect Melancholy. When you sense a black cloud looming, rather than just breezing in and throwing out a quick question about what is wrong, you need to slow down and sit down. Take a breath before saying anything. Then in an FM deejay-like voice—soft, gentle, and soothing—look into their eyes and say something like, "Penny for your thoughts?" Be patient, play the silence. When you do get an answer, don't say the first thing that pops into your mind. It is usually the wrong thing to say. Instead, try to look at the situation from their perspective. Make a real effort to understand where they are coming from and why or how they are hurting. This will take some work on your part, especially in the beginning, but remember that every relationship takes work. The Perfect Melancholy may take some time to adjust to your new approach and may at first believe you are insincere, so do not expect instantaneous results. With continued discipline on your part, you will see changes. Hopefully, once you take that first step and make the changes (it is usually easier for the Popular Sanguine to adjust their behavior), the Perfect Melancholy will follow suit as the relationship begins to take on a healthier posture.

Like the opposites in the Perfect Melancholy and Popular Sanguine marriage, the Powerful Choleric and Peaceful Phlegmatic marriage also faces similar, yet different, dilemmas—the very thing the partners need is the exact thing that is unintentionally withheld.

Powerful Cholerics need appreciation and a sense of accomplishment. They need to accomplish tasks for their own self-worth or identity. At the end of the day a Powerful Choleric goes through a mental checklist to insure that they have accomplished more than anyone else they know. Assuming they have, they can sleep well. But if they have been forced to spend the day on a family outing, for example, their mental checklist may come up short. In such cases, Powerful Cholerics have been known to get back up out of bed and go complete some task. While they typically do accomplish more than anyone else, they also need others to appreciate them for all they do. One of the best things you can ever say to the Powerful Choleric is, "I don't know how you do everything you do. This place would just fall apart without you."

However, the Powerful Choleric is usually married to the Peaceful Phlegmatic. With what you already understand about personalities, think about Peaceful Phlegmatics for a moment. Production or accomplishment does not carry the same value for them. Peaceful Phlegmatics value peace, harmony, and stability. Just once they would like to take a vacation without a schedule. They enjoy the luxury of lying on a beach reading a good book. Knowing this, how does the Peaceful Phlegmatic feel about everything the Powerful Choleric produces, about their whirlwind of activity? I ask my audiences, "What do the Peaceful Phleg-matics wish their Powerful Choleric spouses would do?" The answer is always the same: rest or sit down. Then I ask, "How does all this activ-ity make the Peaceful Phlegmatic feel?" Tired or worthless is the stan-dard answer. Feeling like that, is the Peaceful Phlegmatic who does not understand the other personalities ever likely to give the Powerful Cho-leric spouse enough appreciation for all they do? No! They feel threat-ened by it, so they will not acknowledge it in a positive way.

Since the Powerful Choleric needs this appreciation, which they are not likely to get from their spouse, their first reaction is to try harder. Subconsciously, the Powerful Cholerics think if they do more, that people will have to notice. They become workaholics in hopes of being recognized. The professional world usually does notice these good workers; in fact, it counts on the presence of these Powerful Choler-ics who will happily carry far more than their share of the load. They usually do get their needed appreciation in the workplace, making it easier and easier to spend more and more time at work—ever widen-ing the gap between themselves and their spouse.

So what's a Peaceful Phlegmatic to do? Realize that because you withhold needed appreciation, your Powerful Choleric spouse will work harder, do more. By noticing what they do, you are not draw-ing attention to the fact that you have not done nearly as much. The Powerful Choleric isn't looking for competition, just compli-ments. Like the Perfect Melancholy, the Peaceful Phlegmatic also needs to learn that compliments cost nothing. Make an effort to observe both the big and small projects the Powerful Choleric does. Notice them and comment favorably about them. This will go a long way toward the Powerful Choleric loosening up their to-do list and being willing to do some of the things that are important to the Peaceful Phlegmatic.

Peaceful Phlegmatics need respect and a sense of self-worth. Unfor-tunately for their emotional needs, the Peaceful Phlegmatic is usu-ally married to the Powerful Choleric. What does the Powerful Cho-leric respect and see as worthy? PRODUCTION! Is the Peaceful Phlegmatic ever going to produce enough to gain the respect of the Powerful Choleric? No! The Powerful Choleric holds back respect, waiting for the Peaceful Phlegmatic to accomplish something Pow-erful Cholerics value, basing the approval on tasks and production. However, in the Powerful Choleric's mind, the Peaceful Phlegmatic is in a production deficit, and even if they suddenly got active today, they could never make up for years of living on the sidelines.

The Peaceful Phlegmatic personality is not reinforced in childhood or adult life in our current society. Accomplishment and earnings are valued over patience and traditional values such as simplicity. A Peaceful Phlegmatic man said, "I would rather be happy than successful." Without missing a beat, his Powerful Choleric wife said, "If I am successful, I will be happy!"

As children Peaceful Phlegmatics didn't get voted anything and weren't awarded anything, but they didn't stand out for negative reasons either. They slipped through the cracks. Therefore, they grow up to be adults who need respect and a feeling of self-worth not for what they do, but for who they are, or just because they are. This is a difficult concept for the Powerful Choleric to grasp, given the fact that their values are based on production. I remember a Powerful Choleric woman asking me at a seminar, "How do I give my Peaceful Phlegmatic husband respect and a feeling of self-worth when he doesn't do anything?" Therein lies the problem.

The Powerful Choleric is as far from the Peaceful Phlegmatic as the East is from the West. In dealing with the Peaceful Phlegmatic, the Powerful Choleric needs to "think Japanese." In Japan questions are phrased to allow for a positive response. You do not go into a store and ask, "Do you have any bananas?" forcing the proprietor to say no. Instead the Japanese ask, "Do you not have any bananas today?" allowing the shopkeeper to say yes in either case—"Yes, I do have bananas" or "Yes, you are correct, I do not have bananas." Westerners in this regard typify the Powerful Choleric, who will control a conversation and try to force the desired answer out of the Peaceful Phlegmatic, as if in a court of law. The Powerful Choleric is always seeking to establish absolutes, while the Peaceful Phlegmatic sees infinite variations of shades of gray and is left feeling as if they have to make a case before the Choleric listens. The Phlegmatic Japanese will never tell you you are wrong. Instead they offer options. Instead of saying "No, I don't want to go to the movies," they will say "Yes, but have you considered the symphony for this evening?" Powerful Cholerics need to learn this approach when communicating with Peaceful Phlegmatics. A Powerful Choleric might respond, "But you don't like comedies," immediately shutting off any further communication. Above all else Peaceful Phlegmatics hate people to tell them about themselves. All the while the Powerful Choleric is being frustrated by the Peaceful Phlegmatic's seeming unwillingness to clearly communicate their entertainment preference.

Peaceful Phlegmatics will get the feeling that they are respected and important or valued when Powerful Cholerics notice what is important to them and cheerfully engage in that activity, even if it is only resting beside a river or having a picnic in a park. Doing things that are important to the Peaceful Phlegmatic without prodding and without making them feel guilty goes a long way toward meeting their needs of respect and self-worth.

One Square in Common

While it is true that opposites attract, at least in a first marriage, we have found that the marriages that take the least amount of work are those that have one personality square in common. Each chapter of this book features a set of squares, a chart displaying certain strengths and weaknesses of the personalities as they apply to each topic area. These squares are laid out so that opposite personalities are opposite each other. However, those marriages that have both an opposite personality type and one overlapping square usually work most smoothly and take the least work. The shared square gives both parties something in common. For example, I am about fifty-fifty Popular Sanguine and Powerful Choleric. Chuck is mostly Perfect Melancholy with some Powerful Choleric. We are opposites in that I am Popular Sanguine and he is Perfect Melancholy. But we also both have some Powerful Choleric. In our marriage that benefits us in that neither of us ever really wants to rest. On any given Saturday, we both have more to accomplish than is humanly possible. We both have our mental checklists, and we view the weekend as an opportunity to accomplish those things that we cannot get done during the work week. With the Powerful Choleric square in common, our marriage is one of action. Vacations are for seeing and doing new things, not for resting.

One of my best friends, Rachel, is a Peaceful Phlegmatic with some Popular Sanguine. Her husband is a combination Powerful Choleric and Popular Sanguine. Together they share the Popular Sanguine square. As a couple they are lots of fun. Rachel asked me how this would play out in marriage. I told her because they both share an optimistic, fun-loving outlook, they are not likely to ever have any serious marriage problems. Having fun together allows spouses to overlook many other problems. However, since neither of them has any real quantity of the Perfect Melancholy, they may never get their finances in order. I painted the following scenario of what might happen in a marriage of their personality combination: You have a bad day at work. You come home and look at Rudy with those big eyes and say, "Rudy, I've had a bad day. Let's go out to dinner and to a funny movie. I need to be cheered up." Knowing that finances have been a problem area, you two have tried to create a budget and are trying to stick to it. So Rudy says, "We can't. It's not in our budget." You say, "But I really need to go out. We have credit cards. Let's go." Being a Popular Sanguine himself, Rudy doesn't want to see you unhappy, so he agrees. Some form of this scenario repeats itself frequently over the years, and while you may not be horribly in debt, you are unlikely to ever get ahead. Rachel looked at me wide-eyed. My creative scene was exactly right. I told her the good thing about their combination is that they will not really care since the comfort of a huge savings account is not an issue to them. (Although for the in-laws, it might be a whole other story . . .) Couples with the Popular Sanguine square in common are lots of fun. You don't want to have a party without them!

Chuck and I used to have next-door neighbors who have the Perfect Melancholy square in common. She was a Powerful Choleric/Perfect Melancholy, and he was a Perfect Melancholy/Peaceful Phlegmatic. In contrast to the couples with the Popular Sanguine square in common, those with the Perfect Melancholy in common are the picture of success. They are both well educated, they drive the right cars, and they have a lovely, large home. They have retirement funds and have their future fully mapped out. Before they bought their dream house and moved away, our neighbors would invite us to their home for dinner or other social events. We always had a lovely time. When we left, we would say to each other, "That was nice," and it was. We didn't leave bursting with excitement, slapping our knees, and exclaiming over what a "blast" it had been. The Perfect Melancholy home isn't that way. As a couple, those with the Perfect Melancholy square in common are pleasant and enjoyable, but fun and exciting are not the first words you would use to describe them.

The household with the Peaceful Phlegmatic square in common will be a very comfortable home. Brenda is a Peaceful Phlegmatic who used to live with my family. She married Ken, who is also about 50 percent Peaceful Phlegmatic. In their home comfort is a priority. They value harmony and stability. They do not panic if a guest drops by unannounced. They do not frantically throw things in the closet in an attempt to make a good impression (as the Popular Sanguine does). The house just looks the way it looks. They are very content with each other and with their life together. They do not feel a compulsion to conquer anything. These attitudes in common help their marriage work. Without that common denominator, one might constantly be trying to light a fire under the other. When both parties in a marriage share that comfortable quality, everyone relaxes with them. The couple with the Peaceful Phlegmatic square in common may find that they have many projects that are unfinished, but like the Popular Sanguine marriage, they don't mind the personality weaknesses that they share.

I find the marriage that takes the most work and the most adjustment is the marriage in which one spouse is the top two squares on the chart, the Popular Sanguine combined with the Powerful Choleric, and the other spouse is the bottom two squares, the Peaceful Phlegmatic combined with the Perfect Melancholy. The top two squares are the outgoing, optimistic people, the ones that are energized by people. When both of these personalities are combined in one person, you get someone who is supercharged, really high-strung, and overwhelming to others. The bottom two squares are the more pessimistic and reclusive people, people who are drained by others and recharged by solitude. When both of these personalities are found in one person, that person can easily slip into being the true couch potato—someone who is hard to get moving or motivated. When these two different combinations marry, not only are they opposites, but they do not have the benefit of sharing one square in common. Their marriage can work, but it will take work. In any relationship, if both parties are willing to try, if they will put forth that extra effort, and if they understand each other's personalities and corresponding emotional needs, the relationship can work and truly be fulfilling and enjoyable.

Even if only one party in a marriage understands these personality concepts, amazing changes can take place when that person cares enough to take the first step and make a difference. Even though I had an ingrained understanding of personalities, Chuck had no real knowledge of them when we got married. With only one of us being aware of and using the benefit of the Personalities, they still impacted our relationship positively. Now Chuck uses these concepts daily in his practice as a marriage and family therapist. If you need to see Chuck, or someone else trained in these concepts, please get the help. But, better yet, apply these truths now, and you may never need a therapist!

Single Again

What Makes Us Attractive to Others?

GRACE "ROCKY" GRAZIANO

Sixteen years after her marriage of twenty-five years ended in divorce, Grace "Rocky" Graziano shares her story with people at her workshops and seminars. Having learned many of the bittersweet intricacies of relationships, Rocky now teaches others how God created us equal but very different and how understanding the personalities will enhance their lives.

hen Christian churches first began divorced singles ministries, they had in mind a support structure to bolster up the spiritual and emotional self-worth of the hurting individual. Some churches have started divorced singles programs for general education, some have Bible studies, and some have hired staff members specifically trained to aid in emotional healing. Social events give newly divorced individuals a safe place to go to ease the pain of loneliness.

All these avenues lead toward rebuilding people's lives, but we must refrain from turning the church into a marriage brokerage. The purpose of a divorce/recovery ministry should be to bring people to emotional stability and enable them to make rational choices in their next relationship.

Florence and Fred Littauer point out that we marry people of opposite personalities who are on the same level of emotional pain as we are. But if we base a new marriage on our mutual pain, we soon find ourselves in another damaging situation. Teaching about personalities in our divorce/recovery groups would allow us to see what went wrong the last time and to make sure we don't make the same mistake again. Such study would be eye-opening and would help people avoid jumping into a new marriage before they have healed from the previous one. Then we would see that two broken individuals do not make a whole marriage.

Because I have been through divorce, I have a personal passion for helping others in similar situations. During my married life I didn't know anything about personalities. Therefore, I spent twenty-five years in a marriage that displayed immaturity, insecurity, imperfection, and most of all miscommunication. What happened to the white picket fence and living happily ever after?

I have been divorced for sixteen years, and it is only during the last five years that I have come to terms with the differences that caused my divorce. After attending a Florence Littauer presentation, it all came home to me. It was as if a light bulb went on and I instantly understood the simple concept of the Personalities.

Why does it take us so long to realize that we are all born equal but very different? God intended it to be this way so we could learn from each other. Our different personalities are a gift rather than a hindrance. We need to understand and accept that we all have strengths and weaknesses. Seventy percent of surveyed singles placed investing time and effort in close friendships and relationships as their top priority in life. Yet in this quest, they generally interpret differences as negative because of their resistance to change. Studies have shown that 47 percent of all Americans strongly resist change. But that resistance fades when people are introduced to a commonsense explanation for their so-called differences.

Let us take a familiar scenario of a recently divorced or never married single. Singlehood is filled with new challenges, things to do, and places to go. It is the "wild" time. For a divorced person, one of the hurdles to face is letting go of old things. The single life, we tell ourselves, is great, yet we keep yearning to have that one special relationship. The desire of almost everyone is to have that perfect relationship. The prob-

Your Personality Profile

On the chart below, review the strengths of each personality. Identify the strengths you have in column A and which strengths your ex-spouse had in column B. How many are similar? How many are different? In looking toward the future, what traits would you want in a spouse? Identify those in column C. Now check the weaknesses of both you and your ex-spouse. Can you see where your problems came from? Finally examine the possible weaknesses of your new "Hope." Whatever strengths he or she has will be accompanied by comparative weaknesses. Can you live with these?

Popular Sanguine
The "Fun" Marriage

Strengths	A	B	C
animated	—	—	—
playful	—	—	—
sociable	—	—	—
convincing	—	—	—
refreshing	—	—	—
spirited	—	—	—
optimistic	—	—	—
spontaneous	—	—	—
funny	—	—	—
talker	—	—	—

Weaknesses	A	B	C
undisciplined	—	—	—
forgetful	—	—	—
haphazard	—	—	—
naive	—	—	—
talkative	—	—	—
disorganized	—	—	—
loud	—	—	—
restless	—	—	—
changeable	—	—	—
show-off	—	—	—

Powerful Choleric
The "Active" Marriage

Strengths	A	B	C
adventurous	—	—	—
persuasive	—	—	—
resourceful	—	—	—
positive	—	—	—
sure	—	—	—
independent	—	—	—
decisive	—	—	—
leader	—	—	—
bold	—	—	—
mover	—	—	—

Weaknesses	A	B	C
bossy	—	—	—
resistant	—	—	—
impatient	—	—	—
unaffectionate	—	—	—
headstrong	—	—	—
proud	—	—	—
workaholic	—	—	—
domineering	—	—	—
manipulative	—	—	—
short-tempered	—	—	—

Peaceful Phlegmatic
The "Relaxed" Marriage

Strengths	A	B	C
peaceful	—	—	—
controlled	—	—	—
reserved	—	—	—
satisfied	—	—	—
patient	—	—	—
friendly	—	—	—
diplomatic	—	—	—
consistent	—	—	—
inoffensive	—	—	—
listener	—	—	—

Weaknesses	A	B	C
unenthusiastic	—	—	—
fearful	—	—	—
indecisive	—	—	—
plain	—	—	—
aimless	—	—	—
worrier	—	—	—
timid	—	—	—
doubtful	—	—	—
slow	—	—	—
compromising	—	—	—

Perfect Melancholy
The "Organized" Marriage

Strengths	A	B	C
analytical	—	—	—
persistent	—	—	—
considerate	—	—	—
respectful	—	—	—
planner	—	—	—
orderly	—	—	—
faithful	—	—	—
detailed	—	—	—
idealistic	—	—	—
perfectionist	—	—	—

Weaknesses	A	B	C
unforgiving	—	—	—
resentful	—	—	—
fussy	—	—	—
insecure	—	—	—
hard to please	—	—	—
negative	—	—	—
withdrawn	—	—	—
moody	—	—	—
skeptical	—	—	—
critical	—	—	—

lem is that I said perfect, and that is where the fallacy begins. Because we have visions of a princess riding with a prince on his white horse in the midst of a perfect union, the "in love" couple is blinded by the idea that if a difference pops up, their love will fix everything. This is what we have been programmed to think as children growing up—that the princess always gets the prince and the prince always gets the princess. Then they live happily ever after. (This notion generally stays with us until we are involved in a close relationship. Then if we go through the trauma of a divorce, a separation, or the breakup of a relationship we may keep the resulting anger and hurt for a long time, since the "tape" of the prince and princess has gone awry.) If we think this out intelligently we can change the tape to say that differences are okay: I can accept myself with peculiar behaviors and I can accept those of my mate, future mate, children, and other people in my life.

Opposites Attract . . .

While attending a seminar on relationships a few years ago at a local church, I learned that opposites attract. The principle is that whatever you might have missing in your own personality, this other person exudes.

You are introduced to someone or meet them at a dance, networking group, or just about anywhere. Your eyes lock with theirs and you become captive and enamored. This is the *one*. You know it this time for sure. You begin telling everyone about this most perfect, most intelligent, cutest person in the world. Recently divorced, you both believed your first marriages to be complete disasters, but now God has smiled on both of you. You just love the fact that the person is organized, time-conscious, punctual, and dresses smartly—certainly a no-nonsense personality.

Now look at the person who might be attracted to this Perfect personality. He or she is one who is gregarious, dresses in lots of color, is nonconservative, and certainly is talkative, bubbly, and happy. You can see where these differences would bring some excitement into the encounter of these two individuals.

You start with the "in love" stage, move on to the friendship ring, then the engagement ring, and finally the wedding ring. Sometime after the honeymoon, you ask the question, Do I really know this person? You soon get irritated with his or her timeliness or the constant nagging about how you're not doing everything to his or her standard of perfection. The other party soon loses patience too with the inevitable lighthearted personality who just wants to have fun. Without understanding or communicating, you quickly recoil and withdraw from each other, causing separation or divorce. You just don't understand how this could have happened again, and having come with some baggage from previous relationships, you still are not equipped to handle the same kind of problems you had with your first relationship or spouse. If we stop here, however, and discuss a way to recognize the different personality types, we can learn how our personalities can mesh. This is precisely the time when real love can blossom and grow.

Harmony through Understanding

The foundation can be set for long-lasting love if two parties can come to understand that their differences are assets. Start by being willing to expand and learn more about your own personality and that of a possible mate. Mother Teresa said, "To keep a lamp burning, we have to keep putting oil in it." We can oil ourselves through education. It will be the springboard to healing. Understanding another's personality as well as our own will do wonders for our personal growth, and will better the quality of our lives. It can be life changing when we learn how to share our lives with others, learn all that we were meant to be, and leave others to become all that they were meant to be. As Charles Swindoll says, "Let God do the shaping."

Learning to master your own personality and to understand others will create a recognizable harmony for you to enjoy. Mark Victor Hansen says, "The Law of Life is the law of growth and we have that capability to grow onward, upward and Godward." Socrates said, "Know yourself." Hippocrates wanted to know his patients better and devised an easy method of identifying their personalities. His method can be used as a simple tool enabling you to identify and explore your strengths and weaknesses and those of the people around you.

As Marita mentioned in chapter 1, Popular Sanguines are always wanting fun. They are great motivators, are creative, love people, and generate excitement. They make great salespeople and storytellers, and have an all-around dramatic and magnetic personality. Taken to the extreme, Popular Sanguines can be loud and too cutesy. They generally are not good listeners, as they are always dominating conversation. They are touchy-feely people wanting affection, attention, approval, and acceptance from all. In most cases the Popular Sanguine is attracted to the Perfect Melancholy, and vice versa.

Perfect Melancholies want perfection at all costs. They thrive on everything being perfect, and if something should go awry they can go into depression or become so stressed it immobilizes them. They love electronic gadgets and can pick things apart and put them back together better than any other personality type. They are immaculate, meticulous dressers, with hair in place, shoes shined, and styles conservative. Highly sensitive, they feel deeply. Although short on showing emotion, the Perfect Melancholy needs emotional support and space. You will never find them without lists, charts, and an organizational DayTimer. Once I understood this, it explained my life.

As a Popular Sanguine, I married a Perfect Melancholy/Powerful Choleric. I can remember when after being married only a few days I decided to cook spaghetti for my new husband. Since we are both Italian, you would think we all cook alike—not so. My family always broke the spaghetti in half; his family put the spaghetti whole into the boiling water. As I proceeded to break the spaghetti in half, I heard a loud voice say, "DON'T DO THAT! You never *break* spaghetti!" As a new wife desiring to please my husband, I was completely crushed by his disapproval. I burst into tears. That incident introduced a theme of perfection versus inadequacy that lasted many years.

It was 1957. I was twenty and came from an era of "you made your bed and now you lie in it," and that's what I did. After masking my Popular Sanguine personality growing up—I had strict parents whose philosophy was "speak only when spoken to"—I grew deeper into masking in my marriage. Subconsciously I became a Peaceful Phlegmatic, not risking input for fear of ridicule and rejection. I didn't know how to communicate my feelings and was not aware of any hope or help for our marriage problems. Old-school mentality and irreconcilable differences ended my marriage of twenty-five years. In retrospect, if I had had the opportunity to learn about the personalities years ago, I would have understood my husband's personality and could have reacted differently.

After my divorce, with the old tape still playing, I proceeded to enter into the same type of relationship with a Perfect Melancholy. I knew when we met that this person was *the one*, the best thing since ice cream. We soon began to date. However, sometime after the first year, I started noticing his idiosyncrasies and he started noticing mine.

His closet was an unbelievable sight. I thought he had a clothes fetish. All of his trousers were neatly in a row: black, blue, gray. His shirts, divided by short and long sleeves, were separated in color rows: short blue, short white, long blue, long white. His shoes were neatly polished in a row. In contrast, my shoes were clumped in a heap on my floor. My dresses, blouses, skirts, and slacks were all mixed together. The rainbow of this jumble was certainly colorful and delightful to me but disturbing to a Perfect Melancholy.

While I was still dating my second Perfect Melancholy, I put on my gold Western hat to wear to a wedding with him. He shrieked, "You're not wearing that hat, are you?" My sweet, smiling reply was, "Of course, honey, it matches my outfit." "I will not go anywhere with you in that hat!" he cried out. I had to remove my hat, which caused me to change my whole outfit; otherwise Mr. Perfect Melancholy would have been moody and sulked. Not knowing the Personalities, I could see I'd made another mistake but wasn't sure how. This relationship also ended.

One story with a happy ending is the tale of my good friends Sadie and Mac. Sadie is a strong Popular Sanguine and is married to Mac, a Perfect Melancholy. He is a master with notes, charts, and lists, and is filled with organizational skills that just leave Sadie smiling. Married twenty-three years, they understand each other's quirks and have accepted their weaknesses as well as their strengths. Sometimes, when she is giggling, he rolls his eyes in utter amazement that she could find something so funny. When she talks too much at a party, he gently tugs at her in order to communicate that it's time to go home. Both Sadie and Mac have placed great value on their marriage and have committed to taking the time, effort, and energy to make it work.

The other opposite attraction of personalities is the Powerful Choleric and the Peaceful Phlegmatic. Powerful Cholerics' strengths are that they need to be in control, are great leaders, take charge before they are asked, are very outspoken, and are decisive. Their weaknesses are that many times they come on too strong, expecting everyone to perform on their level. They can be rude and tactless, and hurt people's feelings at the drop of a hat. Not concerned with frills or fluff, their life is always rushed, and vacations are viewed as a waste of time.

Peaceful Phlegmatics take the middle road in life, dress casually, won't attract attention, are very congenial, and will not put themselves in confrontational situations. Their weaknesses are that they are pro-crastinators, are indecisive, and can easily be pushed around.

In this relationship combination, Peaceful Phlegmatics typically get beaten down by their Powerful Choleric mates. Their loss of self-esteem and confidence happens over a long period of time, often leaving Peaceful Phlegmatics devastated.

Take the example of my friend Cathy who is a Powerful Choleric. She was married to Carl, a Peaceful Phlegmatic. Cathy told him what, where, and how to do everything. When he occasionally voiced his opinion it was shot down and he was told he was wrong. After years of this behavior, Cathy did seek counseling—only to tell the counselor that her husband was lazy, unmotivated, too quiet, unex-citing, and she had had enough. Carl finally fought back to try to save the marriage, but to no avail. Another divorce! Some months later I asked if she regretted not trying harder to repair this marriage, and she simply said, "No, we are too different." Could this marriage have been saved? In my opinion, yes. With willingness, more edu-cation about workable relationships, and recognition that differences are okay, not right or wrong, we could lessen the number of divorces and lonely singles.

While babysitting my newest granddaughter, Isabella, I saw Mr. Rogers on television. This particular morning Mr. Rogers was teach-ing his audience of children about differences. He taught that men, women, and children are different, and that since we are all good human beings, we need to get along together. Being different is per-fectly okay. If we could instill this in our youngsters early enough, we could perhaps prevent some future divorces.

On my recent trip to Europe, I met many singles because they are a focus of my personal ministry. In talking with them about the dif-ferent personalities, I learned that Americans, Europeans, and people from all other parts of the world put a high priority on relationships and face the same personality differences.

In Amsterdam I met a twenty-three-year-old woman who had never been married, and when I explained the personalities, she imme-diately understood the downfall of her recent relationship. She iden-tified herself as a Peaceful Phlegmatic and her fiancé as a bossy Pow-erful Choleric. Their differences pulled them apart. After our chat, she decided to contact him and work on repairing their relationship.

Hooray for her! We all need to recognize that we can agree and disagree without injuring each other. In the May 15, 1995, issue of *Bottom Line,* in Carl Mays's article "Strategy for Winning," he says, "Accept yourself and your worth. You must know yourself and accept yourself for what you are."

Planning for the Future

On the chart on page 41, review the strengths of each personality. Identify the strengths you have in column A and which strengths your ex-spouse had in column B. How many are similar? How many are different? In looking toward the future, what traits would you want in a spouse? Identify those in column C. Now check the weaknesses of both you and your ex-spouse. Can you see where your problems came from? Finally examine the possible weaknesses of your new "Hope." Whatever strengths he or she has will be accompanied by comparative weaknesses. Can you live with these?

Let's take a hard look at ourselves and others to reveal what God has created and look to Him to guide us. Let's resist the urge to judge, manipulate, coerce, and expect the impossible from personalities different from our own. You are a most magnificent, remarkable, splendid being whom God has created, and being single is great—but being in a loving, lasting relationship has the potential of being greater.

For those of you who wish to remain single, perhaps this explanation of the Personalities will give you insight into healthier relationships. For those who wish to share their lives with someone, this simple understanding of the Personalities will enhance your life tenfold. Every day is a new beginning. Let this information be a springboard for healing and love.

I love this quote from Billy Graham: "A keen sense of humor helps us to overlook the unbecoming, understand the unconventional, tolerate the unpleasant, overcome the unexpected and outlast the unbearable."

Divorce and Remarriage

Why Couldn't He Be More like Me?

ROSE SWEET

Rose Sweet has experienced both the bitterness of divorce and the sweetness of a second marriage. As a first wife, second wife, and stepmom she has known the difficult issues divorced and remarried couples face. At her "New Queen" seminars, Rose teaches couples in second marriages how to redefine their roles, rights, and responsibilities through new principles, priorities, and practices, including the Personalities.

Oh No, Not Again!

Sally pulled into her garage, turned off the engine, and told the kids to carry their book bags into the house. When the door to the house slammed shut and she could no longer hear her children, Sally stayed in the driver's seat, staring blankly at the tools, tires, and toys that were hung on the wall in front of her. Within seconds, she let her head drop to the steering wheel as she crumpled into silent sobs.

Alone and crying in her car, Sally dreaded going into the house and facing her husband. She let herself think the thought she'd been avoiding all day: Will this marriage fail too? She and her new husband, Bill, had argued bitterly this morning, their first real fight. Maybe things weren't really as bad as she thought; maybe her hormones were just raging again. Sally wasn't sure.

She was sure of one thing, though, and it had bothered her all day—the pain in the pit of her stomach was very familiar. The trip to the mall, lunch with the girls, and the bounty of department-store bags in her car couldn't erase the memory of this morning's argument. She had never seen Bill act like that before, but it was familiar behavior. Sally hated to even think it might be true, but Bill seemed to be turning out just like her first husband!

Sally had been divorced for almost two years before she began to date Bill. When Sally met Bill, he seemed so different from her first husband, Jerry. Jerry hadn't been a Christian, he'd barely finished high school, and he could never get motivated to do much of anything. Sally had ended up taking care of most of the household, paying the bills, and watching the children, along with her full-time job. Jerry rarely had anything to say, and Sally usually had to call her sister or a friend for any in-depth conversation! When it finally dawned on them that their marriage was in trouble, Jerry had at first resisted going with Sally to counseling. To keep Sally happy, though, he'd finally agreed.

"Jerry," the counselor asked him, "this afternoon you've been hearing your wife express quite a long list of what she needs from you in this marriage. Are you able to give her those things?" Jerry had hesitated only briefly and then announced to his wife and the counselor that he'd been thinking about it for a long time and realized he'd bitten off more than he could chew when he married Sally. He wasn't sure he was really ready for a lifetime commitment to one person or the responsibilities of a family. "I wasn't prepared for marriage. I've tried and tried, but I can never live up to your standards, Sally. I just can't stay in this marriage any longer. I need some space."

Later that week, Jerry had moved in with his brother. It wasn't long before Sally heard the news that Jerry was dating other women, and her hopes of reconciliation began to fade. After a year of Jerry's constant refusal to even discuss their situation, Sally had decided to file for divorce so she could at least start receiving some financial support. All Sally ever wanted was to have a long and happy marriage, a lifetime commitment. She was angry that Jerry's passivity had forced her into initiating the legal proceedings. Sally felt somewhat justified by the fact that by his withdrawal during the marriage, Jerry had really been the first to "divorce" her.

When some of the pain of the divorce had subsided, and Sally had reconciled her own bitterness, she was able to remember why she'd married Jerry in the first place. He'd been a kind and gentle man, patient with the kids, and was a good listener. Jerry had always been supportive of Sally's goals and had gone along with how she thought their home should be run. Although he never seemed to have goals of his own, Jerry had always been obliging when it came to letting Sally call the shots. For Sally, that was important.

Her new husband, Bill, had swept her off her feet just when she thought she'd always remain single. She'd met Bill at her church and had been delighted that he was a Christian, was educated, enjoyed some of the finer things in life, and that he shared her love of all types of music. Careful not to make the same mistake twice, Sally made sure to find out more about Bill before they started dating. He owned his own business, had a college degree, and it didn't hurt that Bill looked like every girl's dream: tall and muscular, with calm, green eyes. Sally remembered thinking how happy she'd been at falling in love again and remembered the hope she had that this time everything would work out. Thank goodness, Bill was nothing like Jerry!

At least that's what Sally had thought until this morning's screaming argument. She and Bill had had some tense moments in their first year of marriage, but it was now almost two years and this was their first "big" fight. Bill had been procrastinating on something Sally had been asking him to do for months, and now Sally was demanding some definite timing from him. As their voices began to rise and the tension flared, Sally was suddenly overwhelmed with a sickening sense of déjà vu. It didn't matter what they were fighting about, Bill was refusing to listen to her. The more she explained and reasoned, the more Bill became silent and withdrawn. He deliberately was not responding and busied himself in some minor distraction. This only made Sally angrier and more desperate to get her point across. The hotter she got, the colder he became. The more she pursued, the more he retreated. Sally realized even her tears of frustration were doing nothing to soften her husband toward her. Finally, Bill said sarcastically before he walked out the door, "Sorry I'm not able to live up to your high standards, but it's the best I can do!" Bill's words struck Sally squarely in her gut: They were the same exact words Jerry had repeatedly used in their arguments!

The queasy feeling that had disappeared for a short while at the mall was back. Sally was sick with confusion and hopelessness. In a few minutes she'd have to wipe away the tears and walk in with her

Personality Problems
in Divorce and Remarriage

Popular Sanguine *The "Fun" Marriage*	Powerful Choleric *The "Active" Marriage*
Divorce • considers divorce when the fun stops • gets depressed, but bounces back quickly • is optimistic about finding someone new • begins dating sooner than other personalities	**Divorce** • considers divorce when unable to control mate • usually initiates the divorce proceedings • tends to rush through the grief process • is optimistic about finding someone new
Remarriage • hasn't spent time identifying root cause of divorce • tends to remarry too quickly • can easily put old marriage behind	**Remarriage** • may not date for a while due to lack of need • decides to work harder at changing new spouse • doesn't waste time thinking about old marriage
Peaceful Phlegmatic *The "Relaxed" Marriage*	Perfect Melancholy *The "Organized" Marriage*
Divorce • thinks about divorce as the easy way out • rarely if ever initiates divorce proceedings • doesn't spend too much time analyzing problems • may not begin dating again for years	**Divorce** • agonizes over and analyzes the failed marriage • goes through extended depression • doubts there's anyone new available • may not date for a long period
Remarriage • continues to look for someone to take care of them • fails to initiate or continue counseling	**Remarriage** • usually has to "settle" for someone less perfect • brings unresolved emotions from old marriage into the new

usual sunny smile so the kids would not suspect anything. *Oh,* she thought, *how I hate this marital merry-go-round!*

Christians Get Married, Christians Get Divorced

While divorce is not in keeping with God's instructions for us, many of us nevertheless find ourselves with failed marriages, myself included. After the initial shock of my divorce, I learned from Scripture that the sacred covenant between a man and woman could sometimes be invalidated depending on their circumstances. Although that didn't ease the pain, I was comforted by the fact that I was nevertheless loved and accepted and that there was still a plan for my life!

When I remarried, I never imagined I might face the same problems I'd had before. The story of Powerful Choleric Sally and Peaceful Phlegmatic Bill is a composite of many second marriages. Like Sally, I'd often compared my new husband to my first one, hoping to justify why I had made a much different, if not wiser, choice this time around. Many remarried women think at first that their new husband is quite different from the last, when most times the two are very much the same! When I learned about personalities, I realized that most of the men to whom I'd been attracted (all the way back to little Ralph in second grade) were a combination of the Perfect Melancholy and Peaceful Phlegmatic personalities, the opposite of my own Powerful Choleric/Popular Sanguine combination. I'd always been drawn to the generous and thoughtful Perfect Melancholies and was comfortable with the yielding, cooperative Peaceful Phlegmatics. I remember little Ralph had never even batted an eye when I turned on the charm and practically ordered him to hand over any goodies in his lunch every day!

Like Sally, I became depressed when I began to see patterns of negative behavior in my new husband that were similar to those of my previous spouse. I was sure it meant this marriage was headed for the same divorce court, and I was terrified of another failed marriage and the emotional upheaval I knew it would bring.

Learning about personalities came in the nick of time for my husband, Tom, and me. We began to understand ourselves and each other better, and we established a new mutual honor and respect for each other's natural strengths. We also learned that the problem isn't our personalities, the problem is our response to those personalities! For those of you who have divorced and remarried, or who have loved ones in this situation, I'd like to offer insight, words of encouragement, and four practical tips to using the knowledge of personalities for healing and hope!

1. Focus on the Problem, Not the Personality

If you have remarried or are dating someone with the same personality as your former spouse, don't panic. It's possible to have a very successful marriage with many different blends of the personalities, as long as both partners are mentally and emotionally mature. Instead of focusing on the personality differences, you can begin to identify the attitudes that result in personality weaknesses.

Most divorced people can readily identify their former mate's weaknesses. The Powerful Choleric wife who leaves her Peaceful Phlegmatic husband may blame the failed marriage on the fact that "he was never highly motivated, rarely talked, and was just happy living on the couch. The kids and I needed more than that." She's definitely describing some typical Peaceful Phlegmatic weaknesses. However, the weakness was not in her husband's actions, which were the symptom. It was rooted in his immature attitude. Peaceful Phlegmatics will always tend to be less motivated in life than Powerful Cholerics, but if they have a mature attitude, they will be more likely to function in their strengths, not their weaknesses. What is maturity? Simply stated, maturity is taking responsibility for our own attitudes and actions, without blaming anyone or anything else for our circumstances. The Powerful Choleric woman who fears marrying another Peaceful Phlegmatic may miss out on a wonderful relationship with a second steady Peaceful Phlegmatic man because she has incorrectly identified outward actions as the problem rather than the inward attitudes. A mature Peaceful Phlegmatic acting on his strengths will behave much differently than an immature Phlegmatic functioning in his weaknesses.

Perfect Melancholy Max divorced Popular Sanguine Susan because he found out she'd been having a series of affairs, a frequent weakness of immature Popular Sanguines in troubled marriages. When he felt ready to date again, he vowed he would only look for the opposite of Susan: a serious, down-to-earth woman who wasn't likely to flirt with other men. He eventually chose his new wife, Perfect Melancholy Mona, but soon discovered himself in another unhappy marriage. Not only did his second marriage lack the joy and sparkle that his former wife had often brought to their relationship, his new wife was even more depressed than he was! After the honeymoon period, Perfect Melancholy Mona constantly pointed out his imperfections, could only live on a very structured schedule, and worried endlessly about everything. This unhappy man realized too late that the "perfect" personality—as far opposite from the first spouse as possible—doesn't guarantee the perfect marriage.

Tip: With new partners, look for attitudes of self-centeredness, failure to take responsibility for themselves, or a tendency to blame outside people and circumstances for their problems. Remember

enhanced personality weaknesses are only the symptom of an immature attitude.

2. Don't Bring the Old Problems into the New Marriage

With any marriage problem, our tendency is to blame others, and we
fail to take our own fearless moral inventory. Serious soul-searching
is a painful process—who wants more pain after a devastating divorce?
Tragically, if divorced or remarried people don't take the time to do
this, though, they are bound to repeat the same mistakes in their new
relationship.

After a divorce, Popular Sanguines just want to have fun again and
frequently fail to dig deeply enough into what really caused their marriages to fail. They tend to remain optimistic that someone new will
bring them happiness, or that new circumstances will fix everything.
They bounce back on their feet and start dating, or tend to remarry
more quickly than Perfect Melancholies or Peaceful Phlegmatics.
Because they failed to identify and eliminate the root of their first set
of problems, they will usually repeat the same mistakes in remarriage.

Like Popular Sanguines, Powerful Cholerics tend to be in a hurry
to end the pain and get on with life; they usually initiate the formal
divorce proceedings. All too quickly they will identify what they think
were the causes of the divorce so they can wrap it up, case closed. Like
Popular Sanguines, they are confident there's someone new out there
for them. They don't waste too much time mourning and frequently
begin to date and/or remarry in a relatively short period of time. They
are determined that if their new mate has "rough edges," they will just
work harder or find some new way of changing them.

After a divorce, Perfect Melancholies may spend months or even
years analyzing and agonizing over the old marriage until they are so
thoroughly confused and depressed they lose hope that anyone will
ever make them happy again. They continue to search for the perfect
mate but have little confidence they'll ever find them. Dating again
comes only after an extended depression. Even in the new marriage,
Perfect Melancholies have a hard time letting go of the past.

Peaceful Phlegmatics, as the passive-aggressive partners, rarely initiate divorce. Although they may frequently, or even constantly, think
about divorce as an easy "out," they fear the emotional, financial, and
physical upheaval that would occur. When they are served with divorce
papers, they rarely contest them, hoping to quickly end the conflict.

They tend to minimize the pain and don't really like to think about the divorce. While they are not too sure, they do hope there's someone new out there who will come and find them and make them happy.

All of the personalities have the same basic human weakness—failure to consider how our own response to the situation may be the real problem, not the other person or the circumstances. If we don't learn to identify and eliminate our individual personality's basic fears and attitudes that keep us in emotional bondage, those of us who are divorced will find ourselves repeating history. If you need to do some soul-searching in this area, see the chart "Personality Problems in Divorce and Remarriage" on page 51 for a helpful summary of the attitudes and tendencies to watch for in your own life. Even if you were in counseling during the marriage or through the divorce period, continued individual counseling to help the maturing and healing process is the best preparation for any future relationship.

Tip: The new marriage can't thrive while the old is still alive. If you're still carrying unresolved bitterness, fear, guilt, or other emotions from the old marriage, including a negative attitude toward certain personalities, you will need to resolve those issues through prayer and counseling before you can be free to build a healthy new marriage.

3. Start Thanking God for Your New Spouse's Personality

I had heard for years about the elusive "meek and quiet spirit" I was supposed to develop as a Christian wife, but as a Powerful Choleric personality I had no idea what it really was or how to get it. I know now! One of the reasons we should honor our spouse is that he or she may be the personal "tool" God is using to build character into us. God blessed me with a stubborn, slow-moving, tortoise-to-my-hare husband, with a personality much like my former spouse's. The choice was simple. I could either end up divorced again or learn new ways to respond to his Peaceful Phlegmatic traits. As a Powerful Choleric, I was always in such a rush to get going places and doing things. Frequently I would react to Tom's much slower pace with great disdain. "Can't you please hurry up!?" I once hollered to him from the car when we were leaving for a weekend vacation. He was still in the house checking the windows and doors and making sure we hadn't forgotten anything.

When he got to the car he asked me, "Do you have the theater tickets?" "Yes, of course I do," I replied rather scornfully. "What about the kids' dress clothes?" "Yes, yes, yes! I have everything. Now let's go!" I practically screamed. "What about your hair dryer?" he asked. I froze.

The last time we'd been out of town and ready to attend a big event, I'd gotten out of the hotel shower with long, wet hair, only to find I'd been in such a rush to pack, I'd forgotten my hair dryer! I panicked and tore around the hotel room searching through our luggage for what I knew was not there. I screamed, yelled, cried, and begged Tom to go find me a hair dryer. He did, thank goodness, but he never wanted to go through another emotional explosion like that again. He had learned from my mistake, but I hadn't. This time the hair dryer was still in my bathroom—again.

I raced in and back out of the house with the hair dryer and sheepishly grinned at Tom while the kids sat in the backseat of the car and watched. "Oh, thank you, thank you, THANK YOU, honey!" I declared as I covered him with kisses. "Please forgive me!" Tom rolled his eyes and the kids giggled. That day I truly began to honor Tom's slow, methodical Peaceful Phlegmatic/Perfect Melancholy pace and to see the weakness of my own Powerful Choleric/Popular Sanguine impatience and forgetfulness.

I changed my attitude toward my husband's "weaknesses" and began to see them as a challenge to help me grow emotionally. God had conveniently used my husband, Tom, as the chisel that chipped away at my self-righteous Powerful Choleric pride.

Tip: Look for strengths in your mate's opposite personality that you could cultivate in your own.

4. Never Compare Your New Husband or Wife to Your Ex-spouse

More often than not, remarried couples will find their new spouse has some, if not all, of the same personality characteristics as their former mates. Not only do opposites attract, they continue to attract! When troubles crop up in the new marriage—and they will because we're all still learning—be careful not to compare your old and new spouses. While their personalities may be similar, their attitudes, moral reference points, and emotional maturity levels may be completely different.

My husband, Tom, was attracted to my Powerful Choleric leadership qualities. When we had our first argument, however, and I responded with my firm, assertive "I'm not gonna take this garbage!" attitude, he was overwhelmed with the old emotions he'd felt when he'd argued with his Powerful Choleric ex-wife. He told me later that he'd feared I would turn out to be just like her, and being Perfect Melancholy, he clung to that depressing thought for days! It wasn't until we talked through his fears that we both realized we'd married personalities similar to our former spouses, but that neither of us was really "like" them. If Tom had continued to carry his conviction that I was just like his ex-wife, he would have set himself up to repeatedly reject me.

Another benefit of studying the personalities is the ability to love those whom we may not feel like loving, especially ex-spouses. Instead of concentrating on their weaknesses, we can shift our focus to an ex-spouse's personality strengths, resulting in a more loving attitude. When my husband and I began to distinguish between personality strengths and the immaturity that causes weaknesses, we were able to look at our former spouses with less negative emotion and more positive objectivity. Despite the disappointment, I could look back and see that my former husband had special strengths in his Peaceful Phlegmatic personality. My husband tries to remember the positive aspects of his ex-wife's Powerful Choleric personality. When God calls us to love all people, even those who have hurt or disappointed us, we can use our knowledge of the personalities to appreciate and honor their strong points.

Tip: "Finally, brothers, whatever is true, whatever is noble, whatever is right, whatever is pure, whatever is lovely, whatever is admirable—if anything is excellent or praiseworthy—think about such things" (Phil. 4:8 NIV).

Christians Get Married, Christians Stay Married!

Let's go back and find out what happened to Sally and Bill. Sally had finally gathered her belongings, gotten out of the car, and started into the house when Bill was already coming toward her. He grabbed her and held her tight. "Honey, I'm so sorry about my attitude this morning. Will you forgive me?" Sally longed to melt into his arms but didn't want to let her guard down too quickly. She pulled away slightly and looked into Bill's eyes. "Do you really think my standards are so high, Bill?"

Bill squeezed her once, took her hand, led her down the hall into their room, and closed the door. He motioned her to sit next to him on the bed, and he continued to hold her hand. "Honey, what I did this morning was let my emotions rule me. Instead of responding to you, I reacted to you. I blamed your standards for my failure. Look,

I take full responsibility for my behavior and I promise I will work hard on my habit of procrastinating. Since we learned the personalities, I realize now it's a way I try to control, and I also know I can stop doing it. It helps me when we work on a schedule, and if you'll work with me and be patient, I know this won't happen again. Okay?"

Sally couldn't believe what she was hearing. Maybe Bill wasn't like her first husband, Jerry, after all. Jerry had rarely taken responsibility for anything and had resisted any problem-solving sessions.

"It will never happen again?" she asked half seriously. Bill laughed. "Okay, maybe it will. How about once a year?" Sally smiled as she closed her eyes and buried her face in her husband's chest. She felt safe and warm in his arms, and she let herself cry a little.

Sally's thoughts drifted slowly as Bill continued to hold her. Suddenly she remembered all the packages in the trunk of the car. "Bill," she said slowly, "after we argued this morning I went to the mall . . ." Her voice trailed off. "Uh oh!" said Bill in mock reproach. "Well, Miss Sanguine, did you get me anything?" Sally smiled and knew there just might be hope for this marriage after all!

Parenting

Understanding Your Children's Personalities

CHERYL KIRKING

Cheryl Kirking draws upon her background in teaching, psychology, public relations, and parenting to present workshops and inspirational Keynotes to church and business groups nationwide. She is a graduate of the University of Wisconsin-Madison and a member of the National Speakers Association. In 1989 she founded her company, Mill Pond Communications, Ltd., which specializes in personal effectiveness workshops and inspirational Keynotes. She enjoys small-town life with her husband and seven-year-old triplets.

Most of us are like snowflakes trying to be like each other, yet knowing full well that no two snowflakes are ever identical. If we were to devote the same amount of energy in trying to discover the true self that lies buried deep within our own nature, we would all work harmoniously with life instead of forever fighting it.

William E. Elliott

Our children are unique individuals, with behaviors that delight us, amaze us, infuriate us, and confound us. Predicting, understanding, and responding effectively to our kids' behavior is often a daunting task.

Have you ever wished for the secret recipe to raising well-behaved, happy children? A foolproof recipe that, if followed precisely, would result in emotionally secure children who would grow up to be well-adjusted, successful adults? Such a recipe unfortunately doesn't exist, but by understanding the personality of your child, you can help your child become the best that he or she can be. And by understanding your own personality, you can better understand the dynamics of your relationship with your child.

Nature and Nurture: Using Both to Your Advantage

The purpose of this chapter is *not* to discount the importance of environmental factors in shaping who we are. Regardless of personality, there are basic environmental circumstances that benefit all children. Loving parents who are committed to raising their children. Parents who share their faith in God. Opportunities for physical, spiritual, emotional, and intellectual growth. Open, honest lines of communication. Lots of praise. Laughter in the home. Nutritious food, plenty of sleep, and exercise. Established family traditions. The opportunity to learn responsible behavior through required household chores. Good books to read. Being shown the joy of serving others. A safe, nonviolent environment in which as much consideration is given to what the children hear and watch as to what foods they eat. All of these factors shape who we are and what we become.

> There is no such thing as an average person. Each one of us is a unique individual. The beauty and the bloom of each human soul is a thing apart—a separate holy miracle under God, never once repeated throughout all the millenniums of time.
>
> Lane Weston

When I teach groups of parents and describe the four basic personality types, I am often asked, "How do we know it isn't just circumstances that cause our children to have different personalities?" and "Doesn't birth order determine a lot?" Environmental factors are often used to explain children's behavior:

"He is such an easy baby because his mother was so happy during her pregnancy."

Popular Sanguine
Parent/Child Relationships

Popular Sanguine Parents with Popular Sanguine Children	Popular Sanguine Parents with Powerful Choleric Children
Strengths: They share a zest for life, sense of humor, and optimism that can bind them together.	**Strengths:** Parents and children share an optimistic outlook, and a Sanguine parent is a good "cheerleader" for a Powerful Choleric child who thrives on praise for achievements.
Pitfalls to Avoid: Since organization is not a strength for either parent or child, parent must make an extra effort to instill a sense of discipline and responsibility. Parent must be careful not to compete for the spotlight with Popular Sanguine children particularly around their friends during the teen years.	**Pitfalls to Avoid:** Those children will fight to get their way, and a Popular Sanguine parent may give in just to avoid conflict. Being a parent means you will not always be liked by your headstrong Powerful Choleric children but if boundaries aren't established and enforced, your roles as parent/child may actually be reversed.
Popular Sanguine Parents with Peaceful Phlegmatic Children	**Popular Sanguine Parents with Perfect Melancholy Children**
Strengths: You share a relaxed attitude and an appreciation of wit.	**Strengths:** You share a creative spirit and artistic nature. Although you are very different in personality, you can share a very complementary relationship if you work at understanding one another.
Pitfalls to Avoid: Don't expect your Phlegmatic children to express excitement over the things you think are fun. Encourage them, but in a loving, quiet way, for they will likely retreat if pushed. You both need to work on organization, so demonstrate self-discipline in your own life.	**Pitfalls to Avoid:** Don't expect these children to be as demonstrative and bubbly as you. Be quiet and take time to listen to them. Offer lots of positive reinforcement for accomplishments. Encourage them in their pursuits, and provide private space and quiet for refueling. Respect their need to be prompt, to stick to routine and schedules.

"He was such a fussy baby because his mother was so tense during her pregnancy."

"She's such a shy child because her older brother is so overbearing."

"She's such an overbearing child because she's had to be in order to be heard in such a big family."

These observations often have great merit. Indeed, we know that birth order within the family and other varying environmental circumstances all play a tremendous role in affecting behavior. Yet long before I had studied personalities, I knew that my three children, each very different from one another, were born with their basic personalities. How can I state this with such certainty? I have fraternal triplets. Three peas in a pod? Hardly. Because they are fraternal, they developed from three separate eggs and genetically are no more alike than any other brothers or sisters.

Although my children share a unique bond as triplets, their personalities are very different and have been since before they were born! Because I was limited to bed rest during most of the pregnancy, I had lots of quiet time to become acquainted with my babies, then known as A, B, and C. Even though they developed in utero under identical circumstances, they reacted quite differently to stimuli such as music, noises, and movement. Soon babies A, B, and C were born, and we named them Bryce, Sarah Jean, and Blake. I didn't know the personality terms back then, but years later, as I reread my diary that journals their development, it is very clear that Bryce has always been a Popular Sanguine, just as Sarah Jean has always been a Powerful Choleric, and Blake a Perfect Melancholy.

A delightful example of their different approaches to the same circumstance occurred when they were four years old and were decorating gingerbread men at Christmastime. Three pairs of little hands were washed. Three little aprons were tied around three excited "bakers." I divided the cookies equally and placed dishes of colored frosting, gumdrops, candy sprinkles, and M&M's on the table. Popular Sanguine Bryce immediately began slathering frosting with wild abandon, cramming as many candies on his cookies as possible, as well as sneaking several into his mouth. This display of uncontrolled behavior was very distressing to Powerful Choleric Sarah Jean, who began wailing, "Mommy, make him stop! He's using all the candy up! Stop him! Make him give me the pink and purple gumdrops! I get the pink and purple gumdrops 'cause I'm the girl!" I quickly intervened, dividing the candies equally. Meanwhile, Blake hadn't begun his decorating. "Blakey, how are you going to decorate your cookies?" I asked. "I need help," he said. "Well, what do you need help with, honey?" "I need help making the face right." In true Perfect Melancholy fashion, Blake wasn't about to jump into this project until he was sure it would turn out "right." "Blake," I said, "just decorate it any way you want to. There's no right or wrong way to decorate cookies!" "No," he pleaded, "you help me get the face right." So I guided his little hand and we carefully made the eyes, nose, mouth, and hair. "Now you decorate the body," I insisted. Soon the body was decorated—with just one yellow M&M "button," perfectly centered. "Don't you want to put anything more on your gingerbread man?" I asked. "No," he answered. "Now wipe my hands,

Powerful Choleric
Parent/Child Relationships

Powerful Choleric Parents with Popular Sanguine Children

Strengths:
You share an optimist outlook and enjoy people, as you are both outgoing. Your Popular Sanguine children will likely follow your leadership if offered plenty of praise.

Pitfalls to Avoid:
Don't expect your Popular Sanguine children to have the same intense drive for accomplishment that you have. Allow plenty of time for fun, or your children may seek to find fun outside the home in unacceptable ways.

Powerful Choleric Parents with Powerful Choleric Children

Strengths:
Both are self-motivated, outgoing people who share a love of accomplishment.

Pitfalls to Avoid:
If your goals and likes are very different, conflict is inevitable unless you appreciate your differences and truly listen to each other's viewpoints. Establish ground rules for dealing with conflict, which may require that you both have a "cooling down period" before any discussion. Teach the art of compromise by developing the ability to do so in yourself.

Powerful Choleric Parents with Peaceful Phlegmatic Children

Strengths:
There can be a natural balance in these relationships, with children willingly following the parents' lead. Your natural ability to organize is a skill that children can model.

Pitfalls to Avoid:
Although it might seem easier, don't do everything for these children or make all their decisions for them. If the Powerful Choleric parent doesn't foster responsibility, children may never "grow up" and assume responsibility for their lives. Use kind words to motivate them. Help them get organized, but don't do the work for them. Create an area in which they can relax and have "down time."

Powerful Choleric Parents with Perfect Melancholy Children

Strengths:
Your ability to motivate others can bring out the best in these creative children if you take a quiet, positive, encouraging approach.

Pitfalls to Avoid:
Don't insist on quick, decisive action from these children. Give them time to mull things over. Allow them to express themselves without being judged, ask for their opinions, and then listen, listen, listen before offering your own advice.

please." "What about the rest of the cookies?" I asked. "Don't you want to decorate the rest?" "Nope," he answered happily, "I like this one. Now I have work to do." And off he scampered to his "work" of building with his Legos. After all, he had created his perfect cookie—to make any more would simply be redundant! "I'll take his candy!" Bryce immediately volunteered. "No! Mommy! Divide them!" Sarah Jean squawked. "And I get all the pink and purple gumdrops!"

My children were born within minutes of each other and for the first five years shared a bedroom, wore each other's clothes, ate the same food, came into contact with the same people, listened to the same stories and music, breathed the same air. Because they happened to be part of a four-year medical study of premature babies, evaluations reveal that they are very similar in their physical and intellectual development. They continue to live by the same basic schedule and are even in the same classroom at school. Yet their personality differences delight and sometimes amaze us! My husband and I have found that, while we strive to be consistent and fair, we are most successful at parenting each child when we take into account his or her natural temperament.

> The deepest principle of human nature is the craving to be appreciated.
>
> William James
>
> Education is the leading of human souls to what is best, and making what is best out of them.
>
> John Ruskin

The purpose of using the Personalities is not to label your children or to place them in an unyielding box without opportunity for growth or change. To simply dismiss a child's bossiness by saying "Well, she was born that way," or to fail to help a child overcome his shyness because "He's just naturally shy" would be doing a tremendous disservice to the child. The purpose of understanding personalities is to help us bring out the best in ourselves and our children, building on the strengths and working on the weaknesses, resulting in a well-rounded individual. For example, by understanding that your Powerful Choleric child has a tendency toward bossiness, you know that it's important to help her develop patience and gentleness toward others. By understanding that your Peaceful Phlegmatic child often feels shy, you can help him develop confidence by providing situations where he can feel safe to express himself and thereby gain self-assurance in a variety of settings. By recognizing your Popular Sanguine's constant need for attention, you can help her find creative outlets for expression, as well as help her learn the importance of being quiet sometimes to listen to others. By realizing that your Perfect Melancholy has a deep need to be understood, you can remember to "draw him out" in order to keep the lines of communication open.

> The greatest of all rules for human happiness is talking things over. Half of the trouble in life comes from not understanding each other, and the other half from not trying to understand.
>
> Source unknown

Peaceful Phlegmatic
Parent/Child Relationships

Peaceful Phlegmatic Parents with Popular Sanguine Children	Peaceful Phlegmatic Parents with Powerful Choleric Children
Strengths:	**Strengths:**
Both possess a good sense of humor and enjoy a good time. Parents are delighted by entertaining children, and children enjoy the appreciation.	These two personalities can complement each other, but only if the naturally reticent parent establishes control from the very beginning, and relinquishes areas of control only when the child has matured to appropriately handle them!
Pitfalls to Avoid:	**Pitfalls to Avoid:**
Since neither possess natural organizational skills, parents must develop these skills first, in order to model them to the children. Develop a set of guidelines for discipline and stick to it, or Popular Sanguine children may charm their way out of deserved consequences and shirk responsibilities.	Establish appropriate guidelines for discipline and stick to them. You'll do your Powerful Choleric children no favors by letting them run the household. Offer them plenty of choices whenever possible so that they are able to exert some control over their lives. Praise them and give them credit for accomplishments.
Peaceful Phlegmatic Parents with Peaceful Phlegmatic Children	**Peaceful Phlegmatic Parents with Perfect Melancholy Children**
Strengths:	**Strengths:**
Peaceful Phlegmatics can enjoy a relaxed, easygoing relationship.	Neither needs a lot of "chatter," so these two personalities can enjoy just "being" in each other's company.
Pitfalls to Avoid:	**Pitfalls to Avoid:**
Avoid falling into a rut of noncommunication. You must put energy into these relationships or they might become nonexistent. Parents must develop self-discipline to model to children. Motivate your children, help them set goals and develop steps to meet them. Praise often.	This combination can result in a severe lack of communication if the naturally quiet parents fail to "draw out" the naturally withdrawn child. The children, feeling misunderstood, may withdraw further, while discouraged parents may give up trying to communicate.

Parents who learn to identify the personalities of family members can begin to recognize some of the roadblocks that may exist in the paths of communication with their children. Following are some examples that participants in personality workshops have shared with me. A mother of four recently told me:

> I now understand my third daughter so much better. My first two girls (Popular Sanguines) tell me everything, yet Janet has always seemed uncommunicative. I now know that she is a Perfect Melancholy, and that I can't expect her to share with me as readily as my first two. . . . I believe this understanding will help us both, especially as she enters her teen years.

Parents of twenty-one- and twenty-four-year-old sons wrote:

Thanks to our new knowledge of the Personalities, my husband and I have been able to "figure out" our older son much better, and have established a rapport with him that was sorely missing. You see, my husband and I are both Perfect Melancholies, as is our second son, Jason. We three like order, consistency and structure. Our first son, John, is the exact opposite, and I realize that for much of his life we tried to "correct" his "flaws." We now see that John is a Popular Sanguine personality. Behaviors in John that we often thought were silly are really what make John fun-loving! We often complained of his lack of focus, always flitting from one thing to another. I now understand that it is this spontaneity that makes him quite appealing to others, and will serve him well as an elementary teacher. Although we see now that we could have handled our relationship with John better, we are encouraged to realize that being raised with a bunch of Perfect Melancholies has probably taught him skills that are naturally "lacking" in his Popular Sanguine personality . . . like organization and perseverance. And we decided the rest of us need to lighten up a bit, and could use a dose of John's zest for life!

Another mother offered a similar account, but with different personalities involved:

I believe that I learned about the Personalities just in time. I'm a combination Powerful Choleric and Popular Sanguine and realize that I have been trying to turn my fifteen-year-old daughter into something she is not. She is a great kid . . . smart, loving, attractive, and respected by her peers. Lately, though, she has been rather sullen, and we've really been at odds a lot. I know that is to be expected in the teen years, but I worry that she is lacking in self-worth, and I think that I may have added to that problem. I always said that I wanted my children to be themselves, and yet I fear that I have let my disappointment show that Ginny hasn't pursued the things I wanted her to, especially in extracurricular school activities. High school for me was a nonstop whirlwind of activity, and I couldn't understand why Ginny didn't want the same. . . . It was hard for me to believe she could be happy without all the activities that made me happy in school. With my newfound understanding of the Personalities, I have come to really appreciate her quiet, relaxed nature and hope that I can let her know that I truly love her sweet personality and wouldn't want her any other way!

Perfect Melancholy
Parent/Child Relationships

Perfect Melancholy Parents with Popular Sanguine Children

Strengths:

Perfect Melancholy parents can help Popular Sanguine children develop needed organizational skills, and children can inject humor and fun into the home.

Pitfalls to Avoid:

Recognize that your personalities are quite opposite! If you don't let these children have fun at home, they'll find it elsewhere. Whereas you are naturally organized, Popular Sanguines are not, so help them learn how to develop discipline without nitpicking or criticizing. Instead, reward jobs well done with praise and opportunities for creative fun. Allow some messiness in a designated area. Encourage participation in the arts, but don't expect your Popular Sanguine children to master each skill perfectly. Allow them to learn just for the joy of learning, not to be perfect.

Perfect Melancholy Parents with Powerful Choleric Children

Strengths:

These two share a natural ability to organize and keep to a schedule.

Pitfalls to Avoid:

You want these children on your side! Powerful Choleric children want to get credit for their hard work, so don't reserve your praise for only those tasks that were done "perfectly," or you'll have an adversarial relationship. Be flexible and offer them choices whenever possible so they feel that they have a sense of control in their lives.

Perfect Melancholy Parents with Peaceful Phlegmatic Children

Strengths:

These two can enjoy sharing a quiet, low-key atmosphere.

Pitfalls to Avoid:

These children need a great deal of encouragement, which Melancholy parents are not used to offering. Remember to take time to guide them while offering lots of praise, encouraging them to reach their potential. Don't let them "slip through the cracks" or be forgotten just because they are quiet.

Perfect Melancholy Parents with Perfect Melancholy Children

Strengths:

Both enjoy order, neatness, sticking to a schedule, and often a deep appreciation of the arts.

Pitfalls to Avoid:

Recognize that just as you have definite ideas about the right way to do things, your children have equally definite ideas, which may or may not coincide with your own. Encourage your children in artistic pursuits of their choosing, not only in the areas in which you want them to excel. Don't take normal rebellion personally, or you both may end up withdrawing from each other. Help these children learn to express feelings by developing your own ability to do so. They have a deep need to be understood.

> It is difficult to make a man miserable while he feels he is worthy of himself and claims kindred to the great God who made him.
>
> Abraham Lincoln

When we help our children recognize and value their unique talents, we are equipping them with confidence and a sense of self-worth. Most parents know that we shouldn't compare our children to one another in a disapproving manner: "Why can't you get good grades like your sister?" or "When are you going to grow up? . . . your brother didn't act like that when he was your age!" The sting of these hurtful remarks often stays with a child forever. Another common tendency is to try to make our kids be just like we are. In her book *Your Personality Tree*, Florence Littauer asks, "Doesn't Proverbs 22:6 tell us 'train up a child in the way he should go' not in the way we dreamed up?" I highly recommend this book, which offers practical suggestions on how to improve family relationships through increased understanding of the personalities. Another excellent book by Florence Littauer, *Raising Christians, Not Just Children,* contains solid parental advice.

> God has put something noble and good into every heart which His hand created.
>
> Mark Twain

It has been fascinating to observe how differently my children play. When they were three years old I gave them a pail full of sidewalk chalk. Popular Sanguine Bryce immediately began to haphazardly fill the entire driveway with color, while Powerful Choleric Sarah Jean was concerned that they each have the same amount of chalk, and hands on hips, expressed loud concern that Bryce was using it all up. Meanwhile, Perfect Melancholy Blake was off to one side, systematically lining up the chalk pieces, organizing them by size and color.

People often ask if our children fight over toys. Although they do sometimes argue over playthings, I have found that their preferences in toys differ as greatly as their personality types. As a Popular Sanguine, Bryce enjoys art supplies, costumes, and music, which encourage him to move, create, and perform. He loves all toys—for a while. Perfect Melancholy Blake, on the other hand, can play with the same toy for hours, even days. Due to his analytical nature, he enjoys puzzles. He particularly enjoys building things, and made Lego creations as a toddler that were better than anything I could make as an adult! Powerful Choleric Sarah Jean likes to do what grown-ups do. Rather than toy pots and pans, she wants to play with the real things. Real jewelry (acquired at garage sales) makes her happier than plastic "kid" jewelry. And she loves to mother her dolls. (I have a hunch she'll soon run the household much more efficiently than I do!) I do feel that it is important to expose children to a variety of play experiences and to encourage them to play with many different types of toys. Yet their preferences in playthings clearly reflect their personality types.

Train up a child in the way he should go—and walk there yourself once in a while.

Josh Billings

Stop, Look, and Listen

One afternoon four-year-old Blake sat on the floor beside me, happily bending pipe cleaners into various creations as I plugged away at the computer. "Look at my invention, Mom!" he'd chirp. "Uh-huh, Blake, that's nice," I would answer. Every minute or so, he'd have a new invention for me to admire. "See, Mommy, this one's a windmill!" "Uh-huh," I'd murmur, "that's nice, honey." He continued to describe all the unique features of his latest invention and finally asked, "Did you hear me, Mom?" "Oh yes, honey," I answered. "I'm listening. . . . sometimes Mommy does two things at once, but I'm listening." "But I want you to listen with your face!" Blake remarked. That got to me . . . bull's-eye . . . straight to the heart! I need to listen with my face, because what he has to say is important.

Attentive listening remains critical to good parent-child relationships as children grow older too. Years ago, when I taught junior and senior high school, one of my eighth-grade girls stopped by my room after school wanting to discuss some very personal matters. "I think perhaps you need to talk to your mother about this," I suggested. "Why?" she asked cynically. "She doesn't know anything about me . . . but she thinks she does."

Many parents are tempted to throw up their hands in despair, declaring, "I've given up trying to understand that kid." Or, equally hurtful, they think they know their children better than they actually do. Children are in a constant state of change. Knowing and using the Personalities as a way to understand our children is a valuable tool, and in addition we need to stop, look, and listen to our kids. We need to find out where they are at today, which is a different place than they were yesterday or will be tomorrow. We need to take time to "listen with our faces."

Home Schooling

What a Difference a Personality Makes

SHERYL ARTHUR-HANEY

Sheryl Arthur-Haney's passion for teaching about personalities stems from the daily changes she witnesses within her own family and professional relationships. Married with two sons, Sheryl and her husband, Lee, share the joys and frustrations of their hectic lives. Sheryl focuses much of her time and effort on home schooling, also serving on the executive board for MADD Texas. Her three-story Greek revival home serves as the site for her engaging defensive driving courses and her highly entertaining Personality Plus classes.

An estimated 1.5 million children are home schooled in the United States, with that number growing each year. I have found that an understanding of the personalities is imperative to educating our children at home. Whether we have elected to home school after months of prayer, after years of consumer dissatisfaction with the prevalent academic standards, or because of the lack of safety in today's schools, an insightful look into each of our children's personality windows will make a day in the life of a home-school parent much easier, hopefully without the need for prescription medication!

Our children are only under our roof for about six thousand days. In that time all that they are and will become stems from our guidance and direction. As the parent you may be best suited to teach your children. Who best understands their academic strengths and weaknesses? Who can inspire them toward independent studies without the bell ringing ordering them to go to another room and subject? Where else in the real world besides school does society have a group of individuals all the same age trying to communicate, gain knowledge, and fight for attention? Meanwhile, each one also feels pressured to act and dress like everyone else in the group.

Institutional public and private schools in the United States are rapidly being scrutinized and coming up woefully short in the global arena of learned and applied knowledge. Home schooling is a fast-growing entity in our society today. Colleges and universities eagerly recruit home school graduates. They are more independent thinkers, are less subject to peer pressure, are self-innovative starters, and not surprisingly, score higher on standard college entrance exams. By college age, most home school students have real jobs, can already balance a checkbook, and have a keen skill or talent they market successfully. At eight years old, one Powerful Choleric home school student began a grocery purchase and delivery industry. Serving an old folks' home with a little red wagon, the student made upward of eighty dollars a month.

Preparation Can Be Your Panacea

Home school lesson plan preparation can stretch into the late hours of the night while the little student darlings are fast asleep. A simple project such as finger painting requires planning, preparation, and cleanup afterward. I find simply lowering the dishwasher door and squirting some nontoxic finger paint on its surface creates a convenient toddler creative playtime. When the finger painting is complete or the tykes have grown weary, just wash them off, shut the dishwasher door, and start it. This method also works in the bathtub and shower. This technique should appeal to any Popular Sanguine or Peaceful Phlegmatic student or mom—especially moms who find planning is not their forte. However, this format will nonplus the Powerful Choleric and Perfect Melancholy toddlers, because they can't control the ends and corners of the paper and have no finished product to display on the refrigerator.

Planning can be much easier than you might think. A little ingenuity, handy bookmarks, audiotapes, cassette players, and workbooks open to pages assigned go a long way toward making the day a success. The personality squares on page 73 offer specific planning helps for moms of each personality. Additionally, they feature tips for teaching children of each personality.

Prescription for Math

Mothers often hack away at teaching how to count by twos, threes, fives, and tens. One day I simply grew weary and put masking tape up the stairs. With a magic marker I stepped off the twos, threes, and so on. Within three weeks the entire family could recite their number lines backward and forward. As a bonus, the stairs were terrifically clean under that tape once it was finally removed!

My second-grade son was continually struggling with the multiplication of nine. I finally broke the secret code of math teachers' ethics and showed him how the sum of nine times any number will equal nine: 9 x 2 is 18 and 1 + 8 = 9; 9 x 3 is 27 and 2 + 7 = 9; 9 x 4 is 36 and 3 + 6 =9; and so on. His smile and the delight in his sparkling Popular Sanguine eyes made that day's home schooling one of the more memorable blessings in my life.

Break a few of the rules and make math fun. Use cards, beans in egg crates, frozen peas in ice cubes, or anything tangible to teach these abstract concepts. One bit of advice is to hide the calculator from even the smallest children. One complete math workbook was mysteriously completed in three days with the use of solar-power calculations and the nimble fingers of a seven-year-old. A calculator may be added to the child's math program after basic math skills have been mastered.

Reading . . . and Are They?

The rapidly changing world of technology, including spellcheck, complete encyclopedias on CD-ROM, books on audiotape, and educational television challenges parents trying to instill a love of reading in their children. I was horrified recently to hear leading scholars question whether reading is all that necessary today.

At times I announce that an oral book report is to be given to a real live audience and the book had better be read and presented in such a way that others can enjoy and learn from it. When it comes to book reports and seeking out an audience, I gather a group of home schoolers and cart them to a nursing home to relate their latest reading adventure. I insist they wear costumes depicting a character in their book.

Homeschooling with the Personalities

Popular Sanguine

Reading

Be sure you promise them they can wear a costume to do their book report. Make sure they read the book in its entirety.

Math

Let them learn multiplication tables by stepping on stairs with the tables written on masking tape. (They will need three weeks.)

Social Studies

Learn the states and capitals by audio memory tapes. Learn the countries by memory tapes and learn to point at them to the rhythm of music.

Penmanship

Tell them funny stories about each cursive letter with which they have problems so it will be fun. These students will have good penmanship because they like what they can do best—entertain.

Powerful Choleric

Reading

Make sure that they read what they are interested in and when reporting on the same that they not be so droll. These children can be talked into reading for money.

Math

Math is the stronghold for these children and they will relish it. Give your student a house to chart or plot by way of a measuring tape and don't be surprised how fast he or she learns the multiplication tables in less than a week.

Social Studies

These children will be able to work up entire units on any subject without provocation. They will read a book, do a complete costume with intricate folding, discuss geometric forms, and tell of all they have learned in a succinct, matter-of-fact way.

Penmanship

These children balk at any cute or clever way to teach cursive. Make sure they have lots of practice tracing over difficult letters and talk to them as if they are already adults. "Trick" these students into teaching younger students how to write in cursive.

Peaceful Phlegmatic

Reading

Books on audiotape and in large print will be best for these children who like everything the easy way. Make sure they follow along with their books as the audiotape "reads" it to them.

Math

Flash cards work best for teaching these children the multiplication tables. Sometimes row memorization will be necessary, but they catch on faster than their Sanguine counterparts. Try some hands-on manipulatives here.

Social Studies

These students will shy away from any book reports done before the public. Oral or written reports will be best in small groups. Audio memory tapes work well, but this group will not want to go the extra step to point out where the capitals and states actually are on the map. They will bluff a lot in this area.

Penmanship

They do not like to have words shoved at them, and any nonsensical examples such as "The quick brown fox . . ." will drive these little ones into an angry mood. The lowercase alphabet is best done by not picking up the pen except to dot and cross after they have written their ABC's with one connecting stroke.

Perfect Melancholy

Reading

These students need lots of attention and love and will be naturally avid readers if you offer attention. Introduce them to reading other than mysteries. They will be passionate readers for life.

Math

These children will easily understand the abstracts of math and can apply them long before their counterparts. Math will not be hard for them, but staying challenged will be tough. Begin learning algebra with these students in fifth grade.

Social Studies

Encouragement is necessary here. These students will like special holidays that are celebrated around the world and will not take kindly to audio memory tapes. They have an uncanny perception and fascination with the obscure and the forbidden. Science will be their forte.

Penmanship

These young people will not have the time nor the fortitude to give good legible handwriting an attempt. They are thinking in higher realms, and only by strong discipline will you be able to produce legible handwriting from them.

They must dress for that particular time period. Just the mention of this activity sends all the little Popular Sanguines scrambling for the most colorful costume to be found in the family closets and then searching for a book depicting their character. This is definitely the cart-before-the-horse sort of thing, which is nothing new to this group. The Perfect Melancholies find this assignment childish yet challenging and usually take three weeks of intensive origami lessons to fold themselves a regulation costume of the Revolutionary War, complete with the three-cornered hat. If you don't watch them, they are more than willing to take up the time teaching the octogenarians in the audience how to fold their own.

A Powerful Choleric in his power and control frame usually picks up a pair of eyeglasses, a briefcase, and a fake mustache on the way out the door, and tells the old folks he is Atticus in *To Kill a Mockingbird* and then bellows, "Any questions?" The Peaceful Phlegmatics usually hang on the outskirts of the group and wait for me to drag them to center stage. Then they beautifully recite their reports, leaving the ending summarized as "You'll have to check this book out of the library and read it yourself to know the ending. I wouldn't want to spoil that for you" (which usually means they have not finished the book). This is also a favorite ruse of the Popular Sanguine. I find that classics in large print for the elderly serve as excellent readers for the elementary school child and his baby-boomer parents whose eyesight is not what it once was.

To encourage readers, I suggest making a really big production each time a family member has a library card bestowed on them. This can make for a new family tradition. Photograph and videotape the momentous occasion of the predictably Perfect Melancholy library lady handing the card to those chubby little hands. Mark it in the baby book. Of course, the children of a Popular Sanguine mother may never have this entry in their baby book since the book was lost long ago. We celebrate by having banana splits for the family supper. This may end up being one of your child's fondest memories and might lead him or her into a lifetime of gratifying reading.

Inspiring the little ones to read is somewhat tricky. I have a Popular Sanguine child who finds the world around her too much fun to just sit. Once during a walk I was struck by the idea to let my little-miss-marvel-at-everything-and-comment-on-it child sit under a lawn sprinkler, hold an umbrella, and read. It was an hour later and many gallons of water down the street when her book was completed. The Perfect Melancholy and Peaceful Phlegmatic children will always enjoy reading because they can hide from people behind the pages of a book. My children know that while they are reading, I very rarely ask them to help with the out-of-routine chores. My Choleric eleven-year-old, however, would rather be building a dirty-laundry delivery system out our third-floor window to the backyard washhouse using pulleys and ropes than be reading. He has an excellent memory, though, and frequently watches the true learning documentary channels and retains a surprising amount of information. The rest of the family reads avidly, and we are sometimes frustrated by his lack of interest in reading.

Spelling . . . a Natural or Not?

Too often spelling is taught by rote memorization. There are basically twenty-nine rules in the English language that will allow even the foreigner to spell most words in our very complicated system. Some rules we have been exposed to for years, such as the "I before E except after C" rule, and others we have not been so fortunate to have had pounded into our memories. For instance, it is a little-known fact that in the English language there are only two words that should ever end in the letter *U: you* and *thou,* both pronouns. However, there are commonly used words derived from French or other languages that do allow *U* as an ending. Examples are impromptu, menu, emu, guru, Honolulu, Zulu, and so on. However, if the elementary speller can recall this rule, "no word should end in *U* in English," then they will know how to spell the following words if dictated in a spelling test: argue, tissue, issue, venue, rue, cue, due, flue, glue, hue, and sue. A simple rule to teach is the "All" rule. If in one syllable, "All" will always have two *L*s, but add another syllable and one of the *L*s is *always* dropped off. Easy enough, but infrequently shared with a listening and retentive mind.

The Perfect Melancholy child will thrive on these seemingly tedious rules. The Powerful Choleric child will actually become empowered by them. Equipped with this new knowledge, they tell total strangers these rules and incorporate them in everyday conversation. The Popular Sanguines and Peaceful Phlegmatics, however, find these rules rather frightening concepts to retain. For them, I switch into the military march mode. I take a rule and set it to a marching cadence. We march around the house until it is learned, making learning more fun. For instance: "Left, left, left, right, left, . . . *Y* not *I* is at the end of a word. That is the number five rule I have heard. Except for *taxi* and *macaroni*—these two Italian words are really easy—left, left, left, right, left," and so on.

Some of the twenty-nine rules are complicated. In our home school we are taking three years to truly learn them. This sometimes requires spending two weeks on one rule. The rule "every syllable must have a vowel" is easy enough and helps to explain words like *little*. My Machiavellian Perfect Melancholy child actually told me he felt he was cheating by using these rules that even adults usually do not know.

Learning the Greek and Latin roots is very important. We listed them on index cards and used them to play bingo. By making it fun, even my friable Peaceful Phlegmatic child was enthused. We played into the wee hours of the morning. The winner amassed piles of shredded wheat as his reward, and I served him his spoils of victory for breakfast. Vocabulary building is the key to enjoyment of reading and comprehension. Through the study of the roots we mastered the meaning of such obscure words as *photochronograph* and *synchronoscope*. The simpering Popular Sanguines may find *micro, macro, hydros,* and *aqua* a little challenging to keep straight, but learning as a family or group is great fun.

Playful Positive Penmanship

A nicely flowing cursive handwriting is very impressive, yet most children find it difficult to learn. Conventional schools tend to teach block printing first, but I have found the musculature in the hands and arms of six- and seven-year-olds is not developed well enough. After weeks of the start and stop movements of block printing, my six-year-old skipped straight into cursive handwriting. I began with the little rhyme, "Pussycat, pussycat where have you been . . ." and all the circles stacked to form a cat. Once this rhyme is recited over and over the child has a cat smiling back at him and a smile on his own face that will light your heart for a week or two. Next we moved to the entire lowercase cursive alphabet by not picking up the pen until reaching *z*. Once my sunny Popular Sanguine had done this about fifteen times he looked up and asked me, "Now when are you going to teach me to read what I've just written?" I was ever so astonished. It never occurred to me I would have to do that. Did anyone teach me how to read cursive? After two weeks he was able to read his handwriting, and I must say it is among the best in the family.

I didn't know at the time why our teacher made us write and type the infernally long and perplexing sentence "The quick brown fox jumps over the lazy dog." I now know it contains all the letters of the alphabet and then some. Don't misunderstand, I still intend to teach my child block printing, because many forms being used today, such as employment applications, require it. And I sure intend for him to be gainfully employed someday. However, it should be understood that a child's interest and pleasure in the flow of cursive is much higher than in the halting motions of basic printing.

The end rolls of paper from a newspaper printing press make a marvelous medium on which to practice large, flowing movements of the arms and hands. With classical music playing in the background, I have the children close their eyes and feel the waves of the music. "Feel the waves of the music. Feel it flow through your ears into your hands and fingers and out onto the paper. Flow and circle, and flow and circle," I whisper. The neighbors think we are a little strange and possibly holdbacks from the sixties, but the penmanship is coming along quite nicely, and the large movements inspire great freedom of expression. Sometimes you can use sidewalk chalk, garden hoses on low pressure, and silly foam in a can to inspire the Peaceful Phlegmatic and the must-have-fun Popular Sanguine children in your family. Just set them up on a hot summer's day, turn them loose on the sidewalk or the driveway, and let them write.

Another way to stimulate their little fingers is an exercise I have added recently—scrunching a complete sheet of newspaper. I hand the child a sheet of newsprint and have him grab it in the middle at the fold. With only one hand, he must pull it into his palm until the edges disappear. At the exercise's completion, he should have a wadded-up piece of paper about the size of a tennis ball. Little hands will be blackened with newsprint and hands and arms will be tired, but it is good exercise. Try it yourself. It is a lot more difficult than you can imagine! This is also a good exercise for piano-playing fingers.

Instead of writing in mundane penmanship practice workbooks, we write letters to policemen, firemen, soldiers, and other civic workers. Half the fun is getting to mail or deliver them. Children will work much harder if they actually have a manuscript that will be significant to them as well as to others, despite its being less than perfect.

History

I have tried to find a meaningful and memorable way to teach history. I have found it best to incorporate vocabulary, art, map skills, math, and music to make the unit an all-encompassing study. The inexperienced home school teacher will purchase prefab units on

Columbus Day, which have a colorful display of the *Niña,* the *Pinta,* and the *Santa Maria,* but leave the teacher with a hollow feeling of incompletion. I try to use books of poetry, speeches of the time, videos, and colorful books. It's fun to make a time line, but ours usually ends up running up on the baseboards and over the transoms and ceiling molding before it even reaches the seventeenth century. One must have foresight for this simple project and use tiny paper people.

The early-reader biographies are a pleasure to read and have read to you. We read Lincoln by candlelight, wrote on the back of a shovel using charcoal, made stovepipe hats out of posterboard, memorized the Gettysburg address (known as the most important speech in American history), and employed math in the kitchen making spoon bread. We learned Civil War songs from tapes and visited a farm where we learned to chop wood. I find this teaching method appeals to all personalities. My Powerful Choleric eleven-year-old created his own self-study of Ben Franklin. With the aid of my father, he arranged a family motorboat outing on an area lake. I was flabbergasted when he pulled a monstrous kite out of a bag, stripped down to his swimsuit, put on a life preserver, jumped overboard, and commanded, "Meet me two hundred yards down the lake!" Once the massive kite was aloft, it dragged him through the water as he reenacted one of Ben Franklin's kite experiments. He also thoroughly cleaned between his toes!

Geography

As a Popular Sanguine teacher and mom, I have only had success in teaching geography by using musical audio memory tapes. The minute we are in the car the tapes go on. In about two weeks we know all the state capitals, countries of South America and Malaysia, and the entire world. Even at the age of three, little ones can learn the countries of Europe and the globe. Finding them on a map presents another aspect of the subject. Studies have shown that the average citizen cannot name even five state capitals. I solved the problem with tear-off disposable paper maps of the United States and the globe with continents divided into countries. I found these at a teaching aids store. Whenever we eat out or have to wait for an appointment or lesson of some sort, or before a concert, we whip out our paper maps and study—making a game out of who can find the capitals. I must say this is great fun and leads to tremendous decibel levels in our voices, so be forewarned. (P.S. Neither Sydney nor Melbourne is the capital of Australia—it's Canberra. This cost me a piece of pie.)

Social Studies

One of the advantages of home schooling is that city council and school board meetings, county and district court proceedings are all under way during school hours. I encourage all to visit the work area of a post office, a local sign and billboard shop, a radio station, and the drafting and engineering area of the highway department. I find that the general public is very positive toward home schoolers, and nearly everyone knows someone who is currently home schooling.

There are numerous free videotapes available from the official travel bureaus of most states and countries. Some commercial travel agencies also loan free videos. The meticulous Perfect Melancholies can order these and keep a record of when they are to be returned. Your Popular Sanguines can politely charm travel agents for posters and booklets depicting out-of-date or expired promotions. Use these in your studies.

Did you know these people were home schooled: Florence Nightingale, Booker T. Washington, Thomas Alva Edison, Andrew Carnegie, Teddy and Franklin Roosevelt, Pearl S. Buck, and Agatha Christie? These are just a few of the more famous home schoolers in history. Home schooling is much easier day in and day out with the help of daily inspirational study. Home schooling offers a healthier and more relaxed atmosphere conducive to real learning than any conventional school. Your children will grow into quite erudite citizens of their communities.

After you analyze your children's personalities, you can enter the home school arena with a minimum of surprises, and your school year should be astonishingly fruitful. Be forewarned, though, when there is any kind of a discipline problem, emotional hurting, or insecurity in any of the family members, home schooling will magnify the situation. You should go into the dedication and disciplinary facets of home schooling prayerfully and thoughtfully. You must consider what truly matters in the life of a child. Children are constantly trying to give meaning to this life and to "make sense" of the world around them. They are more likely to achieve great heights of academic and personal spiritual happiness when they have been hand-fed the three things we *all* strive for: approval, recognition, and significance. What better way to do this than to dedicate our waking hours to teaching our own children?

Attention Deficit Disorder

Disability or Misunderstanding?

JoAnn Hawthorn

JoAnn Hawthorn has been a public educator in the field of speech and language for the past fifteen years. Working in close contact with students who have been labeled or diagnosed with ADHD (Attention Deficit Disorder with Hyperactivity) has given her the unique opportunity to combine her understanding of personalities with the practical experience she has had with children. Presently, JoAnn is conducting workshops in which she shares with educators the relationship between student personalities and their achievement in the classroom.

o teach is to touch a life forever." Those words are etched in an oversized wooden pencil that sits on my bookcase in my classroom. They are the first words that I see in the morning when I enter and the last words that I see in the evening upon leaving. What an opportunity we have as educators to make a difference in so many lives. In order to make this difference, however, we must never stop learning ourselves. We must always keep the door open to new ideas, opinions, and any information that we can use to help the child as a whole. As a speech and language pathologist, I come face-to-face with over forty students per week on an individual basis. This gives me a wonderful opportunity to get to know them as unique individuals, a privilege that most classroom teachers do not always have since their caseloads are high and working with children individually is generally next to impossible.

While attending a Personality Trainer Workshop to become certified in teaching the Personalities, the proverbial "lightbulb" came on. The discussion focused on understanding children's personalities. As I scanned the diagram representing the personalities, their strengths and weaknesses, and the emotional needs that all children have, I saw a startling similarity between the personality weaknesses described and the symptoms that I knew to be representative of a child with attention deficit disorder with hyperactivity (ADHD). (ADHD is now the accepted acronym that covers both attention deficit disorder and attention deficit disorder with hyperactivity.) I had never stopped to think about the symptoms and how similar they were to the weaknesses shown by the individual personalities. Let's take a brief look at how the personalities relate to children and then focus on those characteristics that appear most often and are the most visible to those working with children who have an exceptional need.

Personalities in the Classroom

Popular Sanguines love being the center of attention. They accomplish this through their ability to talk incessantly and monopolize conversations. They are fun-loving, enthusiastic, daring, and quite spontaneous. Florence Littauer's book *Personality Plus* describes Popular Sanguine children as being "energized by people." The weaknesses of this personality are demonstrated through the children's inability to follow through on tasks and to organize their minds or their materials. It is also quite easy to spot the difficulty they have in paying attention for any length of time. They are very easily distracted by any movement or noises. These students are the answer to a teacher's prayer when role playing and spontaneity are required. I am reminded of a student who volunteered to try out a new toy in front of the class. She not only did not know how to use it, she fell down several times in an attempt to accomplish the task, but she wouldn't give up. The class doubled over in laughter—and she loved every minute of it. However, taken out of the limelight and placed back in reality, she didn't know where she was, where she was supposed to be, nor did she really care. She was having too much fun!

The Powerful Choleric is also daring but generally has a goal in mind. This is in contrast to the child who takes the plunge, not knowing what the consequences of their actions might be. Powerful Choleric children are generally self-sufficient and quite competitive. In contrast, these same children can be very manipulative and insistent on getting their own way. They tend to argue, many times for the sake of arguing, and one would think they invented the word *stubborn*. You haven't experienced personalities until you have dealt with a Powerful Choleric kindergartner!

Every teacher has a student who "makes their day." I was blessed with such a Powerful Choleric student several years ago. She took charge of me from the minute I walked into the classroom. She had the day planned from beginning to end—the activities that would be used, the rules that we would follow, and how I should organize my desk and room at the end of the day. She would argue that black was white, and believe me, stubborn took on a whole new meaning for me. In spite of her take-charge attitude, she was a delightful young lady and has always had a special place in my heart.

The strengths of Perfect Melancholy children appear very desirable on the surface. They are deep thinkers and quite intense. They are perfectionists by nature. They not only can be entrusted with duties and responsibilities, but they will do them as they were told. Unfortunately, Perfect Melancholy children who cannot achieve perfection become easily depressed. They will resort to severe mood swings and host some sad pity parties for themselves. They are extremely sensitive and hear only the negatives from others. They will often just "shut down" and do nothing. I have a Perfect Melancholy nephew who, because of his ability to concentrate, tunes others out in order to complete a project. He has gotten into trouble many times for not following the teacher's directions, which he didn't hear. Perfect Melancholy children must complete what they start, and they can't be bothered by teachers telling them to go out for recess or to finish their project later. They need to finish it now!

Now to the Peaceful Phlegmatic—since I am this type, you can understand why I enjoyed the Powerful Choleric child so much—I didn't have to do anything! She took care of me. But the Peaceful Phlegmatic children are delightful too. They cause little or no trouble and will avoid conflict at all costs. They are easily entertained, dependable, agreeable, and win others over by their ability to get along with almost everyone. They follow the rules of the classroom because they are obedient and are afraid of getting in trouble. However, the nursery rhyme describing the little girl with a curl in the middle of her

ADHD Characteristics and the Personalities

Popular Sanguine	Powerful Choleric
Weaknesses	**Weaknesses**
• no follow-through • disorganized • easily distracted • short interest span • forgetful	• manipulative • temper tantrums • constantly going • insistent • stubborn • argumentative
ADHD Characteristics	**ADHD Characteristics**
• doesn't finish tasks • difficulty getting organized • easily distracted • effort fades quickly • excessively forgetful	• demands attention • short fuse • constant motion • difficulty waiting for turn • obstinate • bossy and sassy
Peaceful Phlegmatic	Perfect Melancholy
Weaknesses	**Weaknesses**
• avoids work • lazy • quietly stubborn • retreats to be alone • fearful	• moody • hears negatives • avoids criticism • won't communicate • overly perfectionistic
ADHD Characteristics	**ADHD Characteristics**
• procrastinates excessively • criticized as being lazy • difficulty getting started • keeps to self socially • sensitive to criticism	• depressed mood • can't let go of negative feedback • sensitive to criticism • difficulty expressing emotions • overly perfectionistic and needs extra time to do work

forehead says it all. When Peaceful Phlegmatics are good, they are very, very good, but when they are bad, they are terrible. The weaknesses of the Peaceful Phlegmatics are demonstrated by what appears to be a very lazy and selfish attitude. They avoid work if at all possible and feel that if they procrastinate long enough, someone else will do the job. The Peaceful Phlegmatic can be inappropriately withdrawn and quiet. In fact, the word *comatose* has entered numerous conversations dealing with the Peaceful Phlegmatic personality. Unfortunately, I have a difficult time recognizing Peaceful Phlegmatic students because my attention is always drawn to the children who are causing trouble or making all the noise!

ADHD Characteristics and Personality Weaknesses

As I returned home from the Personality Training Workshop and delved into the information I had on ADHD, I was amazed to find such great similarity between the personality weaknesses and the characteristics present in ADHD children, both those with and those without the hyperactivity. For those with the hyperactivity, some comparisons are:

1. *Inability to attend.* The child has difficulty following directions, completing tasks, and is unable to stay seated for any length of time. The ability to listen and follow directions is sometimes next to impossible. This is similar to the Popular Sanguine child's description—they wiggle, tap pencils, and lose everything.
2. *Impulsiveness.* The child blurts out answers or comments without thinking. Most of the time the responses are not even related to what has been asked. There is an old saying, "Think first, act later." Children with ADHD will do it in reverse. They act with no forethought as to what the consequences might be. For example, rushing out into a busy street to retrieve a ball would be quite common for them. Children with ADHD have a difficult time when things don't go their way, are very intolerant of other people and situations, and use temper tantrums as an attention getter. These traits are also typical of the Powerful Choleric.
3. *Need for attention.* The difference between the normal need for attention and that of a child with ADHD is the child's intense desire for stimulation. These children become the class clowns, monopolize conversations, and thrive on being the center of attention for the sole purpose of keeping active. They accomplish this through falling off their chairs, making strange noises, constantly talking to themselves or others, getting physical with other children, or partaking in some unusual act, such as eating a goldfish or hitting their head against a wall—anything to keep them stimulated and keep attention on them. The Popular Sanguine child may behave this way too.
4. *Inappropriate social skills.* Children with ADHD have a difficult time complying with others. For some it is simply the inability to remember, while for others it becomes a stubborn unwillingness. P. H. Wender, in his book *The Hyperactive Child, Adolescent, and Adult: Attention Deficit Disorder through the Lifespan* (Oxford University Press, 1987), says that "parents often describe their ADHD children as obstinate, disobedient, stubborn, bossy, sassy, and uncaring." These children have a need to be leading—

to be first! It is no coincidence then that these children have a difficult time socially—similar to the Powerful Choleric child.

Perhaps by now you are beginning to see some similarities among the personalities and ADHD when the "H" component is visible. However, before we look at what all this means for us, we must give equal attention to the similar characteristics present when hyperactivity doesn't exist.

1. *Ability to attend.* Children who do not exhibit hyperactivity react quite differently to listening. They do not have a problem with sustained attention, but rather with *how* to attend. Words like *spacey, daydreaming,* and *tired* are often used to describe someone with these tendencies. They are the children who appear to be "lost in a fog." Teachers many times feel like they are interrupting a wonderful nap when they call on these students! These are also traits of the Peaceful Phlegmatic and Perfect Melancholy.

2. *Movement.* Lethargic, sluggish, and hypoactive well describe someone with nonhyper ADHD. These children are not as active and they exhibit a much slower processing time. They will probably be the last ones out the door when the fire alarm goes off, the last to complete their work, answer a question, or get in line. I had a student several years ago who was so hypoactive that he actually slid right off his chair and onto the floor in the middle of our session—as a Peaceful Phlegmatic might do.

3. *Need for attention.* Again, unlike the hyperactive child, this one doesn't seek attention and will generally go unnoticed because of his lack of involvement in the environment. The only time attention is drawn to him is when he is not keeping up with the others or when he fails to respond in class. Because of difficulty with memory recall, he does poorly on comprehension tasks. These are the children who are reprimanded for not paying attention—like the Peaceful Phlegmatic who is so often lost in his own world.

4. *Social skills.* These children tend to withdraw from others. They are shy and are not generally willing to take risks. They act very much in contrast to the children with hyperactivity because they are rarely, if ever, aggressive, and as a result they are not rejected by others. Also in contrast, these children never want to be in charge and therefore do not lay claim to being bossy or con-

trolling. They are accepted by others because they are peaceful and won't talk back—like the Peaceful Phlegmatic and Perfect Melancholy.

So far we have briefly looked at each personality type in relation to the classroom, as well as the characteristics of ADHD with and without hyperactivity. What does all this mean? Where do we go from here, and what can we do with this information? Learning about and understanding personalities has made such an incredible difference in my life that I feel quite strongly about the need for people in education to become informed. Also, having been a part of many Building Consultation Teams (as they are called in my school district) in which classroom teachers, special educators, guidance counselors, school psychologists, and administrators look at possible interventions that will assist students who are struggling, I am aware of the signs and symptoms that educators look for when identifying students who are having difficulties and need more individualized attention.

When I assimilate current research in ADHD and the Personalities, I sense a common thread connecting the two issues. I feel it is worthwhile to look at the similarities and consider some possible interventions that might be tried before referring children for an ADHD diagnosis.

Emotional Needs and Helpful Interventions

Let's consider the emotional needs of the individual personalities so we might better understand how important they are to the performance of the child. Only through educating ourselves are we able to meet these emotional needs.

The emotional needs of Popular Sanguines include an almost desperate desire to receive attention and have constant approval for everything they do. They need to be among people, in the middle of activity, to feel accepted as they are, and to receive affection. They thrive on being told they are cute, adorable, and precious.

Powerful Choleric children need to know they are appreciated for their achievements. They like to be placed in roles of leadership and should be allowed to be in control of something that they can call their own in order to function at their best. They need constant challenges and praise.

In contrast, the Peaceful Phlegmatic personality begs not to be put in leadership positions. However, they can be in charge if forced into it. They function best if they can be placed in quiet and peaceful situations. They do well receiving attention and praise like the Popular Sanguine, and they thrive on positive encouragement from others. Unlike the Popular Sanguine, the Peaceful Phlegmatic will not seek center stage to get the attention, and they will avoid anything that would leave them taking the responsibility or blame.

The emotional needs of the Perfect Melancholy are sensitivity to their inner thoughts and a feeling of support. They like their space and thrive when they can separate themselves from messes, noise, and disorganization, and get their work done correctly. They are easily hurt and want others to appreciate how well they do.

As one can clearly see from the above descriptions, all of the personalities need appreciation and approval. These are emotional needs found in all profiles. However, each personality responds differently when those needs aren't met. For instance, the Popular Sanguine gets easily distracted, tells lies, and can become very forgetful and disorganized. The Powerful Choleric becomes manipulative and argumentative. He can quickly flare up in anger and have temper tantrums. The Peaceful Phlegmatic will withdraw and avoid work. She demonstrates a lazy attitude and can become quietly stubborn. The Perfect Melancholy becomes moody and extremely sensitive. He hears only the negative side of things and will become noncommunicative. Perfect Melancholy people control quietly by their moods or even by the threat of bad moods.

Prior to looking at special programs, medication, or discipline measures for children having difficulties, it makes sense to consider whether or not their emotional needs have been met. For example, being a Peaceful Phlegmatic myself, I can attest to the fact that if someone tried to give me medication for ADHD because I was lazy, avoiding my work, stubborn, and fearful, it would not be very beneficial because "that is who I am." Those are basically the weaknesses of a Peaceful Phlegmatic child. They are not neurological disorders, but rather traits of my personality. Contrast that to the same symptoms appearing in a Powerful Choleric child. In this case medication might be extremely helpful, since the symptoms are not at all consistent with a Powerful Choleric personality.

Perhaps one of the reasons that medication does not work for every child is that in some cases we are trying to fix something that is inherent in a child's personality. I am not implying that ADHD does not exist. I have personally witnessed the changes that have come about in testing children who were diagnosed with ADHD. When they were put on proper medication it, was like night and day. However, now that I understand more about personalities, I question whether or not all the children who appear to have ADHD tendencies are, indeed, in need of medication. Looking at the strengths and weaknesses within each personality and the emotional needs identified with each, we have another avenue to consider before looking for a medical diagnosis. It is a cost-effective approach that can be done right in the classroom with little or no training. One must only be willing to acquaint oneself with the Personalities and observe the child daily from a personality standpoint first. Try to establish what the child's personality is before focusing on his or her "misbehaviors." Once their personality is known, it is quite simple to look at the behaviors in question and plug them in. If the behaviors one sees are indicative of their personality type, it is very likely that some or all of their emotional needs have never been met. As a result, rather than their strengths being the most obvious, the weaknesses surface and cause the parent or teacher to question that behavior. However, if the misbehaviors are not at all those of the child's particular personality type, then consideration of ADHD would appear to be a very valid move.

Some of the interventions that might be tried with the Popular Sanguine child would be to reduce the number of routine and boring activities that are presented. They need to have some degree of spontaneity in their daily lives and should constantly be challenged. Focus on details should be kept to a minimum, and criticism, although it is necessary in all of our lives, should be given—as with all personalities—in a constructive way. Inappropriate behaviors will surface if a Popular Sanguine child is constantly faced with boredom and/or harsh criticism. A perfect opportunity for this child would be to partake in any activity that puts him in front of the class, like role playing, or to allow him to volunteer for various activities that involve being with people. Popular Sanguine children love applause and prizes for achievement. If Popular Sanguines do not have their emotional needs met at home, they will act up in school. Parents should be encouraged to give these children eye-to-eye attention instead of sending them to their rooms to be quiet. Praise everything possible, minimize criticism, and see if the behavior improves.

Powerful Choleric children will become behavior problems when they are bored or have too much free time on their hands. They need to be busy and challenged. Although learning to lose is a very important lesson in all our lives, a Powerful Choleric does not do well when placed in a "no-win" situation or in one where he can't possibly be successful. Cholerics refuse to play games they can't win. A dream come true for Powerful Cholerics would be to keep them busy at all times. Put them in charge of the classroom when you have to leave for a short time, or send them on errands. Let them hand out papers, books, or art materials. Let them feel in charge of something that is important but won't necessarily cause too much upheaval in the classroom. They love to hear "I can't believe you did that so quickly and so well. I can't believe how smart you are!"

When Powerful Cholerics' needs for control, action, praise, and approval aren't met at home, they easily become the bullies on the playground and would rather draw negative attention than none at all. Try to explain to the parent that what this child needs is something to control—his room, the garage, the garden, the dog, and some chores with responsibility—setting the table, emptying the wastebaskets, sorting laundry, along with praise for everything he does. If he feels he's a winner at home, he will become one at school.

Keeping in mind the direct contrast between the Powerful Choleric and the Peaceful Phlegmatic, those aggressive needs of a Choleric child would literally "do in" a Phlegmatic. The quiet Peaceful Phlegmatic child needs to avoid conflict and confrontation. Situations that cause tension should be kept to a minimum. These children are also overwhelmed when faced with too much work, having to make quick decisions, or taking the initiative to do something. They are faithful followers and will do almost anything they are told. To put them in positions of leadership and tremendous responsibility will bring out their weaknesses, and they may tune out whatever is going on. These quiet children frequently fall through the cracks at home and school because they don't demand attention. They tend to feel they are unimportant, and left by themselves, they can easily spend their lives on television. They are not self-motivated, and the parents need to check on their assignments to see that they do them and also that they pass them in. These Phlegmatics are often single-interest children. The parents need to try different subjects, hobbies, or sports to see what jolts them into action. If a Peaceful Phlegmatic child has a Powerful Choleric parent, they need to get attention or praise often—not only when they achieve some great feat. Their emotional need is for a feeling of worth whether or not they are accomplishing something. Without acceptance as they are, they feel insecure and not part of the family. When this happens at home, they carry a defeatist attitude to school and think there is no hope for them. They love to hear, "You are such a special child. I'm so glad you don't give me trouble like some of the others."

Perfect Melancholy children have a deep desire to do everything correctly. They are the teacher's dream, the ones schools are made for, dependable, serious, and conscientious. They sit quietly and keep their desks in order. The only time they become a problem is when they become depressed and seem to withdraw from social relationships. Adults try to "jolly them up," but this approach only shows them how everyone is happy but them, which makes them more depressed. This doesn't mean they need mood elevators, but rather that the source for their low feelings needs to be found. It's always easier to give a pill than to spend time talking to the child, so encourage the parent to start by setting aside an hour for that child alone at least once a week. The parent should ask questions and listen, even if there are silences while the child is thinking. It is also important to resist jumping in or lecturing, and to resist the urge to let the child know a "normal" child would answer more quickly. Because the Perfect Melancholy child is sensitive, they pick up on family problems and internalize negatives and fears. Many times their moods in school are related to problems at home.

Medication or a Modified Approach?

As you can see, there are numerous similarities among the ADHD characteristics and those of the four prsonalities. A look at the chart entitled "ADHD Characteristics and the Personalities" on page 83 shows at a glance what the ADHD characteristics look like when compared to the weaknesses in each personality. If the symptoms of ADHD are the same as those weaknesses exemplified in the personality, perhaps some other interventions should occur before a diagnosis of ADHD is made. If there appears to be little or no connection, then a look at ADHD would probably be advisable.

Because I have raised two children who are now in their twenties and have worked to diagnose problem children for ten years, I have dealt with a wide range of symptoms. As I teach Active Parenting classes and come in contact with numerous parents who relate horror stories about their children and their behaviors, I find that once the parents see their children's personalities and begin to meet their emotional needs, the behaviors begin to change. I do not want to suggest that ADHD does not exist and that it should not be pursued when such tendencies present themselves. Rather, I am suggesting an inexpensive and simple test that could be applied to first rule out the possibility that you might be dealing with a personality weakness rather than a medical problem.

There is not a medication available that will permanently change your child's personality—nothing changes Popular Sanguines into Perfect Melancholies. The only change that comes about within one's personality is when the strengths begin to manifest because the emotional needs are met. And when the weaknesses are recognized, then, and only then, can one begin to work on those weaknesses and turn them into strengths before resorting to drugs to "fix" the child. One school nurse explained that she has so many children on Ritalin that she needs charts to take out the pills at the right time. "I'm not allowed to give them aspirin, but I must see that they get their medication on time," she explains. "They depend on their Ritalin so much that they come in early begging for their next capsule." Is it possible we are producing addictive natures in many children who don't need drugs along with those who do?

Because there is no definitive blood test or X-ray to show who will benefit from Ritalin, the decision is based on behavior, lack of attention, and inability to focus for a concentrated period of time. In a nation fixated on television, with the attention span the length of a commercial, it's difficult to evaluate who really needs the drug. One young working mother called her doctor to ask if he would prescribe medication for her two-year-old "who is driving me crazy jumping all over the place." Obviously the child probably isn't a Peaceful Phlegmatic, but "jumping all over the place" doesn't mean an automatic diagnosis of ADHD either. Could a knowledge of the personalities help this mother?

We as educators have a wonderful opportunity to make it a point to understand the students with whom we work, recognize their weaknesses, and help them develop their strengths. Sometimes this will

result in the help coming from a bottle of Ritalin or Cylert. Sometimes it will come from simply understanding their personalities. We
have to learn to recognize the difference, however. The Serenity Prayer
used in Alcoholics Anonymous is so appropriate for many of the situations we find ourselves in today. It could well be applied in this situation:

> Lord,
> Grant me the courage to change the things I can change,
> the serenity to accept the things I cannot change,
> and the wisdom to know the difference.

Part 2

In the Workplace

Job Preparation

Finding the Right Job
for Your Personality

Mae Harbor

Mae Harbor's invaluable knowledge and training have come from her experience in the approximately thirty jobs she has held. She has worked literally in cotton and bean fields, in management, and is now a successful entrepreneur. She has a B.S. in Human Resource Management and a certificate in Substance Abuse Counseling. Mae uses her education and experience to teach others professional job etiquette and how to successfully prepare for a job based on their personality needs and talents.

nticipation, innovation, and excitement are strong influences as we enter the twenty-first century. The subject of employment is an area of heavy debate. Profuse rhetoric regarding our work arena is abundant, confusing, sometimes even complicated and misleading. Many questions add perplexing variables for us to consider as we ponder our survival in the next century. Human survival has always been partially dependent on the ability to handle our respective job assignments. Job assignments were uncomplicated in the early stages of humankind. We were hunters or gatherers depending mostly on our sex, and the primary goal was to satisfy our three basic needs of attaining food, providing shelter, and maintaining safety for our family group. Many more factors than these affect our job-related decisions today, and yet our primary motivation to work still rests in satisfying our basic needs. The apostle Paul reinforced this motivation when he wrote, "If a man will not work, he shall not eat" (1 Thess. 3:10 NIV). Our perception of work, the state of having a job, has expanded to include more than just the physical task at hand. Our educational requirements, physical attributes, mental stimulation, emotional fulfillment, and personality are among the things we must now consider when preparing for and accepting a job assignment.

Personality

Work is an essential part of our existence, so it is unfortunate that we do not pay more attention to factors that have an impact on job assignment. Factors like the enjoyment, fulfillment, and satisfaction we derive from our jobs play a dominant role in how well we perform on the job. In turn, our performance on the job affects how well we are able to satisfy our basic needs. We relate to these factors through our perception, how *we* see it. It does not really matter how it is, it's how *we* see it that determines our level of job satisfaction. The impact of our personality on how we see reality gets less attention than it deserves.

As we grew up, many of us were responsible for specific chores within our family. Sex determined the assignment of jobs at my house, much like early humankind. My brother had the outside chores, and I was assigned chores inside. I do not consider those chores jobs. I define *job* as a specifically defined task completed for an agreed-upon compensation. It may or may not be a task that is satisfying or desired. But job satisfaction—or the lack thereof—is a major consideration and often the source of many problems when entering the workplace. We do not always prepare or plan for a job. We fall into work through external circumstances and the dictates of others. It did not occur to my parents that I enjoyed outside work and probably would have dispensed my chores more efficiently if assigned to outside chores. The insightful Russian author Maxim Gorki said, "When work is a pleasure, life is a joy! When work is duty, life is slavery."

Getting the Most from Job Preparation

Popular Sanguine *Excitement Out Front*	Powerful Choleric *"Real" Responsibility*
Preparation Pitfalls • impulsive, surface consideration • easily bored and poorly educated • needs a crowd to exercise **Job Goals** • contact with others • adequate pay and periodic new assignments • find an exercise group	**Preparation Pitfalls** • ego-driven selection • overeducation and impatience with lack of activity • needs to physically excel peers **Job Goals** • some measure of responsibility • adequate pay for knowledge • spaced projects • exercise accountability
Peaceful Phlegmatic *Respect*	Perfect Melancholy *Structure and Definition*
Preparation Pitfalls • search for the easy responsibility • tries to make do with poor education • overwhelmed with activity • views exercise as work **Job Goals** • periodic outside contact • pay that meets needs • few stress assignments and exercise that is not regimented	**Preparation Pitfalls** • seeking the perfect field • sense of inadequate education • irritated with sudden changes • needs perfect time/place for exercise **Job Goals** • well-defined job • pay that adds value appreciation • specific, timed projects and exercise periods

Somehow, I think my mother knew she would endure long-term resistance from me regarding my assigned chores. I disliked dishes, sweeping, ironing, and such. I fell into my first job as a result of her attack to overcome my resistance. I was nine or ten years old. I was not part of the decision-making process, nor did I have any say in determining the rate of exchange for my labor. I was hired out by my mother to a "slave master" who had a giant bean field. The plants were easily ten feet tall and each of the fifty rows *had* to be ninety feet long. It sounds ridiculous, but that's the reality of how I remember it. My mother did not know about personalities. She knew about work. She thought a child should learn to work early—particularly her child. Mother observed that I was only happy when I was doing what *I* wanted and referred to me as a hardheaded child. She did not call me a child with a personality. No, I was a hardheaded kid, determined to do what I wanted.

I carried that label until much later in life when I became familiar with the personalities. I recognized in myself the Powerful Choleric and some parts of the Popular Sanguine personalities. It was important that I have some sense of control and fun, and that was nearly impossible at the time—I know because I now realize my mother was a combination of the Perfect Melancholy and the Powerful Choleric. She was an extremely sensitive lady who had an intuitiveness that was uncanny. My devil-may-care behavior and attitude distressed her. She decided early on to change me, make me more responsible and serious about life. Her solution was to put me to work with no planning or job preparation—just the edict that I was going to the bean field. Of course I balked and pouted, but to no avail. My Peaceful Phlegmatic father added his vote to mine, but as you might imagine, we lost! It's no surprise that the slave master found me asleep in the bean field about two hours after the clock started. My acceptance of working with bugs, sun, and dirt had not been a part of the job description.

Have you ever taken a job assignment and found that the job required duties that were not part of the job description? It was not my decision to pick beans and *they could not make me*. My slave master fired me and marched me home, in what she thought would be disgrace, to my mother. She told my mom I was lazy and did not want to work. She was half right: I did not want to work. Daddy and I had won! Mother would not encourage me to work again for five years. Since that first job experience, I have observed that a large percentage of workers slave in a "bean field." We fall into a job or we are given a job assignment without any preparation. It's a bean field! How we respond will define our survival. What will we do?

Bookstores and libraries abound with books on jobs available today and tomorrow and wages projected based on various trends. Volumes describe the legalities governing job searches and interviews. Companies, learning institutions, and governmental agencies teach the employer how to hire employees and the employee how to seek employment. We endure a myriad of tests when going through the job-hunting process. An employer hires based on the needs of the company. Therefore, it behooves us as employees to be cognizant of selecting the job that will satisfy our basic needs. The factors of educational requirements, physical attributes, mental stimulation, and emotional fulfillment are also issues for evaluation. Unfortunately, too many of us are taught early in life to look for a job that pays well monetarily. This is a one-dimensional view. The assumption is that if we get the money, the rest will come or will not matter. But after my first bean-field assignment, I decided I would never go into another bean field I did not like. That decision alone is sometimes not enough to motivate preparation. I did not prepare for a job sufficiently, and as a result I fell into several jobs—all in bean fields I did not like. My work life threatened to end as a job fatality.

To avoid becoming a job fatality you must prepare yourself. It is never too late to start preparing for a change. I followed five fundamentals that helped me prepare. I found that personality, educational requirements, physical attributes, mental stimulation, and emotional fulfillment were all pertinent factors. I first determined which bean field I thought would satisfy me and supply my basic needs. I started my first phase of preparation in high school. I decided I wanted to become a registered nurse. I made that decision because I liked the little caps the nurses wore. I also liked taking care of people. My mother told me nurses were important people and they made *good* money. Her emphasis on the *important people* is what really excited me. What excites you deep within? Any drudging job assignment needs examination as a candidate for replacement—as Henry Ward Beecher said, "Work is not the curse, but drudgery is."

Newsweek magazine interviewed the father of prodigy golfer Tiger Woods. Tiger's father observed that Tiger was a child obsessed with getting low golf scores. He encouraged his nine-year-old son to relax and just enjoy the game. Tiger responded, "That is how I enjoy [the game] and am happy, shooting low numbers." At nine years old this child had a passion, and he is living it today. It provides his basic needs and includes the other factors of proper job preparation. Tiger's obvious intensity and perfection at golf, coupled with his forceful demeanor, indicate that he is a combination of the Perfect Melancholy and Powerful Choleric personalities. His interviews are short and pointed, yet he is intensely sensitive toward his "subjects," the golf admirers. First Timothy 4:14 (NIV) instructs us: "Do not neglect your gift." Have you found a job assignment that enhances your gift? If you are doing something you love, the money will come.

I was sure I would enjoy being a nurse. I visited a counselor at a nursing school, and I am positive she knew nothing about personalities as she counseled with me. I am not sure why she discouraged me from being a nurse, but she did. She suggested I complete nurse's aide training, then if I still wanted to be a registered nurse, I could enroll in nursing school later. I heeded her advice. I was not enthusiastic about being a nurse's aide, but I thought it was necessary to get into nursing. I learned much by completing the training. Be careful whom you ask for advice is the number one lesson I learned. In retrospect, this nurse advisor was a Perfect Melancholy. She talked about the money my parents would have to spend, the grades I had to make, and the rigid schedule required. She did not mention the positive feeling of being a competent nurse. Which personality advised you as you prepared for your ideal job assignment? Who is advising you now?

I graduated with top scores from the nurse's aide program. During my personal interview with the instructor, she, too, passed judgment on me. "You made very good scores," she said, "but when you walk into a room, you make the patient feel that you do not care whether they are sick or not." I was devastated! I had come across as uncaring when I was trying to be cheerful—how did they interpret my advice to "tough it up" as insensitive?

I was unaware that personality played a role in how people interpreted my approach to them. No one offered me counseling on how to adapt my approach to patient care for different personalities. Had my advisors had training about personalities, they would have been able to teach me how to enhance my strengths and transform my weaknesses. That would have helped me effectively change my approach to individuals. Instead, I was judged to have a demeanor that was not suitable for nursing. What a disappointment!

I fell into numerous jobs after that experience. One bean field assignment lasted for more than twenty-five years. It has taken almost thirty-five years to rediscover the bean field that satisfies and fulfills my spirit. Ecclesiastes 2:24 (NIV) gives me encouragement and freedom: "A man can do nothing better than to eat and drink and find satisfaction in his work." Our heavenly Father knows how important it is to our spirits to feel good about what we do to earn our living.

The chart on page 97 shows how each of the four remaining areas of job preparation we are about to cover apply to each of the personalities.

Emotional Fulfillment

As believers, it is to God's glory that we must seek the bean field that will supply our basic needs and also satisfy our need for emotional fulfillment. Now that you know your own personality from reading the opening chapter of this book, from reading the other books on this subject such as *Personality Plus,* or from taking the Personality Profile test, use that knowledge as your guide. You may still do time in an undesired bean field, yet you will be able to avoid a sense of doom. You will not find it necessary to sleep through your job assignment as I first did. An ignorance of our innate personality traits can cause negative reactions. We might engage in destructive behavior such as ignoring the weaknesses of our personality, which can easily lead into abusive activities such as drugs and promiscuity. Strive to recognize and accept your personality strengths in order to grow and mature emotionally. Knowledge of my personality traits helped me become an emotionally secure person with a purpose. I found myself asking the Lord for guidance. I prayed for a conscious awareness to use in conquering my weaknesses. A Powerful Choleric tends to be too indignant to ask for help, and if you are a Perfect Melancholy, you may not ask, because needing help is a sign of imperfection. Similarly, a Peaceful Phlegmatic may not ask for help because they seldom want to make a commitment. The one personality that will ask for help quickly and easily is the Popular Sanguine. In their case help is useless though, because they tend to conveniently forget, thus ignoring the advice!

Serving time in a bean field we do not enjoy will cause us to be emotional dwarfs. Eleanor Roosevelt said, "When you cease to make a contribution, you begin to die." This is true regardless of personality traits. The results tend to be universal. Emotional insecurity and immaturity are sure to be the source of deep anger and resentment. Be sure you examine whether the job you are doing or preparing to do makes you feel uplifted and good about yourself and those around you. Ephesians 4:26–28 (NIV) instructs us: "Do not let the sun go down while you are still angry, and do not give the devil a foothold. He who has been stealing must steal no longer, but must work, doing something useful with his own hands, that he may have something to share with those in need." We must guard against being in or preparing to be in a bean field that generates anger and resentment within us. Acknowledge your personality first. Then determine which field should be the focus of your preparation. Which area of expertise will facilitate your emotional fulfillment?

Popular Sanguines flourish as the recipients of attention and approval. They should prepare for jobs that do not consist of routine drudgery. An appropriate job would have ample opportunity to interact with people, would not require a vast memory for endless details, and would allow the Popular Sanguine to showcase.

If you are a Powerful Choleric, do not prepare for a job requiring you to work closely with sensitive, temperamental people. Stay away from jobs that do not offer change. Seek positions that allow you to advance and be rewarded in proportion to your production. Powerful Cholerics are the most difficult of the personalities to work with when they have become disillusioned and angry on the job. As a Powerful Choleric you may seek to fulfill your emotional need for loyalty, control, and credit for your work through the threat of anger. Few will openly oppose a Powerful Choleric who is in a position of authority. You *will* take control and *run* things. Make sure that as you prepare for work, you are aware of your emotions—let them be the first item you control.

Most personalities relish having a Peaceful Phlegmatic as an employee. As a Peaceful Phlegmatic you must prepare most carefully for a job since you can be stopped cold by lack of respect. Because you are easygoing, you are often perceived as lazy, especially by the goal-oriented Powerful Choleric and the organized Perfect Melancholy. Prepare for your job by learning to recognize the other personalities. Make the effort to evaluate the maturity of others. Are they secure and self-confident enough to interact with your personality? Do you feel they have an arrogant attitude? Depending on how you interpret their attitude, you may find yourself resentful, resistant, or downright stubborn toward your job responsibilities. Too often our attitude toward others is dependent on their attitudes toward us. It is easy for you to procrastinate, so do not seek a job requiring you to constantly meet deadlines. That is stress you do not need. Support and assistant positions may be the ticket for you.

Perfect Melancholies must also choose their profession carefully. Their emotional need for space and silence can be overwhelming. The field of accounting, with its charts, graphs, and checks and balances, offers a system aimed at completion and perfection. Aeronautics also lends itself well to the Perfect Melancholy personality. Though it requires interaction with other people, it has the innate capacity for attention to details. A Perfect Melancholy pilot would not allow a crew to operate in an imperfect manner, nor would such a pilot take shortcuts, give incorrect commands, or ignore safety procedures.

My personal physician operates as a Perfect Melancholy as he goes about his medical responsibilities. Nurses must follow his mandates to the letter, and his associates know he studies everything to the last detail. He functions perfectly in a way that withstands any challenge of imperfection. Make one of your goals when selecting your bean field to select a field that provides sensitivity and support. By selecting a field that causes people to be sensitive to your concerns for them, you'll allow them to support you and help you avoid the overwhelming mood swings that come with imperfections in life.

Educational Requirements

Acknowledging your personality and growing emotionally both come before deciding on your need for education. Education is the third step of job preparation, but it is an absolute must, *no exceptions.* The *Occupational Outlook Handbook* indicates that jobs requiring the most education and training will be the fastest growing and highest paying through the year 2005. Occupations that require a bachelor's degree or above will average 23 percent growth, almost double the 12 percent growth projected for occupations that require less education and training. Whatever your personality or emotional need, a good educational foundation will enhance it properly.

> Blessed is the man who finds wisdom,
>   the man who gains understanding,
> for she is more profitable than silver
>   and yields better returns than gold.
> She is more precious than rubies;
>   nothing you desire can compare with her.
> Long life is in her right hand;
>   in her left hand are riches and honor.
>   Proverbs 3:13–16 (NIV)

Popular Sanguines who have difficulty focusing, Powerful Cholerics who resist instruction, Perfect Melancholies who study to the nth degree for perfection, and Peaceful Phlegmatics who do not want to work that hard all lose much by ignoring their educational needs. None of us will develop our personality strengths without education. I have a friend named Susan whom I admire immensely. She and I were serving time in the same bean field. We often spoke of our unhappiness and job frustrations and what we wished were possible. We each were slowly preparing for our future bean field of choice when Susan made a radical move. She quit her "good" job and returned to school to acquire a second master's degree in an unrelated field. She gave up the security of her present bean field as she made a major career move. Her reason was, "I just was not happy doing what I was doing and I had to make a move. I could not wait and I needed a master's degree to get to where I wanted to be." Since attaining her master's degree, she has taken some part-time jobs to make ends meet. I gave her some unsolicited Powerful Choleric advice, suggesting she seek some related job assignment until a spot in her bean field is available. The financial benefit of her new bean field is promising, and it sounds like fun to me. Susan told me she knew she would not be satisfied doing anything less than her passion, and she was willing to sacrifice while waiting. She knows her personality demands emotional fulfillment from a job, and she has the faith. She has met the educational requirements. There is no doubt in her mind that the position that will provide the fulfillment she needs is just around the corner.

Do not think for a moment that you need a master's degree to achieve fulfillment. Just understand that you *must* have sufficient education, ample experience, or proper training to develop the wisdom that serves as a rung in your ladder to success. Too many people think it is a matter of luck. Luck is preparation meeting opportunity. Too often our education is much influenced by the educational success or failure of our parents or guardians. If our benefactors wanted to be doctors, for example, and did not have the opportunity, they make certain that we go to medical school. This is why many Popular Sanguines become accountants. Pitiful is the Popular Sanguine who could have been educated in the marketing or public relations field, but is sitting in an office crunching numbers all day. Powerful Cholerics, on the other hand, will be compelled to excel at whatever field they choose. It is those around them who will suffer if they operate outside their fields of expertise. Powerful Cholerics must choose a bean field that creates a never-ending realm for learning, some field that requires refresher courses or experiences regular changes.

If you are a Peaceful Phlegmatic, educate yourself in the art of how to make a decision and stick to it, even at the risk of enduring stress. I once worked for a Peaceful Phlegmatic who tried to hold rein on several Popular Sanguines and Powerful Cholerics and one lone Perfect Melancholy. Whoever got to the office first had support. As you can imagine, the office was in a constant state of turmoil amid a few periods of stagnant frustration. As a Peaceful Phlegmatic, *work* to learn your field or job well. You will find that you will receive the respect you need. You are most like a diamond in the rough. The pressure will make your worth shine!

Perfect Melancholy, you will educate and reeducate yourself. That is surely okay. Do not expect any of the other personalities to be as knowledgeable as you. You will be the Perfect expert, remembering all the details and placing value on them. Develop a circle of excellence for yourself so that your education does not take the form of a fishing net. Each new addition to your knowledge bank is a connective thread that catches all the mistakes and imperfections of others. You are ready to snag even the most insignificant mistake committed by another unsuspecting personality. Determine a limit to what you need to know. Even if destiny, fate, or whatever you choose to call it plays a hand, without the proper skills your stint in the bean field will be uncomfortable and unproductive. Additionally, your stipend may not provide for your basic needs.

Mental Stimulation

Sometimes it is difficult to separate the fourth fundamental, mental stimulation, from educational attributes. When I pursued my education, I thought the stimulation was making me mentally sure of myself. Much to my dismay, I found my mind was in turmoil. The facts and figures it contained did not bring a calm assurance to my job search. I hunted for work diligently. I was intelligent and amply trained for the job. Still, I would become so mentally anxious that I did not present myself in a favorable light. I would spout too much nomenclature, or I would ramble incoherently. Consequently, I experienced more anxiety when I did not get the job I sought.

My family physician once referred to me as an intellectual snob. I did not understand what he meant at the time, but I thought about it often. In my analysis, I remembered when I was in the seventh grade. I attended a small school. The seventh grade had more than twice the number of students as the eighth grade. School administrators thought the solution was to allow some of the more advanced seventh graders to graduate into high school with the eighth graders. I was fortunate to be one of those students. Many benefits came with that eighth-grade graduation. Among them was the acknowledgment that I was one of the most intelligent. What a treat for a Powerful Choleric—confirmation that I was intellectually elite! My doctor knew more about me than I did. My intelligence could not fill in for mental security, and education must not be a substitute for mental stimulation.

As we prepare for a job, we acquire whatever education is necessary. We add that knowledge to our mental bank, using it as another rung of the ladder to get us into the bean field of our choice. My personal challenge was that I did not address the anxiety of my mind as commanded by Paul in Philippians 4:6–7 (NIV):

> Do not be anxious about anything, but in everything, by prayer and petition, with thanksgiving, present your requests to God. And the peace of God, which transcends all understanding, will guard your hearts and your minds in Christ Jesus.

That Scripture makes clear that as I seek a job to provide for my needs and fulfillment, I do not need to be anxious. Christ Jesus is my guardian. The bean field I want to be in is already there. I suggest you prepare mentally as I did. Guard the door to your mind and monitor the information you assimilate.

It is so important for each personality to choose a field that provides mental stimulation. Ask yourself these questions: What creates excitement for me when I think or talk about it? Am I getting involved in this field because of someone else? Do I feel accepted, appreciated, respected, or supported? Can I meet my basic needs doing this, or do I need to make adjustments?

Always remember that mental stimulation does not exhaust you or make you tired. Your energy level will replenish itself for present and future challenges. Prayerfully evaluate new information to confirm or change your decisions and choices. You may have to tunnel under or climb over obstacles that disguise the path to your bean field. Read, read, and read more. When the opportunity presents itself, do not rely on luck—be ready. Be mentally prepared.

Physical Attributes

The last fundamental of job preparation is to become physically fit. You have acknowledged your personality traits, met the educational requirements, achieved emotional fulfillment, and developed mental stimulation. These fundamentals relate together best and you function at optimum level when you are physically fit. Being adequately prepared for a job assignment requires that all fundamentals be aligned. Being physically fit is somewhat relative, but even if you are physically challenged, you have a level of physical fitness to attain.

I was mesmerized as I watched the most recent Olympics. Each participant was physically superior to any level of fitness I thought I could attain. I recognized my attitude was one of the barriers to my physical fitness. You or I do not need to run faster or jump higher than everyone else to be physically fit. I am not an Olympian, and I am not willing to make becoming an Olympian my bean field. However, physical training of some kind is as important for you and me as practice is for an Olympian. Physical fitness better prepares us for any job, and we can start getting fit right away. The body's stamina and strength increase as you become physically fit.

Be sure to consult a physician before engaging in physical exercise. When the doctor says you are "exercise ready," focus on some form of exercise and do it consistently. Choose a moderate level of activity to begin. If necessary, buy some instructional books or consult an expert. Refrain from overspending on attire; think twice about joining a health club if you are not currently in an exercise program. If you decide to join a health club immediately, find one that will allow you a trial membership. If you use the membership regularly, the trial is successful, and you can join. If not, you have saved some money.

Whatever you choose, be sure you are consistent. "A small daily task if it be really daily, will beat the labors of a spasmodic Hercules" is the declaration of English novelist Anthony Trollope. What better demonstration of a spasmodic Hercules than the Powerful Choleric who charges into physical exercise trying to do in a few hours what should have been done in a daily lifestyle? The Powerful Choleric must set realistic goals when embarking on an exercise regimen. Enlist the aid of a Peaceful Phlegmatic. I often exercise with a Peaceful Phlegmatic. She holds me back and I pull her forward. She does not allow me to kill myself (or her) and I do not allow her to sit. As a Peaceful Phlegmatic, she realizes she needs prodding because it is so easy for her to procrastinate until tomorrow. Our combination works well. Probably the Popular Sanguine and the Perfect Melancholy would complement each other on the physical improvement trail as well. The Popular Sanguine will help the Perfect Melancholy realize that exercise can be enjoyable and less structured. The Perfect Melancholy will help the Popular Sanguine realize that exercise does have a purpose and that something should be accomplished in addition to having a good time. Getting in shape physically is not the easiest task and is probably the single area where help should be enlisted from other personalities and from a doctor. Supplement your exercise with a doctor's approved diet, 48 to 64 ounces of water daily, vitamin supplements if necessary, and adequate amounts of sleep and relaxation. Additional applications of this topic to your specific personality can be found in chapter 23.

Certainly adherence to the five fundamentals of job preparation is ideal. It is unrealistic to believe that you will fulfill *each* of them *all* the time, at least in the beginning. A Powerful Choleric has the urge to impatiently do everything at once, and I attempted to do just that. Quickly I found the *Revell Bible Dictionary* definition of *hope:* an eager, confident expectation that sustains a person while he or she is waiting patiently for future fulfillment. My hope was a beacon leading me into the bean field of my heart. I was excited, but not prepared for the speaking career I desired. Additional education, improvement of myself through a closer relationship with Christ, and some work to enhance my strengths and strengthen my weakness were details that needed attention. Certification through Florence Littauer's *Personality Plus* program equipped me with essential information I feel compelled to share with others. As I share *Personality Plus,* other doors begin to emerge revealing bean fields that pique my excitement and provide the activity and challenge I need. I find it a daily challenge to help others recognize their personalities and the personalities of others and use that knowledge to enhance their business and personal lives.

Watch for minefields along your way. Impatience held me, the Powerful Choleric, in its grip. The Popular Sanguine is ambushed by the perpetual desire to be adored and accepted. The Peaceful Phlegmatic is buried in the effort to avoid stress and the quest for peace and a feeling of worth. The Perfect Melancholy will always struggle for the elusive state of perfect support. These shortcomings can be a mirage blocking your vision while you try to satisfy your basic needs.

Be aware that if you want to satisfy your basic needs doing something you enjoy, you need to focus on the fundamentals. They work in synchronization to get you the job assignment of your choice. A job that fulfills your needs and that you are happy with precludes many circumstantial and situational problems. French philosopher Voltaire warned that "work spares us from three evils: boredom, vice, and need." As we avoid those pitfalls, Paul tells us in 1 Corinthians 3:8

(NIV), "The man who plants and the man who waters have one purpose, and each will be rewarded according to his own labor." The Scriptures, philosophers, poets, politicians, and other writers all tell us it is important to work at something we enjoy. Our reward will come as a result of making that choice. We often choose based on advice from people who sometimes mean well, but who have no knowledge of the innate gift of our personalities. We must acknowledge personality, emotional fulfillment, educational requirements, mental stimulation, and physical attributes as we prepare for any job.

Properly prepared, we will not fall into a bean field with ten-foot plants and ninety-foot rows like I did at ten years old. In the wrong bean field a Powerful Choleric like me will have no control, a Popular Sanguine will have no fun, a Peaceful Phlegmatic will have too much work, and a Perfect Melancholy will have too many imperfections. How overwhelming this is for us. This knowledge of how personality relates to job choice eliminates the mystery behind many unhappy, nonproductive workers. You and I cannot control the happiness or productivity of others in our bean fields. We must take responsibility for ourselves. "There is only one corner of the universe you can be certain of improving, and that's your own self," said English novelist Aldous Huxley. Improve and prepare yourself!

Education

Managing the Personalities in the Classroom

ARLENE HENDRIKS

Arlene Hendriks has spent many years in various classroom settings during her career as a teacher. She taught a K–8, one-room school for five years, as well as other multigraded classes, which she prefers over single grades. Arlene recently made a career change and currently lives in northern California with her husband, Eddy, where she is now the pastor of the Anderson Valley United Methodist Church in Boonville.

eachers as well as parents often look at the children who seem to be "naturally" well behaved, neat, orderly, and on task as more desirable than those who seem to be scattered, bossy, or unmotivated. If only everyone would just follow directions, sit quietly and do their work, pick up after themselves, and keep their room or desk clean and neat, life would be so much simpler.

In my early years of teaching, I was guilty of this perception as well. My goal was to fit all my students into the mold I had of a "good student." My dream of a well-ordered classroom was one where you could hear a pin drop, where all the students would be quietly on task as I went from desk to desk helping individuals with whatever questions they had. Reality was much different. I often found myself exhausted at the end of the day from trying to make those who didn't follow the script into model students.

I was to find out, however, that the "ideal" class would prove to be much more dull and uninteresting than the one in which each student was taught that he or she has valuable contributions to make, and in which students were allowed to express themselves within the framework of their particular personalities. Affirming each child's strengths gave me a platform from which to work to bring weaknesses into healthy balance so they could become strengths.

When I began to look more carefully at those students who caused me so much trouble, I found that I actually had a vein of pure gold running through my classroom where I thought there was only fool's gold. I took Florence Littauer's statement that "strengths carried to extremes become weaknesses," turned it around, and said, "If strengths carried to extremes become weaknesses, then weaknesses must be strengths that just need some guidance to bring them back into balance so they can operate as they were intended."

This revolutionized my teaching strategy. I looked at my Powerful Choleric students who always wanted to tell everyone else how to do things, but were the least popular kids in class. *Ah*, I thought, *here are my future leaders, if I can figure out how to bring that bossiness into balance.*

I looked at the Popular Sanguines, always talking, ready at the drop of a hat to jump into any conversation, whether it was their business or not. *Ah*, I realized, *here are my discussion starters, those who will argue and contend about ideas, if I can figure out how to keep them from dominating the exchange so no one else has a chance.*

I looked at my Peaceful Phlegmatics who never seemed to get around to finishing assignments, fell asleep during class discussions, and seemed not to have the energy to get started on anything without prodding and pushing. I especially looked at them when I came back into class after stepping into the hall for a moment. While the rest of the class was in chaos, the Peaceful Phlegmatics had stayed calm, not entering into the mischief. *These will be able to exert a great influence over the rest of the group if I can figure out how to tap into their steadiness in constructive ways,* I thought.

Of course I already appreciated my Perfect Melancholies. They were the ones for whom school was designed in the first place. They knew what the assignments were, when they were due, and they put great energy into doing them efficiently and on time. But if my goal was to get all the others to turn into Perfect Melancholies, I could see my teaching career stretching interminably down through the years until the time to retire.

A New Strategy

"Do plants have muscles?" I posed the question to my junior high science class.

"No way!" came the quick response from Brian, my talkative, argumentative, Popular Sanguine pill.

"You seem pretty sure about that," I replied. "How do you know?"

"Everybody knows that. Only animals have muscles."

"How do you know animals have muscles?"

"Because they move."

"So if a plant moved, would you believe it has muscles?"

"Plants don't move."

"Well, then, take a look at this plant. I'm going to set it in the window. You see how its leaves are facing out toward the class. Tomorrow we'll look at it again. In the meantime, let's take a look at today's lesson."

Filing in the next day, my students began to comment on the plant. Its leaves were now all facing the window, having made a 180° turn since the day before. "You turned the plant," Brian accused.

"Can you put a mark on the plant or the container so you could tell if it had been moved?" I asked.

"Sure."

"What does everyone else think?" I queried. "Has anyone else ever seen plants move their leaves to face the sun?"

A few mumbled affirmations, coupled with contemplative expressions, let me know I had engaged the attention of some of the others. The Perfect Melancholies weren't about to commit themselves to the discussion without knowing the "right" answer. Some began to leaf through the textbook, thinking the answer might be found there. The Powerful Cholerics were busy giving Brian instructions about marking the plant so it couldn't be tampered with. The Peaceful Phlegmatics were happy to sit back and watch. After all, as long as my attention was occupied with plants and muscles, they didn't have to work.

With the plant leaves now facing back into the classroom, both the

Treasures out of Trouble

Popular Sanguine

Strengths:
- friendly, funny
- often works quickly
- loves to talk

Trouble Comes When:
- uses humor to gain attention, detracting from class activities or assignments
- finishes work quickly, but does not follow directions and/or work is sloppy
- is out of seat, talking to others instead of listening or working

Treasures Come Forth When You:
- encourage the gift of humor when it lightens a heavy moment or helps the class move in the direction you want to go
- ask for work to be corrected or improved in specific, incremental steps rather than general, nonspecific directions
- plan activities that encourage verbal interaction

Powerful Choleric

Strengths:
- natural leader
- hard worker
- dynamic, active
- usually has right answer

Trouble Comes When:
- leadership style comes across as bossy
- is critical of those who don't work as hard
- manipulates others to get own way
- dominates discussions
- makes decisions for others

Treasures Come Forth When You:
- create opportunities to teach leadership skills
- discuss ways to lead without bossing
- teach leader to use talking skills to draw others out

Peaceful Phlegmatic

Strengths:
- steady
- good listener
- agreeable
- peaceful

Trouble Comes When:
- cannot be moved to work
- prefers listening to participating in class discussions
- allows others to make decisions and formulate opinions
- avoids thinking about controversial issues and ideas
- appeases others to gain peace

Treasures Come Forth When You:
- attempt to motivate out of genuine appreciation of strengths
- express appreciation for calm, steady presence in midst of chaos
- give help in choosing topics on projects assigned
- teach refusal skills to be able to say no peacefully

Perfect Melancholy

Strengths:
- neat
- does work perfectly
- scheduled
- quiet, on task

Trouble Comes When:
- does not cope with schedule changes well
- assignments are not clearly articulated
- does not want to attempt a task (s)he cannot do perfectly
- spends too much time achieving perfection

Treasures Come Forth When You:
- announce schedule changes ahead of time
- give specific assignments with deadlines far enough in advance that no one is rushed
- allow extra time to finish assignments to his or her satisfaction
- gently encourage to make a few mistakes on purpose

container and the plant clearly marked, we once again turned to the lesson for the day.

On day three, as everyone filed into the room, many eyes turned toward the plant. Once again all the leaves faced the window, but this time the markings showed that the plant had not been moved.

"Well, what do you think?" I asked the class.

Brian was the first to venture an opinion. "I still say plants don't have muscles."

"So how did the leaves get turned?" I wondered.

"Maybe they do have muscles," ventured one girl.

"How could you find out if they do?"

We batted that question around for a while, then turned back to the lesson for the day. In the ensuing weeks we periodically came back to the topic. My Perfect Melancholies started to look in encyclopedias and books on plants. The books didn't say anything about muscles in plants.

I brought in a Venus flytrap, a plant that springs shut, trapping even the fast-moving fly between the two halves of the trap. Well, how could the plant move that fast if it didn't have muscles?

Some dissected plants to see if they could find muscles. Some argued fiercely. "My dad says plants don't have muscles." More books were consulted. Some just sat back and watched. When any argument seemed to settle the question, I would bring in another plant or ask another question to keep the ball in the air. By the time we got to the study of plants toward the end of the semester, the interest level had risen considerably.

Discussion Starter

For Brian, the chance to talk and argue legitimately was exactly what he needed. He couldn't believe that I would actually invite him to blurt out the first thing that came to mind, and that he was allowed to challenge me without getting in trouble. But without a Brian in the class, the discussion would not have been the semester-long adventure it turned out to be.

Each time Brian was encouraged and affirmed in his role as discussion starter, I was able to connect with him on a positive note. Our friendly exchanges laid a foundation for me to ask him to attend to task when the format of the class shifted to a more ordered approach. When he blurted out a comment without benefit of information to back it up, I was able to challenge him to think more deeply by either posing a question myself or fielding someone else's response to his comment.

Popular Sanguines often think through ideas by talking about them—often—as Florence says, "with or without information." But what starts as "without information" can be transformed if the Popular Sanguine is not ridiculed or shut up because his way of processing information is noisier than that of the Perfect Melancholy.

In one discussion of different personality styles in a particular college, a comment was made, "We like the Melancholies best, but we're very nice to the Sanguines because they are the ones who make lots of money and come back to give large endowments to the school!"

Why Can't They All Be Perfect Melancholies?

"Today's assignment is on the board," I told my group of fourth graders. "I'd like for you to work on it while the older ones are with me for reading."

"Do we have to read the whole chapter?"

"Do we have to answer all the questions?"

"Do we have to use complete sentences?"

"Do we have to write in cursive?"

"What page are we on?"

"What day is it today?"

After answering all the questions, amid moans and groans, spitwads and paper airplanes, lost books and desks emptied of what seemed to be reams of paper, the class was finally starting to work. Just as I was turning to the other group, now behind schedule because of all the questions, Mary approached me, paper in hand.

"Here's my paper," she informed me. "What should I do now?"

There it was, neatly written in cursive, complete sentences, headed up correctly in all details, and, at a glance, all answers seeming to be correct. "Why can't they all just do their work like Mary does?" I groaned.

If only our classes could be made up of such students, we would get so much more done. If we could even depend on a linear progression toward the goals we defined for them, some detours along the way would be acceptable. But often we feel frustrated because only a few seem to "get it" and move smoothly along the educational path.

Motivationally Challenged Giftedness

Peaceful Phlegmatics can be a challenge to motivate, but I have found they respond well to a mixture of affirmation, challenge, and, at times, direct insistence. Too often children who seem unmotivated are berated as lazy, but since they cause no trouble, they are allowed to slip through the cracks because it is so much work to get them to do anything.

Chuck was one who chronically either turned work in late or didn't turn it in at all. Yet the work he did manage to finish was quite good. I realized that he would be one of my top students if he only made the effort to get all of his work done and in on time. I was having little success with prodding and nagging. After one particularly fine piece of work he turned in late, as usual, I began thinking about "strengths, out of bounds." I realized that I was trying to make Chuck into a self-motivated Perfect Melancholy, rather than looking to his needs as a Peaceful Phlegmatic.

I began to take special time to discuss his work with him, pointing out what a great job he was doing. Often I would spend some time talking with him about a particular assignment to give his creative juices a "jump start." I saw some improvement, but still, as Christmas break approached, Chuck was significantly behind in his work. My working with him had paid dividends, however, in a friendly rapport having been established so that he knew I was not berating him, but encouraging him to demonstrate the talent lying buried inside.

So when I laid down the law that he would be required to stay after school for an hour each day until his work was caught up, although he wasn't happy with it, he knew it would be a time when he would be surrounded with friendly encouragement. After several weeks, he was finally up-to-date, able to go on vacation without a ton of work hanging over his head. I decided this one time to give him full credit for all his work, not docking him for being late.

Awards assembly took place shortly after the students returned from Christmas break. As names were being called for honor roll recipients, Chuck was in the midst of a daydream. He returned to us with a start as his neighbors began to poke him.

"Hey, Chuck, she called your name," they informed him. He lumbered to his feet with a dazed look on his face, then ambled forward.

"Congratulations, Chuck," I told him. "You've made the A-B honor roll."

"I did?" he mumbled in amazement.

Later, on the way back to the room, I caught up with Chuck. "You seemed pretty surprised with your award," I commented.

"I didn't think I would ever make honor roll."

"Well, the only reason you haven't made it before was because you didn't turn in your work. But I could see that you really are a very capable student, and I wanted you to see what you could do when you put forth the effort. Now, next report period, I'd like to see you get on the honor roll again, only this time you go for the gold."

It turned out that the attainable goal of making honor roll was enough to motivate Chuck to get his work done and in on time most of the time. He did make honor roll the rest of that year.

All the problems weren't magically solved, but my willingness to build a relationship from which to "make" him succeed was a powerful help to him to overcome the "I probably wouldn't be successful anyway, so why bother?" inertia and motivate him to work up to his potential.

Calming Center

Leon was another Peaceful Phlegmatic I once had in first grade. I was trying to teach my rambunctious youngsters the rudiments of sitting in a circle for a class discussion. In addition to the usual first-grade wigglers, I had five boys who were like popcorn in their disruptions. I would get one or two of them settled down, only to have the others start a fight, or poke, pinch, or tickle each other, run around the circle, talk and laugh when others were talking—you get the picture. I was working at getting them to evaluate their behavior and make plans to resist the temptation to disrupt the class. One day I had been talking with one of them who had been sent from the circle that day. He had acknowledged that his behavior was unacceptable and that he probably should not sit by any of his friends if he wanted to stay out of trouble. "Who might you sit by?" I asked.

"Leon," he replied, "Leon never gets in trouble and he never talks. If I sit by Leon, I can stay out of trouble."

The next day I approached Leon. "Ricky would like to sit by you today because he's trying to stay out of trouble, and he thinks you would be able to help him because you won't talk to him if he tries to talk to you during the discussion, and since you never get into trouble, he thinks you won't fool around with him. Is it okay if Ricky sits by you?"

"Okay," was Leon's reply.

It wasn't for lack of trying, but Ricky did stay out of trouble the next day. He was absolutely right about Leon. Leon didn't respond to any of Ricky's attempts to "horse around" with him. Since I had affirmed

Leon's value in the class and his role in helping Ricky stay out of trouble, he was even able to "sh-h-h" Ricky, reminding him to keep quiet.

It didn't take long for the other boys to realize that the answer to "What plan can you make to keep out of trouble tomorrow?" was "I'll sit by Leon."

Leon was such a trooper. Each day he stoically endured all the antics that just came naturally to those five boys. Finally, the day I'd been waiting for came. I asked Leon, "Is it okay for Johnny to sit by you today?"

"Nope," he replied, "I don't want none of them guys sitting by me no more." Typically the Peaceful Phlegmatics have apparently endless patience. But when that patience does run out, it's over! Leon had had enough. It was a perfect transition point to lead the boys into thinking about the effect of their actions on others, and to help them make plans to take responsibility for their own behavior. But in the meantime, Leon's steady, unruffled calmness had given them a focal point around which to think about the factors that went into their disruptive behavior.

In fact, within a short time of Leon's declaration, the boys were really responding well to the idea that they could actually control their impulsive behavior. The fact that I let them make plans, even plans I didn't necessarily agree with, and then evaluate how well the plans had worked, let them know I was with them, walking alongside to help them reach their goal of becoming participants in the class rather than disrupters. They became some of my discussion starters as time went on, and they redirected their energy to the topics we were discussing in circle time.

Leon gained some confidence from his valued role of helper too. He had been one who went nearly unnoticed by everyone in the class because he was so quiet and nearly invisible. In his new role, however, I needed to check in with him to see how he was faring with the "fearsome five" rotating around him each circle time. At recess, or during a quiet moment, I would touch base with him.

One of the extras we had in our room was the "reading club," a large decorated refrigerator box. During recess, quiet times when I had other adults in the room, or after school, people could go in the reading club with me to read. No one had to be in it, and everyone could read for as long or as short as they chose, given the time constraints. It was a very popular place, with a waiting list of students who wanted to read extra with me.

Leon had been lagging behind in his reading. When he became the helper for the five boys, and I would take a moment to check in with him as we started our regular reading groups, I noticed he was putting a little more effort into reading. One day I complimented him on his reading: "You know, you really did well today. You might even want to think about joining the reading club."

He made no response at the time, but a few days later he sidled up to me and said, "You know what?"

"What?"

"Iwannabeinthereadingclub," he raced breathlessly through his speech, then ran out the door for recess. I encouraged him to sign his name on the list posted on the clubhouse door when I saw him next. He would often read only a few sentences at first when his turn came, then gradually he increased his time with me. By the end of the year he was well above his grade level in reading.

In Leon's case, his steadiness in the face of chaos was the hook I used to draw him back from his out-of-bounds withdrawal. With Chuck, it was his characteristically fine work, albeit often late, that gave me the opening I needed to begin to relate to him from a stance of approval and encouragement. Later, the relationship we had built provided the foundation from which I could make some gentle but insistent demands.

Often the Peaceful Phlegmatic students need a jump start to begin believing that a goal is attainable and worth the effort to reach. It takes some dedication and faith in the person's inherent worth to observe and study until we find the opening to encourage someone to pursue excellence. Those Peaceful Phlegmatics I have charmed or pressed into success have become some of my best students, even though it seems they often keep on needing an extra dose of encouragement to maintain their energy. It's a small price to pay for the great contributions they make to the class.

Leader or "Boss"?

Amy was a bright first grader who was always trying to boss the others, telling everyone what to do and how to do it. She was quick to remind them that "Teacher said," and quick to point out when someone was breaking the rules. Placed on a team, she knew just who should do what and made no bones about insisting that everyone follow her plans. Needless to say, she was not popular, and if the others had a choice, she was not invited to join their games.

I noticed, however, that her suggestions were most often valid ones, and she really had a natural sense of what was needed for organizing and leading an event. The other kids' response to Amy was, "Just shut up and stop trying to boss us." However, without direction, they often wasted a lot of time arguing about how to do something. Clearly, here was an opportunity to teach some life skills to all of them.

I started by smiling at Amy a lot. Powerful Cholerics often don't get many smiles. I gave her a smile whenever I caught her eye. I smiled when I was disentangling her from a fracas caused by others' reactions to her bossiness. I wanted her to know that I approved of her. Then we talked about how she felt when the others didn't listen to her and why it might be that they didn't. At first she didn't have a clue, but then she began to suggest that she had been "too bossy." Her plan was to stop bossing people.

"But you have such good ideas," I told her, "I would hate for you to lock them all up inside you and never let them out."

"But nobody likes me, and they won't listen to me."

"Well, let's see if we can figure out how to change that around."

We started talking in our class meetings about leadership and what makes a good leader. As we did some class activities where groups of students were led by their peers, we came together afterward to process the activities not only from an academic standpoint, but from the point of what worked and what didn't in getting the task done. Each time the issue of "bossy" came up, we talked about what the person might have done differently. Since the role of leader rotated among all the students, no one was singled out.

In this context we were able to talk about how the group could help someone who was too bossy, how to lead without bossing, and what happened when no one took the lead to get things moving. Of course, in the upper grades the discussions were much more in-depth than in first grade, but I found that even the first graders could begin to distinguish between interfering in something that was not their business and offering leadership when necessary.

As Amy had opportunities to lead legitimately, I was able to help her develop sensitivity to the times when her natural leadership tended toward the out-of-bounds bossiness the others reacted to so fiercely.

The direct instruction I gave the whole class on leadership techniques began to show up in the way they all talked to each other.

One situation that often caused heated confrontations involved the children moving from a general classroom activity to our circle time, when chairs needed to be put in a circle for class discussions. Earlier the class had decided they each would like to have their own personal chair with their name on it. The problem arose when the coveted spots on either side of me or seats near certain friends were taken by those who had grabbed any chair nearby to get in place first.

When the owner of the chair came along to claim his chair, the one sitting on it was not willing to give up the spot he or she had raced to claim in order to go get his or her own chair. The owner of the chair was not willing to allow the other person to sit in his chair, and the one who came promptly when called was not able to convince the owner that the spot remained his or hers while he went for another chair. It wasn't fair that the latecomer got the best seat. Nor was it fair that the one who raced to be there first could grab any handy chair to sit in.

First we tried to solve the problem of one or two people always grabbing the favorite spots. The class decided that those spots must be rotated. So another person had the right to "bump" the one who had the same spot twice in a row.

Then we tackled the problem of the chairs. It wasn't only the coveted spots where chair squabbles came up. Many students didn't care if they had a personal chair and usually grabbed the first one available to get circled up. The Powerful Cholerics, however, were incensed that everyone wasn't obeying the rules.

In the course of the discussion, I was trying to teach the group as a whole to understand and respect the differences between them. Some people didn't care about chairs and just wanted to get there fast so they could choose the spot they wanted. Some wanted to finish something they were working on and didn't care if they got to the circle quickly, but when they got there they wanted their own chair.

In the end, the plan we worked out was that if someone ended up on someone else's chair and that person wanted it back, he or she could bring another chair to trade for his or her own. Before long the bickering and squabbling subsided. I knew the lesson had "taken" when one day I grabbed a nearby chair to sit beside a student's desk to give some help, only to have one of the kids come over dragging my chair from my desk saying, "Excuse me, Mrs. Hendriks. You're sitting in my chair. Could we please trade?" They really started saying that to each other, and the problem of the chairs faded into the woodwork.

One teaching assignment I had was a one-room, K–8, rural public school. I remained there five years, putting into practice many of the principles discussed here. I never did manage to mold the "ideal" class, but by studying my students, watching for their strengths, and encouraging them to develop according to their own natural bent, we created a warm, safe place for the children to blossom and grow.

The freedom to move around, talk quietly when necessary, shift to a different task, or move to a different spot to be able to work better was balanced by understanding and respecting the needs of others. It wasn't perfect, but I found that in that atmosphere many who would not have fared well in traditional classes were able to function out of their strengths, thus adding a richness to the whole class that would have been lost if I had succeeded in producing a group of people who sat at their desks quietly doing their work without talking or moving.

In our classes, in our families, at work, or in social situations, seeing weaknesses as strengths needing to be brought into balance can give us powerful tools with which to offer encouragement, acceptance, and affirmation to those whom many see as afflicted with fatal character flaws, not worth much to society.

In reality, coming to recognize and appreciate the strengths of the various personalities, even when those strengths seem to be weaknesses, opens the door to a new richness in all our relationships. As we practice looking at the weaknesses of others as strengths just a little (or sometimes a lot) out-of-bounds, we find we have new insight into our own weaknesses, as well as powerful tools to nurture and encourage ourselves to bring our weaknesses into balance so our strengths are fully operating.

By the way, are you wondering if plants have muscles? Next time we see each other let's talk about it.

Law Enforcement

Making Order out of Law and Disorder

KURT HARDY

Kurt Hardy has been a deputy sheriff of the Los Angeles County Sheriff's Department for over thirty-two years and is recognized as one of the top instructors at the Sheriff's Training Academy. Kurt and his wife, Patty, were called into prison ministry, and together they have founded H.O.P.E. (Helping Other People Excel) Communications. Kurt and Patty live in Prescott, Arizona, and together they teach seminars on the challenges of marriage, communication skills, and personality differences.

When I was a little boy, my heroes were cowboys like Hopalong Cassidy, Roy Rogers, and the Lone Ranger. They were the defenders of justice, standing between good and evil, wearing a white hat that never got knocked off in a fight.

I remember listening to Red Ryder and Little Beaver on the radio as they rescued Ma Flanders ranch from the wicked Jake Doyle. When the program ended, I put on my oversized cowboy hat, grabbed my trusty cap gun, and rode off through the neighborhood on my bike, searching for Doyle and the rest of his gang.

As I grew up, I knew I wanted to be a lawman. And that's what I've been for the past thirty-two years, as a Los Angeles County sheriff.

123

Officers' Roll Call

Before I understood the personalities, I didn't know why the other officers on the force couldn't do things my way. Why didn't they jump into every crisis or care about the accuracy of their reports? A few of them wrote things down perfectly and worked hard like me, but some had short memories and made up funny stories about all the tragedies they faced in a day. Others felt it was too much work to fill out reports at all—if you were alive at the end of the day, that was all that mattered.

Now that I have studied the personalities and taught these concepts to law enforcement officers, management, and supervisors in the prison systems, I've heard many comment, "Why didn't anyone tell us this before?" Without this information people tend to think of all officers as the same, while those of us in the profession are left wondering why everyone is so different. I'll guarantee that the "if you've seen one, you've seen them all" cliché isn't an accurate picture of your hometown police force. To prove that point, let's look in on a roll call briefing as the officers arrive to start their shift.

The Perfect Melancholies arrive early to check the assignments for the day. The Powerful Cholerics quickly begin to tell others what to do and the Peaceful Phlegmatics pause to wonder what the day will bring. At last, the Popular Sanguines arrive, laughing and telling the latest cop jokes as they enter the room. Although their uniforms aren't crisply pressed like those of the Perfect Melancholies and they don't take the dangers of their career as seriously as the Powerful Cholerics, the Popular Sanguines' charm entices others to like them despite their faults.

I remember when I was a rookie on patrol and my Peaceful Phlegmatic partner suggested we have lunch at the local firehouse, where we could clear our calls, finish writing reports, and rest a while. One of the firemen, known as "Black Bart" for his mischievous Popular Sanguine ways, put black shoe polish around the inside rim of my patrol helmet.

After lunch we went back to patrol, and each time I removed my helmet to take a report, people would snicker and laugh. My partner never said a word. It took me two hours to discover the one-inch black ring all the way around my shiny bald head!

Popular Sanguines should never tease someone with a Powerful Choleric Personality. We don't get mad, we get even.

A few weeks later, while working the late P.M. shift, my partner and I went back to the same firehouse to clear a call. We entered the side door quietly so as not to wake the firemen and discovered they had left on a fire call. I told my partner, "Vengeance is mine, saith me." I poured honey over the inside sheet of "Black Bart's" bed, then saturated his one and only mattress with water. The following night we went back to the fire station to have a cup of coffee and check up on the prank. I saw Bart sitting at the kitchen table. When he saw me he frowned, so I asked him with a big grin, "You don't look well. Did you get a good night's rest?" Being a Popular Sanguine, he said he slept like a baby. His buddies, however, said he yelled for an hour as he hung out his soggy bedding to dry at 3 A.M.

Popular Sanguine cops are often drawn to the Perfect Melancholy personality. It seems they have a secret mission in life to turn wall-flowers into morning glories.

However, the Perfect Melancholy is quite content to sit alone and analyze his fellow officers. He is often awestruck at their surface bab-bling of sexual conquests and foolish dreams of striking it rich in Las Vegas. He is more concerned with the moral injustices of life and find-ing a cure for the ills of humankind. He sees the depth of the situa-tions and is often annoyed that the Popular Sanguine is so superficial.

The Perfect Melancholy is always on time and expects his fellow officers to respond in like manner. Usually his uniform is as impec-cable as his reports, and his spotless locker could serve as a centerfold for *Good Housekeeping*. As a result, what is seen as a serious, no-fun personality is often the butt of station jokes.

While every officer knows when the midnight auto supply shop (auto theft ring) is open in the area or a pharmaceutical salesman (drug dealer) is working the district, "Melancholy Bob" will have all the vital statistics needed to find the bad boys. Often, though, he won't share what he knows because the others have made fun of him and they don't deserve any help.

Almost as easy to spot as the Popular Sanguines are the Powerful Cholerics. The Powerful Cholerics enter the briefing room like angry bulls. They carry every conceivable piece of equipment needed for the shift—a briefcase under one arm, a flashlight under the other, and a patrol box loaded with every type of report form, extra weapons, ammo, and other goodies.

They are the "take charge" type of cops who are prepared for any last-minute assignment changes. They exude confidence and believe there is nothing beyond their capability to handle. And usually their assumptions are correct. However, at times their pride can get them into serious trouble when they attempt to handle dangerous situations by themselves.

Such was the case of a brand-new sergeant we had at our station. He was a strong Powerful Choleric type, constantly jumping calls (arriving at the scene prior to the handling unit and telling both the complaining party and the handling unit what to do—trying to be a hero). Admittedly, he was very good at handling situations, but he was just a little too sure of himself.

One night the sergeant arrived at a disturbing party call involving a crowd of over a hundred people. The sergeant informed us that he would handle the problem, and we were to maintain a low profile outside the location. We knew the type of people inside, and after fifteen minutes we decided we would wander in and have a "look-see" on the sergeant.

What we found was three bikers pressing the sergeant into a corner. When the sergeant saw eight deputies clearing a path to where he was, he let out a sigh of humble relief. From that night on, the sergeant let the deputies handle their calls, and he handled their reports.

The last personality type to enter the briefing room are the slower-moving, calm and collected Peaceful Phlegmatics. They are identified by their appearance—looking like they just got out of bed—often yawning and rubbing their faces, but easy to get along with.

When they sit down in briefing, they don't just sit, they flop down and stretch out completely, folding their hands across their chests. Often they wear sunglasses so no one can tell if they are sleeping or awake—that is until you hear their loud snoring.

Peaceful Phlegmatic officers are well liked by their peers. Even the people they arrest like them because they have no ax to grind, nor do they need to become another "make my day" copper. They always seem to have a willing ear to listen to the concerns and hear the needs of people.

Supervisors often favor working with the Peaceful Phlegmatics due to their flexible personalities. They can be counted on to work any assignment when needed and can be subjected to shift changes on short notice without rebuttal.

Personalities in Law Enforcement and with Troubled Youth

Popular Sanguine	Powerful Choleric
Officer	**Officer**
Best Position: public relations, foot patrol **Best Traits:** dealing with people **By Nature:** expressive, cheerful **Motivated By:** excitement	**Best Position:** special teams, SWAT **Best Traits:** making quick decisions **By Nature:** authoritative, usually right **Motivated By:** danger
Youth and Gangs	**Youth and Gangs**
Reason: needs attention and belonging **Type of Crime:** petty theft, con artist **Nicknames:** The Clown, Happy	**Reason:** chance to be in control **Type of Crime:** daring major hits **Nicknames:** The Duke, Bulldog
Peaceful Phlegmatic	Perfect Melancholy
Officer	**Officer**
Best Position: intervention, mediation (hot line) **Best Traits:** giving calm response **By Nature:** friendly, inoffensive **Motivated By:** fear	**Best Position:** crime lab, statistics, budgets **Best Traits:** dealing with facts, clues **By Nature:** serious, compassionate **Motivated By:** justice
Youth and Gangs	**Youth and Gangs**
Reason: needs acceptance and belonging **Type of Crime:** follows the leader **Nicknames:** The Wimp, Dopey	**Reason:** chance to be understood **Type of Crime:** organized crime plots **Nicknames:** The Brain, Quiet Man

The Peaceful Phlegmatic police officer has many fine qualities, one of which is patience. One day a senior citizen walked into our station complaining that she couldn't find her cat. John, our resident Peaceful Phlegmatic deputy, explained to her at least ten times that the animal shelter was the place to look for her missing kitty. The woman wouldn't leave. Finally, John received permission to take the woman down to the shelter to look for her cat. Only a Peaceful Phlegmatic would take the time to listen and to demonstrate so much patience.

Working Together

Can opposite personalities work together? Absolutely! Social scientists tell us that opposite personalities tend to polarize each other—a phenomenon known as magnetism.

Opposite personalities often work great as a team. I remember working the detective bureau with a brand-new partner who was a combination Popular Sanguine/Powerful Choleric while I was a combination Perfect Melancholy/Powerful Choleric. While we had the Powerful Choleric in common, the other half of our personalities were opposite. One of our assignments was to make a warrant arrest on a man who failed to appear in court on a burglary charge.

Because it was a busy night with several reports to investigate, I thought the best thing would be to get the warrant arrest out of the way so we could return to the field and complete our assignments. Little did I know what was soon to take place.

When we knocked on the door and identified ourselves, a small-framed woman welcomed us and then pointed to a hulk of a man passed out on the couch with a whiskey bottle still in his hand. When we awakened the man and identified ourselves, he rose slowly from the couch like an accordion unfolding. Once on his feet, he towered over us. He was nearly seven feet tall and weighed over 270 pounds. I craned my neck to look at his face (which closely resembled that of a pit bull). His bloodshot eyes narrowed and the nostrils of his *S*-shaped nose started to flare.

I looked at my partner and said, "Maybe we should come back later." That's when the big man blew out a burst of paint-peeling breath and bellowed, "What's ya want?" Wiping the spray from my face, I said with as much confidence as I could muster, "We are here to expedite a court-ordered summons for your incarceration."

The man turned toward my partner (who looked more like a used car salesman than a detective) and asked, "What's he mean?"

My partner said with a big smile, "What he means is, we're going to chauffeur you to the gray-bar hotel for a bed-and-breakfast. We'll pay the taxi fare. The tab is on us."

The man snarled, "You ain't taking me to no jail. You have-ta fight me first." My latent Powerful Choleric personality was immediately challenged as I readied myself for a bad situation, when suddenly my partner stepped between us and began to sob.

"Oh please, sir," my partner cried out, "don't fight us, you don't understand what will happen." The big man took one step back, raised his fists, and with a voice of contempt said, "Yeah, what will happen?" I watched in disbelief as my partner dropped to his knees clasping his hands together and whimpered, "Sir, if we get into a fight my beautiful jacket will get torn, my shirt, pants, and tie will be ruined, and my brand-new two-tone 'Dapper Dan' shoes will get all scuffed up."

The man swayed slightly and then regained his balance. Saliva sprayed from his mouth as he belched, "That's your problem, not mine."

"That's what I'm talking about," my partner said in a high, trembling voice as his lower lip quivered. "My . . . my wife just bought me these brand new clothes yesterday. When she sees them all ripped up, she's going to beat me good. How would you feel if your woman did that for you, and your clothes got torn up?"

The man looked at the little woman standing in the corner with her arms folded, with squinting eyes like piercing bullets. "Hmmm, I see what you mean," the man said as he slowly shook his head from side to side. "But I still ain't going to jail!"

My partner, still on his knees, bowed his head and wailed, "It's over. For the past two months I've been trying to keep my family together. I gave up drinking, and my two little kids aren't afraid to see me come home anymore. And my wife just bought these clothes for me because she said I'm her new man."

I was amazed at the drama that was unfolding before my eyes. My partner should have received an Oscar for his part, especially since he wasn't married.

My partner turned toward the woman with his arms outstretched and cried, "What will I do now? My wife will think I started drinking and got into a bar fight. I'll lose my family and kids." The woman stomped her foot, extended her arm as she waved her finger in the man's face, and said, "Henry, you better do what's right or else."

The man lowered his fists and said, "I don't wanna be no home wrecker and causing problems. I'll go with ya."

My partner jumped to his feet and said, "Hey man, that's great. We'll get some coffee and doughnuts on the way."

We had to use two sets of handcuffs on the man who took up the whole backseat of the radio car. Luckily my partner kept him entertained with jokes all the way to the booking station.

Later I asked my partner where he got the crazy story. He said he had made it up as he went along. That night it was sure good to have a Popular Sanguine partner!

Law and Order on the Big Screen

Even Hollywood classifies its movies by personality types such as Comedy (Sanguine), Action (Choleric), Drama (Melancholy), and Musical (Phlegmatic). Police stories are big business in the movie industry and have always intrigued the public.

When I think of actors who portray police officers with different personality types, I think of the silent-movie era with Charlie Chaplin. He was always the fumbling, bumbling little funny guy with a unique Popular Sanguine personality. Then there was the ominous Sergeant Jack Webb in the *Dragnet* series. He played the Powerful Choleric detective who always wanted the bottom line—"Just the facts, ma'am, . . . just the facts."

And who could forget the great English actor Basil Rathbone as Sherlock Holmes, playing the Perfect Melancholy? Holmes was so detailed in his investigation that he would find a speck of dust as evidence to convict the culprit and then say to his partner, "It's elementary, Watson, simply elementary."

Finally, there is the affable and frumpy-looking Peter Falk as Columbo, the kick-back Peaceful Phlegmatic who always looks like he just slept all night in his raincoat. Columbo was so mundane in his investigations and so nonconfrontational, the unsuspecting bad guy would inadvertently make an incriminating statement whenever Columbo would walk away and then slowly turn, raising one finger in the air, and say, "By the way, there is just one more thing I'd like to know."

These personality types are not just seen on the movie screen—they're seen in every law enforcement agency throughout the country.

Not Suited for the Job

God has given each of us His gifts and talents for our benefit and His glory. However, few of us take the time to find out what our gifts and talents truly are.

Police officers become "cops" for a variety of reasons. The most prevalent is that they want to help people and make the community a safer place in which to live—a place where children can walk to school unmolested and people can return home from work without the fear of being robbed.

Police officers generally start out with stars in their eyes, seeing themselves as knights of old, protecting the innocent and bringing order to a crime-ridden Camelot.

Soon the realities of life hit home and the officers realize their impact against crime is like removing a grain of sand from the beach and running on foot to the Grand Canyon, dropping the sand in, and yelling, "Hold on, I'm going to fill you up!"

It doesn't take long before disillusionment and discouragement result in burnout. Why does it happen? As I have spent the last number of years in officer training, I have found that the burnout results because many people are locked into a job, or even an entire career, that is not suited to their personality type.

The Popular Sanguine officer would be happiest working at the information bureau, public relations, human resources, or cadet recruitment. That's where the Popular Sanguine officer can exercise what he or she does best—talking and meeting new people.

The Powerful Choleric officer would excel in the administrative services and planning division because of his or her innate ability to quickly assess and identify potential problems. He or she possesses the skill of making fast and accurate decisions about the immediate needs of the department. Motivated by potential danger, the Powerful Choleric would also be excellent on special teams like SWAT that need people who are daring and can make quick decisions.

Perfect Melancholy officers would feel very comfortable working in research and planning or the scientific services bureau because they love to research and analyze detailed information. Their determination to gather accurate data and their suspicious nature make them invaluable as investigators. They are naturally analytical and can piece together clues and gather valuable evidence better than others.

Working for employee support services or the hostage negotiation team is the ideal assignment for Peaceful Phlegmatic officers. There they can use their gift of counseling and listening, or meet the needs and concerns of employees wanting direction for their careers. Peaceful Phlegmatics also work well in mediation and crisis intervention because they remain calm and convincing.

Working with the "Bad Guys"

For several years I was in charge of the lock-up for the Juvenile Court of Inglewood, California. Interviewing the youngsters already in trouble and involved in gangs taught me about their personality differences. I learned that whether or not you know about the personalities, you live out whichever is yours. The young people I interviewed labeled each other. Those whom I identified as Popular Sanguines were identified by their peers by such names as Happy, Smiley, or the Clown. The tired, slouching Peaceful Phlegmatics earned nicknames such as Dopey, Sleepy, or Wimpy. Perfect Melancholies, who were often withdrawn, were known as Quiet Man, the Brain, or the Doctor. And the most respected individuals in the gangs—brash, bold, and brave Powerful Cholerics—were recognized with titles such as the Duke, Sharkey, or Bull Dog.

In general, the gang members are all full of anger and want to take it out on the government, the law, and people who have possessions such as cars, jewelry, or drugs. Because of their insecurities, these kids see nothing wrong with robbing, beating, or even killing one of their perceived enemies. They have suffered some type of deprivation (physical, economic, emotional) in their childhood, and they are out seeking revenge against society.

As I talked with them, I found the average gang member doesn't expect to live past the age of twenty-one, and they accept as a fact of life that they will spend some time in prison. Many of them are misfits by their teenage years and have no respect for themselves or others. The Powerful Cholerics have misplaced leadership abilities and are motivated by anger. They are impulsive, reactive, and controlling. They picture themselves as future Mafia dons and create a godlike aura around themselves. The Peaceful Phlegmatics, who have never fit in anywhere in life and are too scared to take on the world themselves, are drawn to gangs first for protection and then for the feeling of belonging to something bigger than themselves. They feel their families never accepted them, their classmates made fun of them, and finally here is a daring, exciting group that welcomes them. They are desperate for recognition and will do whatever they are told to please their boss, becoming stoolies. The Perfect Melancholies by their late teens have stored up deep resentment for an unfair justice system and have plotted how to get revenge. Few will do it on their own, so the gang gives them an environment in which to develop their plots and to execute them. Because they aren't strong and brave, they're called punks.

Beatrice Dyess, a police officer with the Las Vegas Metropolitan Police Department for twenty-nine years, highlights the way personalities relate to work with troubled youth in the following letter to Florence Littauer:

In July 1996, I was assigned to the Youth Diversion Unit, an intervention/prevention program designed to provide positive alternatives to first time, non-violent offenders. Our primary goal is to prevent youth from reoffense and/or entering into the juvenile justice system. In hindsight,

I guess you could say, I received a blessing. Since with the program, I became a certified J.E.T.T. Stream instructor and was enlightened on a program called R.O.P.E.S. It was through the J.E.T.T. Stream course and the Youth Diversion staff members that I became familiar with the Personality Profile. The R.O.P.E.S. and J.E.T.T. Stream courses are the educational tools utilized with adolescents and parents to increase communication skills, [increase] self-esteem, and develop anger management skills. Your Personality Profile is a key component in both courses and has proven to be instrumental in adolescent development and in altering unhealthy behavioral patterns in the youth and parents serviced by this unit. Most important, it increases communication and teamwork among the family unit. This was accomplished by the youth and parents understanding what type of personality each member of the family has. The Personality Profile gives valuable insight in understanding yourself and those around you. I feel it is this increased awareness and communication within the family that contributes to Youth Diversion's 91 percent success rate. By no means am I attempting to give credit solely to the Personality concept. However, it has played an important role in the positive behavioral changes in conjunction with other methods utilized in the program.

Like Officer Dyess, my wife, Patty, and I are teaching the Personalities to families, troubled youth, and law enforcement leaders. We pray that the Lord will use us to make a difference in these troubled times.

The Living Bible says in Romans 13:4 that the police officer is sent by God to help people. He gives police officers certain gifts and abilities according to their personalities.

God doesn't want us to change our personalities and to jump from one type to another. He's the One who gave our unique gifts to us, and He wants us to use our strengths to overcome weaknesses. What He does want us to change is the way we think by renewing our minds through His Word and being willing to share with others.

Remember, "It's not what you are or what you're not, but what you're doing with what you've got."

Medicine

Patients and Patience

JOYCE WESSELER

Through her professional and personal life experiences, Joyce Wesseler has gained a level of caring that has enabled her to help others. She is a registered nurse with twenty-two years of professional nursing experience, the last ten of which have been spent administering chemotherapy. Known as "The Hat Lady" with a collection of more than eight hundred unique hats, Joyce incorporates her passion for hats in her personality seminars.

One of our greatest fears in life is to hear the doctor say, "You have cancer." Immediately patients start into the stages of "death and dying," even if they've never heard of them. They are in a state of shock, stopped in their tracks. They try denial—*Surely I didn't hear correctly. This couldn't happen to me. No one in my family had cancer. I'm sure the report is wrong.* Some patients stay in denial for a long time, canceling appointments, refusing to tell their spouse, not seeking any kind of treatment. Once individuals get beyond denial, they often become angry, sometimes irate. They're angry at the doctor, the nurse, their mother, and God. They're furious that they, good people, could have a disease when their bad friends are happy and healthy. "Why me?" In the middle of anger, they try bargaining with the God they no longer believe loves them: "If you'll spare me, I'll quit smoking, be a better Christian, give more to the poor. Whatever it takes, I'm ready." When bargaining doesn't bring quick results, the patient often goes into despair—*There's no hope. Once you get this disease, it's over. I might as well give up and just sit here and die.*

When despair becomes too depressing, the person begins to accept the truth and wonder what can be done to prolong life or even beat the invasion. We as caregivers expect and usually accept these stages, but without a knowledge of the personalities, we won't understand why people move on at different paces.

The Popular Sanguines, who love fun and excitement, have the greatest ability to live in denial. From childhood they have made up stories, pretended to live in castles, and expected to live happily ever after. Acceptance of cancer would wipe out the future fun and the castles. Until there is pain, the Popular Sanguine can pretend the fairy godmother will come soon.

The Powerful Cholerics hate sickness in themselves and others because it reveals weakness. Their biggest fear is lack of control over their own lives, and a terminal illness is considered worse than death. They will look for the quick fix, new drugs, or a trip to Mexico. They are angry, they bargain with God, and they will themselves to overcome this obstacle to achievement.

The Perfect Melancholies have always been afraid this would happen. "I knew it. I knew I'd die of cancer." They tend to move from shock right into depression. They read the latest medical journals, find labels for their type of illness, and expound on facts and figures for all who come to visit. Whatever method of treatment they decide on, they will pursue it with diligence and accuracy.

The Peaceful Phlegmatics are the best patients of all. They can avoid some of the anger and depression, and move into a placid acceptance. They appreciate anyone's assistance, enjoy being waited on in the hospital, and don't like to ask for more medication. "I didn't want to bother you. I know you're busy with the others." They don't focus on the problem, and they quietly accept their fate in life.

Patients' personalities, though, are not the only factors influencing the handling of the illness. Caregivers also function out of their personalities, which are frequently opposite of the patients' personalities.

The Popular Sanguine caregiver wants to ignore the person's pain, tell funny stories, and not listen to the chronicle of symptoms while the Powerful Choleric wants people to get up and get moving. "A lot of this is all in your head. If you'd only do something you'd feel a lot better," they decree. One Powerful Choleric wife I know cut her husband's pain medication in half so he could "buck up" and not succumb to dependency on drugs.

Perfect Melancholy caregivers handle problems by recognizing the seriousness of the issue and encouraging discussion about the funeral. They dole out the prescriptions at the right time, minister seriously and deeply to the patient, and won't let friends visit who are too loud, too boisterous, or too happy.

The Peaceful Phlegmatic helpers are a blessing, easily able to fit the mood of the patient. Peaceful Phlegmatics can laugh with those who laugh and weep with those who weep. They won't wake the person up to give them a sleeping pill. They're easy to get along with and flexible.

I have taught Stephen Ministry, "I Can Cope," "Death and Dying," "Getting Well," and hospice classes. I see the personality traits exhibited in the people in these classes, as well as in my patients in the clinic and the hospital.

When we understand our patients' personalities, we need to encourage them to use their God-given personality strengths to cope in times of distress and illness. We must accept them for who they are and not try to make them like us. Rather than dealing with their illness in the ways most comfortable for us, as caregivers we must look for the treatment methods that most support *their* personality type (see the chart on page 137 for help in this area).

A patient of mine with metastatic prostate cancer had been using a cane to walk for some time. Over many months, his condition had become worse. As I was administering his chemotherapy, I mentioned to him that I had overheard at the country club the previous night that he had just been diagnosed with cancer. Never forgetting the confidentiality of our patients, I assured him that I said nothing and only listened. He looked at me and smiled.

"Hadn't you told anyone before?" I asked.

"No, only my wife. I had businesses that I needed to sell and didn't want my cancer to be a factor in the negotiations. I might not have done so well if they had known, but now I have all my business affairs in order."

I then stated, "But you have been walking with a cane for so long."

"Oh, I told people I had arthritis," he chuckled.

Appropriate Interventions
Based on Patients' Personality Needs

Popular Sanguines

Popular Sanguines' basic desire is fun. Being seriously ill says, "Life is no fun." Try to give them some type of fun.

Sanguines Need:
- positive and cheerful personnel
- pleasant surroundings and environment— pictures, flowers, music, satin pillow cases
- good listeners, for they need to talk
- touching and loving support, to feel that you really enjoy caring for them
- people, because they dislike being alone— parties perk them up
- compliments and encouragement
- instructions given more than once (they tend to forget)
- directions on priorities—which pills are essential
- attractive appearance—help with hair or wig, nails, makeup, and a pretty gown or attractive robe

Powerful Cholerics

Powerful Cholerics' basic desire is control. Being incapacitated says, "Life is out of my control." Allow them to make decisions.

Cholerics Need:
- to be allowed to be independent as much as possible because they want to do for themselves
- facts as soon as possible for quick decision making—no cover-up
- intelligent medical personnel (they are bored by repetition and angered by incompetence)
- freedom of movement if possible—it is most difficult for them to be confined
- choice in selection of treatments
- room where they can see the activity in the hall or out of a window
- prompt attention to problems
- procedures done expediently; don't dally around
- sense of loyalty from medical staff
- praise for how well they are doing

Peaceful Phlegmatics

Peaceful Phlegmatics' basic desire is to avoid conflict and confrontation. They will deny serious illness; it overwhelms them. Being sick says, "You've got to face this serious problem and make hard choices."

Phlegmatics Need:
- a peaceful room and surroundings
- time for themselves to think it through
- encouragement to express feelings and fears
- TV, books, and environment where they can "people watch"
- motivation to make decisions and to move into action
- extra time in eating, doing personal care, and decision making
- nonthreatening and congenial personnel
- not to be neglected in their care, due to their congenial ways
- feelings of respect and self-worth

Perfect Melancholies

Perfect Melancholies' basic desire is to have everything done correctly. Being ill says, "Nothing's ever going to be right again." Don't try to jolly them up but allow them to grieve.

Melancholies Need:
- things done right the first time; don't deviate from the tried and true method
- schedule for their plan of care, lab tests, X-rays, treatments, and baths
- things organized and prepared when having blood drawn, IVs started, and treatments
- medication on time and schedule followed
- telephone, call light, personal items convenient and where they want them
- adequate time allowed in eating, bathing, and filling out menus
- ample time to study drug sheets, new information, consent forms before making decisions
- call lights answered promptly
- correct and factual information given to answer their questions
- a good listener and attention to their complaints
- feelings of sensitivity and competent support

If you review the strengths listed in the overviews in appendix C, look at the Powerful Choleric and Perfect Melancholy personalities and you will see this patient's pattern. Here was a man who was in charge, concerned about money, his business, and maintaining control of its disposition. He didn't need sympathy or need to talk about his illness. He kept most things to himself. Strong-willed, decisive, unemotional, and independent, he excelled in emergencies, found creative solutions, and needed to finish what he started. He was well-groomed, always arrived on time or early, came alone, and was very bright and interesting. I always looked forward to his coming for treatment.

A particular Perfect Melancholy patient with breast cancer was a special person to me. Mary always came to the office by herself, meticulously dressed in a tailored suit, briefcase in hand and a pad to take notes on new instructions and lab data. In addition to our drug sheets with side effects and appointment schedules, Mary kept her own records. She outlined times, dates, treatment protocol, side effects, and lab results. Mary had a list of questions outlined for me each time she came. Needless to say, she wasn't one of those quick in-and-out patients. Perfect Melancholy patients are more hesitant, analytical, and detail conscious.

Many times in preparing patients for surgery, we ask them to sign the surgery consent form just before we give the preoperative medication. This may be very upsetting to the Perfect Melancholy patient who requires ample time to read and study the consent forms, whereas the other three personalities may not be bothered at all. Visiting Mary one day in the hospital when she was admitted for additional problems, I asked if there was anything I might do for her before I left.

"Yes, Joyce, get the darn nurses to leave my house slippers beside my step stool. They keep kicking my slippers under my bed," she replied. Perfect Melancholy patients want their personal belongings where *they* want them. Robes, glasses, books, pens, telephone, call light, television and radio controls need to be convenient. They want things to be organized, tidy, and neat.

The Peaceful Phlegmatic patients appear the easiest to care for and the most adjusted. Don't be misled by their calm, peaceful, and agreeable manner, though. They may have many fears and keep their emotions hidden.

I feel this patient many times is the most neglected. As the old saying goes, the squeaky wheel gets the oil first. Especially in a hospital! Perhaps that's why we answer the Powerful Choleric and Perfect

Melancholy patients' call lights first, whereas the Peaceful Phlegmatics may get their call lights ignored and their food trays last, for we know they won't make a big fuss about waiting. These patients want peace at all costs, want their lives to go smoothly, and want their problems to go away. They will try to find the easy way to handle their illness by avoiding the issue and letting someone else take charge.

When we who are in the medical field become ill, we can be the most difficult patients of all. The next most difficult situation might be when we become the primary caregivers to our loved ones. My quiet but witty Peaceful Phlegmatic father had carcinoma of the lung and died in 1977. My Perfect Melancholy mother had been a practicing registered nurse for forty years. My father was the ideal patient who never complained and was always relaxed and peaceful. He allowed, even encouraged, Mother to assume all responsibility. I truly believe Mother thought if she were the perfect nurse she could keep Daddy alive. Mother was very creative at providing enjoyment for both of them. They loved to play golf and duplicate bridge. My father had many friends, and often Mother would drive him to the golf course, help him into the cart, and off they would go—visiting the other golfers.

My mother cared for him at home because she believed she could give better total care than the hospital. His nursing care would be done right and done her way. My father's lung cancer metastasized, and he had to have a gastric feeding tube in his stomach. My mother fed him every three hours, around the clock, through the tube.

She constantly calculated ways to get more calories into his feeding to help prevent his continuing weight loss. She was self-sacrificing and gave 110 percent to his nursing care. She made a medical chart for him at home. Her nurse's notes were precise on intake and output, vital signs, and medications.

Although my father had been bedfast for a long period of time, his skin was in perfect condition at the time of his death due to her constant care. She sterilized surgical instruments and packed and dressed his lung cavity daily in a sterile procedure. It was difficult for anyone to assist her, for there was only one way to do anything, her way—the right way.

My father's illness and dying process was difficult for me as a Popular Sanguine/Powerful Choleric daughter. In allowing my father to have peace at all costs, and allowing Mother to do things perfectly, I felt they both stayed in denial almost up to the very end.

I wanted to talk, share, be honest, have open communications and face the problems—a typical Popular Sanguine/Powerful Choleric choice—but that was not to be done. I teach in my classes that we can never go back and redo a death. However, if my father were dying today, by my knowing the five stages of death and dying and understanding the differences in the personalities, I could give better support. It would be emotionally healthier for both him and for me.

We can never go back. However, we can learn how to handle the next adversity better. Pain is one of our greatest teachers. We need to learn from it and move forward.

Thirty years ago I had a near-death experience. I have read that after such an experience one no longer fears death. That is certainly true for me. I continue to love life, live each day to its fullest in an attitude of gratitude, and have no fear of dying. I truly believe it was one of God's ways of preparing me for the work I have done with cancer patients during the past years in oncology.

In reflecting back on my near-death experience, I found it interesting to see the role my personality played. I was one of five patients with encephalitis. The other four died shortly after hospitalization. I was very ill and mentally made preparation for my own death. One of the issues I wanted to address was a new mother for my children. I had a daughter, Linda, just going into puberty. My two-year-old son, Jeff, hadn't been potty trained. I fought hard to remain on a conscious level until my husband arrived. I wanted to share my idea with him. I thought of a nice-looking, well-educated, spiritual widow who would be a good wife and mother for my family. I was a Powerful Choleric mother and wife moving quickly into action, seeking practical solutions, unemotional, strong-willed, and excelling in emergencies. It amazes me the role our personalities play in good times with good health and in bad times with poor health.

In the last eleven years I have experienced the pain and heartache of two husbands dying with cancer. Ken Keast was a former mayor, city commissioner, retired navy captain, community leader, president, and vice president of companies. He was a Powerful Choleric/Perfect Melancholy and was 6'2", well-built, distinguished-looking, a sea-captain type with a full beard. He was my best friend, and we had such great times sharing our lives.

Ken developed inoperable stomach cancer. Our only hope was for him to be treated experimentally at the Lawrence Berkeley Laboratories in Berkeley, California, with atomic radiation. It was not successful for long-term results but did give us twelve miraculous months more. Ken was only in the hospital a few days during his entire illness. He wanted to be cared for at home. My role was similar to my mother's; however, Ken's personality was different than my father's.

Ken was independent, in charge, and did as much of his own care as possible. He was an excellent patient. Since he was a public figure, the newspaper and radio station did interviews on his atomic treatment. Ken addressed his illness head-on. I think he really enjoyed sharing stories of his fiberglass body suit built for him and having daily upright cat scans. He said it was like *Star Wars*. He quoted the statistics on his recovery. The percentages were not good, but he was always optimistic. He gave 100 percent of himself trying to get a good response to treatment. Here was a Powerful Choleric who thrived on obstacles, exuding confidence, not easily discouraged.

Many people said it wasn't fair that I had to go through the dying process a second time when my second husband, Delmar Wesseler, died two years ago. Life isn't fair, but it was still my privilege to have cared for two men who had given so much love and enjoyment to me. I could use my past experiences and expertise in oncology to help them through a most difficult time in their lives.

Delmar had Acute Myeloid Leukemia (AML), which was not a good diagnosis. He went through a most trying and difficult fifty-nine-day period before he died. His personality was the same as Ken's, Powerful Choleric/Perfect Melancholy, and they were similar in handling their diseases. The difference was that Delmar had to be hospitalized due to his constant blood transfusions, platelets, white cells, antibiotics, and hyperalimentation.

Delmar had two IVs going constantly through his double-lumen catheter—sleep deprivation was a major problem. I asked to have a room where he could view car traffic on the road into the mall. It was very difficult for him to be confined. He was the racehorse and must move or see movement. Delmar once stated, "If you don't get me out of here, I'll die!"

Our doctor, Greg Nanney, was most understanding and allowed passes for Delmar to be out for short periods, thus also meeting my needs as a Popular Sanguine for sociability. Delmar wore a surgical mask, and when we went out, we used good precautions to protect his weakened immune system. Delmar was able to watch our grandson Joey make the winning soccer goal, wrap his Christmas gifts and leave instructions on their distribution, and have his attorney visit our home for final business details.

Prior to Delmar's admission into the hospital, when his blood count was still good, we made a list of things we wanted to do at least one more time if things didn't go right in his treatment. We dined at our favorite restaurants, attended church, went shopping, went to a movie, and had popcorn and soft drinks. He went with his sons, Del and David, to both the farm and the ranch one last time. I am sure Delmar left much advice and many instructions for them.

We attended a fall cancer benefit for a short time, and Delmar purchased a trip to Las Vegas, Nevada. Since he was a world traveler, having been into 204 of the 247 countries, being ill didn't dampen his desire for change and adventure. He made complete funeral arrangements, just in case they would be necessary. As a Powerful Choleric wanting to maintain control after his death, he also gave instructions to his sons for my funeral, even though I wasn't sick!

After reading this chapter, I hope you will be able to use your knowledge of the personalities to help you when you have any kind of illness or when you are the caregiver. Remember to deal with others not just out of your own personality type, but with an awareness of and a sensitivity toward theirs.

Network Marketing

Can It Work for All Personalities?

STEVEN AND TERI OLSON

Steven and Teri Olson became interested in the personalities while they were senior naval officers. When they began their network marketing business they quickly saw the value of making their personalities work for them and using personality concepts to more effectively assist their business associates. They use their knowledge extensively when counseling individuals and couples and while speaking to small groups.

If your idea of network marketing stems from a frightening evening when you went to a party and found you were tricked into being shown a business plan, then let us show you that times have changed, these businesses have grown up, and they provide substantial second incomes for millions of people and full-time prosperity for thousands more. Amway operates in seventy countries and its distributor organizations use *Personality Plus,* translated in twelve languages, as a training tool. Mary Kay has herself become an icon for millions of women who didn't know they could be in business. Network marketing is a great way, at a minimal investment, to find out if you have the drive to be in business for yourself.

In this type of marketing today, the emphasis is on human relationships, getting along with people, and helping them grow. High value is placed on self-improvement, reading positive books, and listening to motivational tapes. A man in his forties said to us recently,

"I didn't read a single book since I got out of high school until I joined this group. Now I read one a week!"

If you are in network marketing or any other business involving people, you know that people can be both your best asset and worst enemy. Considering the options, we find it best to learn to understand and get along with even the difficult people and love them into success.

It is possible to do business without an understanding of the personalities. However, our experience shows that success at the expense of individual worth and attention leaves people with negative feelings toward network marketing. We would like to see attitudes changed and the number of people falling by the wayside reduced. We know that an understanding of the personalities is beneficial to all people in any kind of business, but it is essential in network marketing. No one is sitting around at night saying, "I wish I could be out knocking on doors," but many are wishing for a friend, someone who cares.

How can an understanding of the personalities help you? Chances are you have noticed there are people out there who act differently from you, who see things from a different perspective. A greater understanding of yourself and your associates can help you better communicate all aspects of your business. In *The Seven Habits of Highly Effective People*, Stephen Covey says that you should first seek to understand, then be understood.

Our experience is that most people get it backward—they would rather talk than listen, seek attention than give it. In network marketing, most people are not aware that the benefits that excite one person are just "ho-hum" to another because the different personalities are attracted to different benefits. If you can identify the needs that interest your associates, you can better convey what your business can do for them. On a personal level, most of us tend to respond more favorably toward a presentation that shows us how we can achieve what is important to us.

Remember the sales adage "Find a need and fill it?" A useful modification of this adage for network marketing might be "Identify your contacts' or associates' needs and help them see how a business of their own could help them achieve their desires." While we do not advise using the knowledge of the personalities in an attempt to manipulate people, the information is helpful in applying an organization's system or pattern with each personality's own unique set of strengths and weaknesses. The basic business systems are important in helping new people achieve quick success in network marketing, but an under-

Building Your Business
with the Personalities

Popular Sanguine

Making Contact
- ask about family or friends to establish rapport
- ask about schedule to determine feasibility

Presenting the Plan
- build dreams
- focus on social aspects of the business and recognition
- avoid too many details
- use their name and the names of friends frequently

Following Up
- include social chitchat
- ask questions about them and their dreams
- praise their people skills
- encourage them to make a list of friends
- emphasize the excitement of a new adventure

Building the Business
- help them define, set, and commit to goals
- be sure they have accurate information on leads list
- offer guidance on business skills

Guidance Counseling
- meet over coffee or for lunch
- show how to have fun while building
- offer to help with follow-up
- remind them that books and tapes will help them help others

Powerful Choleric

Making Contact
- ask about line of work and job stability
- ask about their goals, where they want to be in two to five years

Presenting the Plan
- focus on the process of building a team
- stick to the bottom line
- point out their leadership strengths
- offer control of their financial future

Following Up
- plan a specific time frame and offer a meeting overview
- be businesslike and professional
- stress the importance of a tried-and-true plan for success
- focus on controlling their future

Building the Business
- get goals and completion dates on paper
- help them think through potential leads
- remind them that the business is based on numbers of contacts
- encourage them to follow the system

Guidance Counseling
- focus on the process to financial freedom
- remind them that they have control of when they increase income and when they get "promoted"
- emphasize the need to follow the duplication process

Peaceful Phlegmatic

Making Contact
- ask about family or recreational activities
- help them identify what is really important; is there someone special they would like to help?

Presenting the Plan
- emphasize that working now can mean an early retirement
- ask many questions to be sure they are with you
- work with them to find that one dream
- show how patience and ability to get along will help them

Following Up
- know they may be most difficult to read
- tell them of others who are now retired, enjoying the fruits of their labor
- keep the meeting short
- guide them in their goals

Building the Business
- encourage them to listen for people's dreams
- remind them of the value of the opportunity to others

Guidance Counseling
- initiate the session
- push them to be the leader of their group

Perfect Melancholy

Making Contact
- ask about job, organization, and prioritizing tasks
- share a proven pattern for success that is organized and duplicable

Presenting the Plan
- stress importance of organization and sensitivity
- discover an area where more money or time would help make life more perfect
- be sure all your math is correct
- share stories of others in similar places who have done it

Following Up
- be ready for questions
- offer proof of security and income potential
- substantiate claims
- share profiles of leadership

Building the Business
- review their goals and see if they can be sped up
- encourage them to make their lists and actually call the people
- remind them of their dream for financial security

Guidance Counseling
- as a private person, they need encouragement to share struggles
- may become depressed if business is not moving at desired pace
- focus on what they are doing correctly
- be generous with tips for improvement

standing and use of the personalities complements these systems by adding another dimension to help make information more effective.

Some organizations teach that the men function in certain aspects of the business, while the women function in others. However, this may not allow for the best use of individual strengths and weaknesses. Business is no longer a male-only endeavor with the "little woman" passing out the cookies, but rather a cooperative effort based on their individual abilities. There is no free lunch in any business—this is particularly true in network marketing—but when a husband and wife can each work from their own strengths, regardless of gender roles, they can produce results and enjoy the process.

We teach our people that knowing your own personality is not an excuse for poor behavior, not a reason to say, "Well that's just the way I am, and you will just have to accept me." Knowledge of your personality allows you to make changes in your life to capitalize on your natural strengths, and it also gives you a list of your weaknesses so that you can overcome them and achieve the success you desire. You are responsible for you. Don't sit and wonder why others succeed.

If you consider yourself a "people person," outgoing and optimistic, then building relationships is not the problem. However, you may have a more difficult time staying focused or following through on your commitments. Some of you who are more focused on getting the job done may find that relationships aren't particularly important to you. You may even find people to be a bit frustrating. The good news is that regardless of your personality, you can succeed in network marketing if you build up your understanding of the personalities.

We have been involved in network marketing for years while we were both on active duty in the U.S. Navy. We are now retired and in our business full-time. Steve is a combination Perfect Melancholy/Peaceful Phlegmatic, and Teri is Powerful Choleric/Popular Sanguine. Being able to see things from the perspectives of all the personalities has been extremely helpful to us. We hope that our insights will be useful to you in building your network marketing business or in whatever group activity you choose.

Know Thyself

Have you ever gotten frustrated with someone who let you down or dropped the ball? Some people seem to take promises lightly, while others can always be counted on because their word is their bond. You may not have been able to get some people to make a commitment because their schedule seems to run them rather than serve them. Others seem to so overcommit themselves that they end up dropping a ball or two, usually at the worst possible time. Every person has strengths that help them in some aspects of business and weaknesses that hinder them in others. By "knowing thyself," as Socrates suggested, you can greatly improve the likelihood of a successful network marketing business. In the next few pages we will look at how the four personality types function in business, both out of their strengths and out of their weaknesses. See if you recognize yourself. Once you know yourself, the chart on page 145 will help you apply the knowledge of the personalities in your business dealings with others so that you can first understand and then be understood.

Popular Sanguine

The Popular Sanguine's skill in dealing with people is a tremendous asset in network marketing's people-oriented business. If you are a Popular Sanguine, you probably know hundreds of people and are either employed in a job that brings you into contact with people or are involved in activities that involve people. Having a resource pool to draw from is not a problem that concerns you—"I don't know anybody" will never be your objection. Your natural warmth and charisma attract others to you and cause them to want to find out what you are doing, but don't give so much information that they lose interest in what you are saying.

Your comfort with conversation usually results in everyone, particularly you, having a wonderful time, but the primary reason you and a potential associate got together—to conduct business—could get lost along the way. Fun is fine if you are talking with another Popular Sanguine. However, when talking to Powerful Cholerics, be sure to keep your mind on business and get to the point. Be sure to be on time and have your materials organized when sharing with a Perfect Melancholy. If you're talking to a Peaceful Phlegmatic, don't expect them to exhibit excitement and enthusiasm about all the fun you can have. While they are reserved and may appear to reject your thoughts because the whole thing seems like too much work, they will process the ideas presented and make a decision later, perhaps much later.

When you look at your group of network marketing associates, you may wonder if you can pull it all together. One of your biggest challenges will be to admit to yourself that it will take some work to build a network marketing business. Give up your desire to play first, and keep in the forefront of your mind that all the fun you'll have down the road will be worth a bit of focused work right now. We encourage our Popular Sanguine associates to reward the accomplishment of work-related goals with appropriate fun rewards. It is important for you, more than the other personalities, to have fun with your business, or it will become drudgery and you will quickly lose interest. Hang in there, because with your people skills, this business is made just for you. You can be the friend so many are looking for, the magnet that draws people into your group.

Powerful Choleric

Your natural leadership and take-charge drive are tremendous strengths for the network marketing business. They work well for you because this business enables you to be in control of your own destiny. You know how to get the job done and get it done now. Once you believe in your opportunity, your focus and drive will help you achieve the success you desire because you are not afraid to roll up your sleeves and get to work. More than any of the personalities, you need to remind yourself that this is a people business. Be careful that you do not allow your determination to get things done to run over the other personalities. Unlike a traditional business, your associates in network marketing are more like partners. They are not your employees, and you are not their boss. You will need to work to encourage and challenge them without tromping on them. If you have a "my way or the highway" approach, you may lose a lot of friends along the way in your quest to build your business.

When you say you're going to do something, you do it, and you expect the same from others. Prepare for frustration if you rely too much on what people (particularly non–Powerful Cholerics) say rather than on what they do. The Popular Sanguine really meant to attend your meeting but got sidetracked while shopping. The Perfect Melancholy planned on bringing a friend but didn't want to be pushy. The Peaceful Phlegmatic planned on making the calls "tomorrow," but when tomorrow came it was too late to find anyone who could come at the last minute.

Once you understand why these people don't charge forth as you do, you will be able to anticipate reactions instead of being surprised. We have found that once Cholerics develop an interest in the needs of others, they grow faster and have a much better retention of people in their group.

Perfect Melancholy

Since you are not the "leap before you look" type, you will have thoroughly reviewed the business before joining. You understand all the nuances, and once you have made a decision you are committed. Your strengths as the "detail" person, coupled with your great organizational abilities, are wonderful assets for helping people put all the pieces together. You are the one who can be counted on to see the many "little" things that need to be accomplished to have a successful business. These natural skills help you put together a solid and profitable business. Your precise nature and structured business approach add an air of professionalism unmatched by any of the other personalities.

One of your challenges will be to control your tendency to immerse yourself in the details of the business that do not result in productive growth and instead focus on the people who are your future. Contacting, approaching, presenting your marketing plan, and following up are the techniques that, when mastered, result in business growth, but alas, these areas involve people. You are more comfortable when organizing the products, making flyers, and mastering the business manual, but these are things that offer poor financial return for the effort expended. Use your ability to grasp the details to identify the half-dozen things that will give you the greatest reward, and then focus on those six things. And remember, to grow, you, as all others, must get out of your comfort zone and converse positively with the people.

While the Popular Sanguines are the people persons, you are the process person. This is not to say that you can't develop excellent people skills. The fact is you may have become quite accomplished in this area. You can use your tendency toward mastery of a skill to your advantage in your network marketing business by mastering those areas involving interactions with people. Use scripts. With your partner or a friend, role play techniques like approaching and inviting people to look at your business opportunity. This will help you become comfortable with handling frequently raised objections or questions that come up at meetings.

As you share the business opportunity with others, remember that not everyone is interested in details to the extent that you are and resist the temptation to give all your knowledge and insights about the network marketing opportunity. You may lose your audience. Remember that the Popular Sanguines are in pursuit of fun, the Powerful Cholerics want the bottom line, and the Peaceful Phlegmatics need to think about it for a while. When you come across a fellow Melancholy, you can revel in your opportunity to provide more extensive information and insights that will be appreciated and convincing. We have found that mastering the art of asking questions can greatly enhance your opportunity to tell more of what you know by either providing information or gently correcting erroneous perceptions. Feel out what others want to know and provide answers. Don't spend time answering questions no one has asked.

Peaceful Phlegmatic

You bring gentleness and moderation to network marketing. While everyone else is either bouncing off the walls with excitement or down in the dumps because their business is not growing as fast as they expected, you gently ease them down or graciously pick them up. Calm, cool, and collected are adjectives that appropriately describe you. When people present an objection, you are the one who is likely to really hear what they say and empathize with them rather than just blowing off their concern. Not one given to extremes, your sensitive nature makes you ideal to help people survive the difficulties common to network marketing. You may pride yourself in not being swayed by emotion, but at major conference events you appear so low-key, maybe even bored, that others perceive you as disinterested or disengaged. This blasé appearance can be misleading when you are being watched by your other associates who want to emulate you. Many times our leaders have reminded us that people make decisions based on emotion and then justify them with the facts. If you want to be a leader in your network marketing business, you would be advised to practice enthusiasm. We suggest reading Norman Vincent Peale's book *Enthusiasm Makes the Difference,* because it really does!

Your no-pressure, matter-of-fact approaches and presentations are generally viewed as nonthreatening, and you seem trustworthy and believable to many. Yet the Popular Sanguines may find you dull, the Powerful Cholerics may see you as lacking enthusiasm and purpose, and the Perfect Melancholies may not be convinced that you are confident of what you are presenting. Your lack of excitement may not create a sense of urgency to make a decision to join you in your business. Once they see your competent and steady approach to conducting your business, however, and enjoy your subtle sense of humor, they will appreciate the value of persistence in overcoming obstacles and achieving success.

Your desire not to offend anyone could cause you to ignore objections or fail to push for closure. If one of your contacts says they didn't have time to review the marketing material or watch a promotional video, "no problem" erupts from your lips before you can even think about it. One of your big challenges will be to not allow yourself to be a pushover. As a person with some Peaceful Phlegmatic traits, Steve has come to realize that he can be strong without being offensive. He is learning to ask the questions that make others think about what they are really saying, and to take a stand that demonstrates that he is really in control of his destiny. If they didn't review the promotional literature or watch the video, he simply comments that this is apparently not the right time for them and asks if they would like him to check back with them at a later time. Most people don't want to totally eliminate an opportunity, so they ask that he check back in a few months. The important challenge for you as a Peaceful Phlegmatic is to remember to make the next call and to force yourself to do it.

You are probably no stranger to procrastination, and while some may view your hesitancy to pursue objections or push for a decision as a weakness, more than likely you simply did not want to appear pushy or offensive. If you have become involved in network marketing and you desire to succeed, now is the time to answer objections and to gently prod people to make a decision. Remember, your art of negotiation and helping others see both sides of a concern will help you shine in this area. You just need to try a little harder than the Powerful Cholerics who jump into each new venture with innate enthusiasm. It is more difficult for you to define the dreams that will stimulate you to do the necessary things to build your network marketing business. While you might not be the one who makes lemonade when given a sack of lemons, you will readily accept the lemons as a part of life and do your best to love even the unlovely, those whom the Powerful Choleric would drop by the wayside. People see this trait in you and respect you for it. Don't settle into acceptance so quickly that you lose all sense of discernment. Before leading others, you need to identify something that you thirst and hunger for so much that you can't get the thought of it out of your mind. Then you must believe that someday you will achieve that great goal. Napoleon Hill talks about having "a burning desire" in his book *Think and Grow Rich*. You need to find a dream that gives you a burning desire so strong that you will be willing to go for it!

You are great under pressure, and this is a trait that is a strength in this business. People who view you as a pushover are surprised when you won't budge once you have made a decision. You don't make a big fuss about your stand; you just won't move. To the Peaceful Phlegmatic, it's just being persistent. To others, it's being stubborn. This can work to your advantage in the pursuit of your dreams and not letting anyone steal your dream. Dig in those heels and hang in there. Believe that you can achieve the things you hunger for if you're willing to work.

Working with Your Personality

At the beginning of this chapter, we challenged all of you to invest a few minutes of your time, even if you are already successful in network marketing. We suggested that understanding the personalities has value for people at every level of success.

We are convinced that the greatest benefit of understanding the personalities for your network marketing business is knowing yourself. Just as you are much more effective pulling a rope than pushing it, you will be effective in your business when you lead your winning team rather than push from the rear. It's "follow me," not "go get 'em." All the personalities have strengths that help them in certain aspects of their network marketing business and weaknesses that hinder them from achieving their goals. You will be much more effective if you capitalize on your strengths and use your coworkers to fill in your weaknesses. If you are Popular Sanguine, have fun, but use a Perfect Melancholy to explain the plan. If you are Perfect Melancholy, present accurately, but let a Popular Sanguine give some colorful examples. If you are Powerful Choleric, transmit your enthusiasm, but don't overwhelm the group. Have a Peaceful Phlegmatic give a testimony of how the quiet types can be successful. If you are Peaceful Phlegmatic, realize the value of your obvious sincerity, but let the Powerful Choleric give the closing challenge.

We accept that network marketing organizations vary considerably in the way they conduct business. Your organization may have a pattern that has more, fewer, or different steps, but we know that the information we provide will crosswalk to your business pattern with little difficulty. In the charts on page 145 we examine the strengths and weaknesses of the personalities as they affect five critical steps in building a successful network marketing business: making contact with possible business associates, presenting your marketing plan, following up, helping others build their business, and counseling for success.

Ultimately, the usefulness of this chapter will be determined by the level of success you achieve when applying the information we have provided. We wish you the greatest success.

Part 3

Spiritual Life and Worship

Your Church

Pastor's Personality Profile

FLORENCE LITTAUER

Known universally as a leading expert on personalities, Florence Littauer has written more than twenty-five books and is a popular speaker for both church and business conferences. Her best-selling book about personalities, Personality Plus, *has sold nearly 1,000,000 copies. Florence and her husband, Fred, have been married for more than forty-five years and frequently speak at pastors' retreats and leadership seminars.*

When our church needs a new pastor, we form some kind of a committee and begin to have meetings at which we construct a profile of what we want in a pastor. The list usually starts by enumerating the weaknesses of the last dear man and making sure to look for the opposite traits in the new one.

A better approach to selecting a new pastor would use an understanding of the Personalities to recognize that there isn't one perfect pastor. Rather, there are many fine people possessing outstanding strengths and gifts, and they function best when they are assisted in the duties that don't come naturally to them. A search committee that fails to recognize this fundamental fact will search in vain for an individual with the strengths of all and the weaknesses of none and will face disappointment when the pastor they choose is unable to be all things to all people.

Most churches want someone who has charisma in the pulpit and will magnetize every lost soul in the community into the empty pews. He should have stories that will amaze the indifferent, challenge the leaders to greatness, give spiritual food to the deep, and amuse the Amen corner. He should summon the sinners to salvation and charm the children into early confirmation. He should be the life of the party at church socials, joyfully visit each family once a week, and lead evangelistic teams to the shopping malls.

Even more important than his popularity must be his ability to lead. He must take these desperate deacons who don't even like each other and turn them into a loving, harmonious group who will sing while serving tables. He must be dynamic in delivery, controlling of the contentious, and steadfast with the unsteady. He surely will have a vision of tripling attendance within the first year, necessitating an expansion program for the sanctuary. His strength will attract the wealthy men of the world, who will become his finance board in his efforts to raise a million dollars for the new organ to be imported from Germany. He will start more new programs than the government could create. He will pick up all the loose ends left dangling around by the last pastor and will weave them into a carpet for the foyer. In his spare time he will impress the community by being both president of the Rotary Club and chairman of the United Way.

In addition to these overwhelming leadership skills, he must, most importantly, be deep in the Word. He must spend hours a day in Bible study, pray daily for each church member (once a week for those who haven't joined yet), and memorize his entire Scripture lesson for Sunday. His sermons must be scholarly yet simple enough for those who don't grasp truth easily. In addition to all these attributes, he will have the gifts of discernment and mercy and will heal the lame, halt, and blind without getting too emotional about it.

He must be musical: play the piano to bring the crowd to their feet, sing like a cross between the angel Gabriel and George Beverly Shea, and master the marimba for talent night. His wife must have equal musical talent as she is expected to be organist and church choir director at no extra pay. The two of them should sing duets and lead the congregation in a hand-clapping rendition of "Something Good Is Going to Happen" each Sunday night. He should counsel with the combined wisdom of Jay Adams, Dr. James Dobson, Larry Crabb, Howard Hendricks, and David Seamands without offending Dave Hunt.

A Pastor's Personality
for Your Church

Popular Sanguine
Pastor Popular

Initial Appeal:
charming and conversational

Personality Pluses:
charisma in pulpit, storyteller, fun, sociable, loves people, entertaining, energized by responsive audiences, magnetic personality

Personality Minuses:
too dependent on charm, forgets names, lack of preparation, disorganized, not able to keep schedules, appears superficial, exaggerates, spreads rumors

Controls By:
charm and parties, making work sound fun, offering prizes

Finances:
poor manager, overspends, loses track, runs up debts, immature, needs help, should not be expected to keep the books, sees money strictly as means to buy things

Bible Teaching:
joyful, discovering new life, up-to-date, applicable, storytelling, emphasizes the Bible's grace and love

Spiritual Weaknesses:
lust of flesh and eye, easily led into temptation

Powerful Choleric
Pastor Powerful

Initial Appeal:
dynamic and directive

Personality Pluses:
obvious confidence, driving nature, able to take charge and shape people up, highly motivational, sees big picture, exciting personality

Personality Minuses:
too controlling, needs no other opinions, looks down on slow movers, rude, bossy, lack of compassion, feels it is *his* church.

Controls By:
threat of anger, covert manipulation, demanding performance, hot temper

Finances:
takes risks, buys on impulse, needs a finance board, projects too big and expensive, sees money as means to keep control

Bible Teaching:
clear, motivational, demanding action, rewarding, emphasizes the Bible's challenges and hard work

Spiritual Weaknesses:
pride, hard to give God control, needs to do it himself, little time for prayer

Peaceful Phlegmatic
Pastor Peaceful

Initial Appeal:
calm and congenial

Personality Pluses:
friendly, cool charm, brings peace and comfort, avoids problem situations, loves to minister to the hurting, objective counselor, inoffensive, consistent, steady, balanced, pleasing personality

Personality Minuses:
too laid-back, low energy level, not able to motivate, indifferent, lacks excitement

Controls By:
procrastination, appearing helpless

Finances:
not of top interest, conservative, will spend to please people, sees money as means to avoid crisis

Bible Teaching:
simple truth, nondemanding, accepting, personable, peaceful, emphasizes the Bible's comfort and peace

Spiritual Weaknesses:
compromising standards, avoiding confrontation, skirting the truth to keep peace, being slothful

Perfect Melancholy
Pastor Perfect

Initial Appeal:
dignified and deep

Personality Pluses:
intelligent, well-groomed, deeply spiritual, well-prepared, scholarly, truthful, likes facts and statistics, musical, prayerful, serious

Personality Minuses:
too remote; not social; too much time in thinking, planning, and organizing; slow starter; inflexible; too deep; drained by people; easily discouraged

Controls By:
threat of bad moods, sighing, showing disappointment in others

Finances:
gifted money management, counts the cost, balances, projects future finances, works from budget, sees money as means to manage

Bible Teaching:
serious, deep, spiritual striving for perfection, emphasizes the Bible's rules and judgment

Spiritual Weaknesses:
depression, giving up on God, trouble believing God's unconditional love and acceptance

On top of all this he must be a peace-loving man, inoffensive in all his ways, with no thought of stirring up trouble. "Heaven knows we have had enough of that with the last pastor!" He must be calm in the winds of adversity, never take sides in conflict, and keep cool when it's time for *the vote.*

He must counsel the brokenhearted and heal the homes that seem hopeless. He must bring back all those former members who left when the music minister was terminated because of undisclosed indiscretions, and unify the women who are hot and hostile over the competing Bible studies. He must placate the church secretary who is overworked and underpaid and who refuses to run off one more recipe for "tuna casserole with cashew nuts" on the Xerox machine because she was hired for duties of greater depth. Yes, he shall keep peace wherever he goes.

Isn't that what we want for our leader?

> Popularity of the Sanguine
> Power of the Choleric
> Perfection of the Melancholy
> + Peace of the Phlegmatic
> _____
> = One All-purpose Pastor!

What a blessing it is for us who know the personalities that we can stop the eternal quest for a pastor who has the strengths of all and the weaknesses of none.

When we are realistic, what can we expect from one above-average man? If he does have the Popular Sanguine charisma in the pulpit, he may forget to show up at funerals. One Popular Sanguine pastor told me he got into a wedding ceremony before he realized he had forgotten his order of service for this bride and groom and had no idea of their names. He quickly had them kneel at the altar and had the audience close their eyes in silent prayer for the nameless couple. He tiptoed out and ran to his office in the next building where he found his booklet. He raced back into the silent church and proclaimed a grand Amen! The audience loved him, but it was a close call between delight and disaster.

The Popular Sanguine pastor can be the most exciting and dramatic in the pulpit and can be the life of every church gathering as long as he knows himself well enough to have a Perfect Melancholy assistant or secretary to keep his schedule. Any personality can be an effective pastor as long as he amplifies strengths and staffs weaknesses where possible.

The Perfect Melancholy pastor is what we expect of a spiritual leader. He truly cares for the well-being of his people, mines deep truth from the Scripture, and prays with conviction rather than for public effect. He is opposite from Pastor Popular in that he does nothing for show but rather from the sincerity of his heart. He is sensitive to the needs of others and will visit the sick. He can organize committees for maximum results and have an inspired vision for the future. It is difficult for him to bounce back when people fail him by not doing what was expected of them, and he easily gets depressed. He has to learn to lighten up and is helped by an assistant who will encourage him. "They're only human." "It's not the end of the world." "God won't hold you accountable for their failures."

The combination of a Melancholy pastor with a Sanguine assistant, or the reverse, can be outstanding provided they understand the other personalities and realize how much they need each other.

When a church body has the drive to achieve the zeal for growth and the finances potentially available to move ahead, they will do best with the Powerful Choleric pastor. Most of the growing churches I have visited are directed by dynamic, dedicated Powerful Cholerics who have by sheer power, energy, and seven-day work weeks created a masterpiece that becomes subject matter for future church growth conferences. Pastor Powerful can accomplish twice as much in a given day as any other personality, and he can motivate his people to march with him toward an exciting goal. He doesn't seem to need sleep and can wear out those around him. He is energized by people and challenges and loves to surmount obstacles and prove doubters wrong. He makes snap decisions that are usually right and doesn't want anyone to second guess him. Although a Powerful Choleric will no doubt get the church on the move, he may offend a dozen touchy deacons in the process. He will, without even trying, create a power struggle among the ranks, and those who don't see it his way may have to leave. Powerful Cholerics often cause church splits, and the people find themselves taking sides. Although the excuse for the division is doctrinal differences, I've found few people who know enough about doctrine to leave a church over it. Those Powerful Cholerics who keep above disputes are usually caught up in building wings on the church, leaving their personal mark on the cathedral as much as each pope did at St. Peter's.

When Pastor Powerful resigns to revitalize a large complacent church that needs him, the exhausted elders gravitate toward a Peaceful Phlegmatic who doesn't desire to replace the carpeting or raise the height of the steeple. He becomes a restful relief for the weary women of the church who have decorated all the powder rooms they care to for a lifetime. He glues the church splits back together and binds up the broken hearts.

Because Pastor Peaceful does what is required without looking for applause, he often doesn't get credit for what he has accomplished. Healing hurting hearts doesn't get the attention of a dramatic sermon or an emotional altar call. In a world where importance is tied to great achievement, the Phlegmatic individual may not be applauded for his steady, dedicated, behind-the-scenes improvements.

I was called to a large church to assess the pastoral staff to see if each one was in the best position for his or her personality and spiritual gifts. The senior pastor was 200 percent Choleric and had constructed both an imposing new sanctuary and educational facilities that served youth of all ages. He had built an impressive team of support staff motivated by him but given their own areas of responsibility. Many were Cholerics like him and were dynamic leaders of their own mini-churches. The music ministry and prayer pastors were Melancholy while the worship leader and youth pastor were Sanguine. Over all, each was placed in the right position to maximize their other strengths.

The assistant pastor was a Peaceful Phlegmatic custom-designed for this position. When asked, "What do you do here?" he responded, "I follow him (the senior pastor) through life and pick up the pieces." As I later observed, that assessment proved to be true. After church Pastor Powerful, focused on moving from the worship service to the singles luncheon where he was scheduled to give the blessing, quickly dismissed those who wanted to chat with him and left them hanging without response. The Peaceful assistant pastor quietly followed him to pick up the pieces. "He's in a big hurry today (actually every day). Yes, he really likes you. Can I be of any assistance?" He soothed the offended people and kept peace.

When I went back for a review one year later, Pastor Peaceful was gone. I asked what had happened, and the senior pastor said with a sigh, "He just couldn't keep up with me and he took a year off to rest! Can you imagine anyone wanting to rest that long?" This was certainly a foreign concept to Pastor Powerful. Then he added, "When he was here, I didn't think he did much, but now that he's gone, nothing seems to be going right anymore."

Here was a pastor who had chosen the right assistant but who hadn't realized his assistant couldn't function at the same speed and intensity level. What he needed was two Pastor Peacefuls to alternate days and pick up all of his pieces. When we don't understand the personalities, we expect others to think and act like us. Cholerics think that all people should function on their high energy level while Melancholy and Phlegmatic people are waiting for the others to calm down and relax.

Pastor Peaceful is always the "nice guy." He's not out to fight for his own way but to find compromise, keep everyone happy, and pick up the pieces. He is a blessed relief from the problems of the past. Everyone likes Pastor Peaceful, but some wonder if he's too indecisive and not motivated enough. After a few pleasant and refreshing years with him the people begin to mumble, "When is he going to do something? Remember how much Pastor Powerful could accomplish in such a short time? Remember how much we learned from Pastor Perfect? Oh, there was a spiritual man! And remember how much fun we had with Pastor Popular? Perhaps it's time for a change."

Sunny City

Let's take a mythical visit to Sunny City. The troubles all started when Peter Popular came to town after an unsuccessful attempt at seminary education. He'd enjoyed the speech classes and the debate team, but the idea of an in-depth study of Aramaic was worse than all Greek to him. Pete had been voted most likely to succeed in high school and was elected student body president in college. He was bright as well as charming, and he'd always had a magnetic personality. He wanted to be a pastor so he could stand up front and preach. His home church had encouraged him and even took up a love offering to give him spending money for seminary. Pete's denomination was adamant about education and degrees, so it was embarrassing when he failed his first year. He couldn't go home, so he moved to Sunny City and sold insurance.

Peter loved the Word of God and had a knack for making it simple enough and communicating truth to others in such a way that it changed their lives. A friend asked him to start a Bible study, and each week more people came. Pete was thrilled that so many responded to his teaching in spite of his lack of a seminary degree. There were nights when he had flashes of brilliance that electrified his growing group, and there were those times when his lack of preparation was apparent but his charisma kept the people attentive anyhow. He could always come up with a story that drew the people in and plugged any holes in his leaky lesson.

Fun Fellowship

After a year of steady growth, the group decided they wanted to be a church. Pete was the obvious choice for pastor. He hadn't mentioned his lack of a seminary degree lately, and while he never lied, he often ignored the truth and allowed people to make faulty assumptions. Some of his colorful examples were downright fiction, but no one seemed to care as long as they were entertaining. The group rented a school gymnasium on Sundays and named themselves the Fun Fellowship. The townspeople heard that church could be fun, and they flocked to hear Pastor Pete Popular preach.

Pastor Popular became the expected life of the party, although some found him frivolous when he lost a large check for the building fund and later laughed about finding it stapled to his daughter's term paper on sea mollusks. This fun-loving, forgetful, frivolous father of the flock came equipped with a Perfect Melancholy wife who would wring her hands daily over his misdemeanors. She tried to pull him together and got depressed over her failure. Loyal wife that she was, she stood behind him on Sunday mornings and whispered the names of each person as they came up the aisle. One Sunday she went into a visible decline when one bubbly lady effused over how much fun it must be to live with the pastor.

As time went on some of the more serious members wanted committees and deacons, and a few wanted a doctrinal statement and an accounting of the money. Pete had operated things out of his dining room and kept the cash in a shoe box. He could see little reason to count it as it fluctuated daily, and when he ran out of money he took an extra offering. Even though Pastor Popular gave exciting sermons, his reign came to a screeching halt when the new auditor found he'd used church funds to build a pool in his backyard. In the same month the auditor discovered him behind the organ with the church organist. People wanted to believe that they were just checking the tone of the pipes as they claimed, but when the Perfect Melancholy wife was carted off to the local Christian counseling center, this was the last straw. People began to whisper in the parking lot on Sundays, "Do you think this thing is too big for Pastor Popular?" "He's not really very deep and he can't remember people's names." "We need a serious man who is honest, aboveboard, and at the same time into depth."

Suddenly the group talked only of depth. People who were hardly wading in the spiritual shallows themselves wanted to go deeper. As Pete heard rumors of these complaints, he got uptight and lost some of his humor. Then came the day when the self-appointed board of elders voted to ask Pastor Popular to leave. To leave his own church! He was devastated and deeply hurt when they didn't even give him a farewell party.

The hastily created search committee knew exactly what they wanted: a man of depth, a spiritual giant, a prayer warrior, an organized genius, a man of degrees, someone musically gifted, artistic of nature, and meticulously groomed. In summary, a Perfect man. They found him right there in Sunny City at St. Spiritual's where he was the associate pastor of prayer and fasting. The church was thrilled to have a pious pastor, and by the time Pastor Perfect arrived to preach they were ready to get down to business. The first Sunday he announced that they were to become students of the Word, as he sensed their lack of spiritual maturity. "From here on you will bring to church a Bible (the King James Version because it is the only one God honors), a concordance, and a Greek interlinear translation."

The people were so excited about getting into the Word that they rushed to the local Christian bookstore, St. Thomas à Nelson, where Vera Volume helped them make the right selections. She hadn't sold this many Greek-type books since she opened ten years ago. The more affluent members ordered customized zippered book covers to hold the three volumes required for entrance to church on Sundays.

The first Sunday of Pastor Perfect's series on "Diving into Devotional Depth in Deuteronomy" brought out scholars who had never before come to church. The members were all embarrassed that they didn't know many verses and that they couldn't recite John 3:16 in unison. Pastor Perfect could see that he had his work cut out for him, so he extended the Sunday service an extra thirty minutes to increase his teaching time and added a Scripture memory class for Wednesday nights. The studious members liked these changes, but the remaining devotees of Pastor Popular muttered to each other, "This is *no* fun."

Not only was Pastor Perfect appalled at this group's scriptural illiteracy, but he was depressed for days over their lack of financial responsibility. There was no budget and no official bank account. The checks had been from Pastor Popular's personal account. He had always been confused by those pale green ledger pages with little squares and columns.

Once Pastor Perfect got over his despair over the flock's immaturity and lack of fiscal accountability, he set to work on a doctrinal statement. Since this church was not denominational, they didn't have to believe anything in particular; however, everyone had ideas of what they should or shouldn't consider doctrine. Pastor Perfect wanted to write this up himself, but the people wanted a committee. Pastor Perfect prayed, "Dear God, don't let these ignorant people make a mockery of Your church. Please give them divine wisdom."

God gave them so much wisdom that the completed statement took twelve pages full of Roman numerals and asterisks, and no one ever read it in its entirety.

Pastor Perfect had to tread lightly on his next project of changing the name of the church. He could hardly tolerate the "Fun Fellowship" as a serious entity, and by then the most optimistic of the group could see that this was certainly no fun! Meeting in a school gymnasium was unspiritual too, and Pastor Perfect found an abandoned church building that they could afford to buy. Even though it was in disrepair, it did have a steeple, and Pastor Perfect felt this was a start. He didn't ask for ideas from his verbose group, he just had a sign painted:

> *Parish of Piety and Perfection*

No one seemed to care what the sign said. They were all so weary of deep thinking and were so tired of carrying all those books to Sunday service. Pastor Perfect thought a new building would pep them up, but they were depressed over the leaky roof and lack of air conditioning. The attendance had dropped off and donations were down, as was the pastor.

Poor Pastor Perfect had the Spirit of the Lord upon him. He'd majored in the Dead Sea Scrolls at seminary and could pray like the pope with benedictions that left the saints in awe. He spent so many hours in scriptural study that he had no time for visitation, and he personally felt that much of the traditional social activity in the church was trivial and of no eternal value. He gathered people into spiritual cell blocks where they could pray for renewal, but the attendance dwindled when the groups found they had to pray out loud and they were not allowed to have refreshments.

Things got even worse for Pastor Perfect when his Popular Sanguine wife wore false eyelashes to the sweetheart banquet and everyone there branded her as a hussy. She was so hurt when she found they didn't love her that she got a job at a local restaurant as a hostess, causing a few to conjecture as to whether she might be taking a little nip now and then. All these rumors about his wife put the pastor in a deep depression, and some began to whisper in the parking lot, "We need someone who can get this church moving again!"

Before the secret search committee had even two clandestine meetings, Pastor Perfect resigned to teach Greek at the local seminary (which is where he is to this day), and the quest for a dynamic motivator began.

It is not easy to find a successful leader who is willing to leave a successful church. If he has built it up he wants to continue the progress unless the growth flattens out, the people refuse to build one more wing, or he has a fight with the wealthy chairman of the board. When the searchers found Pastor Powerful, he was a victim of all three scenarios. He had built his church from fifty to three hundred in two years, but several families had left town and no one seemed to be replacing them. He had created numerous programs and added rooms to house them, but when he tried to push turning the church lawn into a three-hole golf course for those who had a compulsion to be on the greens on Sundays, the people rebelled. Some would accept the idea if the church charged and used the money for new uniforms for the softball team. Some thought the plan feasible if the sermon was broadcast on loudspeakers and the players promised not to swear when they missed an easy putt. Some felt if the whole plan could be moved behind the church instead of in front it would look less commercial. In general, the congregation believed, after prayerful meditation, that teeing off while trying to avoid hitting the statue of the Virgin Mary was sacrilegious.

Fed up with these narrow-minded people who thought church was only for worship, Pastor Powerful was open to a new challenge. He hated the name "Parish of Piety and Perfection." *It sounds like a funeral parlor,* he said to himself, *and the building looks like death itself.* That first week he had already decided to rename the church.

┌─────────────────────────┐
│   *Power Place*   │
└─────────────────────────┘

Pastor Powerful had the sign repainted and determined to eliminate the word "sermon," calling his words "Moving and Motivational
Messages" to appeal to the yuppies who wouldn't come if church
sounded too spiritual.

When Pastor Powerful preached that first Sunday, he stood up front
with a roll of blueprints under his arm and gave a talk entitled "Building for the Future—God's Way." It was soon apparent that God's way
was the pastor's way. In looking at the plans spread out on the communion table, one elder was heard to say, "If we add all these wings,
the church will fly away!"

In his determination to refurbish the church building, Pastor Powerful stapled paint chips onto the church bulletins and suggested that
anyone opposing his color scheme could write a two-hundred-word
essay on their feelings about why the ladies' room shouldn't be pink
and the steeple done in gold leaf. "I will read each comment and pray
over your opinions," he affirmed to the group, knowing that not one
of them had written fifty words even to their mother in years.

Pastor Powerful could tell right from the beginning that this was
a lazy group. They seemed to feel that showing up on Sundays carrying their three texts was about all one could ask of them. They'd
become jaded about the sorry state of the ceiling, the pathetic plumbing, and the lack of air, causing them to fan themselves with the new
church bulletins. Pastor Powerful was humiliated himself when, after
filling the baptismal tank, he went up with a corpulent convert to find
the tank empty and the basement awash in holy water. However, no
one seemed eager to repair the leaks.

At the board meeting Pastor Powerful was irate at the plumbing
problems and almost blew up when the Powerful Choleric chairman
stated, "This is not our fault but yours. No really intelligent person
would fill a tank with water without checking for leaks ahead of time."
After that comment, another elder suggested Pastor Powerful should
pay for the repairs himself. "After all, we weren't the ones who flooded
the basement."

Pastor Powerful was not accustomed to accepting blame for anything, and he could see his honeymoon with the board was over. He
divided the members into work teams of ten and insisted they show
up each Saturday to work.

The people were also disenchanted with the pastor's Peaceful Phlegmatic wife who had no musical talent and who refused to take her turn at baby-sitting in the church nursery. "Who does she think she is?" Sally Spiritual asked at the meeting of the flower-arranging committee. "Someone special? Too good to work?"

What Sally and the others didn't know was that the pastor's wife was scared to death of them and knew she'd be criticized whether she came or not. She had already developed stomach problems from answering the phone and internalizing all the complaints her husband's aggressive nature had stirred up. She was sad and lonely, and while they criticized her absence, no one came to call on her.

Soon there developed a doctrinal split. Pastor Powerful could see the handwriting on the church wall even though he could hardly believe that the people would turn against a man so dedicated to progress and future plans. When some complained he didn't spend enough time with the people, he explained, "God called me to build a church, not to counsel the people." In fact, he canceled the adult singles group because it was bringing in people with problems. "All we want here," he explained in a message, "is sweet little families who will give to the church."

Well, the sweet little families didn't give enough and the plans for the interactive video wing had to be postponed. When the board voted down turning the church basement into an indoor skating rink, Pastor Powerful knew he was defeated. He should have left right then, but he needed the salary to support him until he could finish his book on church growth and write the seminars to go with the book, complete with colored overheads. By the time he resigned, he had learned how to walk on a bed of hot coals and to drop on one knee like Zig Ziglar, and he was ready to become a motivational speaker. Last we knew, he was working on an infomercial with Kathie Lee.

The search committee was called up to duty and they reviewed their options. "We've seen what a disaster it is to have a pastor with personality," Sam Serious observed. "So let's look for someone who doesn't try to be funny. You can't trust those people with charm."

"But Sam," Steve Silly said, "you were the one who brought in Pastor Perfect. Remember how he made us carry all those books? You can't live long with a man who wants you to pray out loud and who keeps getting you into the Word."

They all nodded at the recall of those endless days of spiritual depth. "Well, we've eliminated humor and Bible study," Bob Bossy bellowed.

"And we surely don't want another one with his own agenda. We have to get control of this church once and for all!"

"That doesn't leave us a lot of options," Floyd Follower said slowly. "I guess we need to find a middle-of-the-road person who's a little bit funny, but who's not overspiritual or domineering." They all agreed with Floyd and set out to look for an inoffensive man with no agenda.

"Before we adjourn," Betty Bubbles added, "could we vote to disband the work groups? I never remember to show up and then I feel guilty when those do-gooders call me the next day."

The vote was unanimous.

Peaceful Pastures

No one knew where to look for a new pastor, so Bob Bossy went to the local seminary for a new graduate. Someone too young to think he knew everything, too inexperienced to pontificate, too insecure to be charming. Bob was thrilled when he interviewed Phil Phlegmatic and found he was right in the middle of the class ranking, had not won any prizes, but had been voted "Mr. Congeniality" by his peers.

"He's the nicest young man I've ever met," Bob Bossy extolled, "And he seems to see me as a father figure." Bob could imagine how easy it would be to control this young man and get the church back on an even keel. Phil was ordained as Pastor Peaceful and moved into the new parsonage Pastor Powerful had built but never got to live in. All the mothers with young daughters paraded them before him and had him over for dinner. "It's not good for man to live alone," Sally Spiritual intoned to Phil one Sunday. "Come speak to the young ladies' Gracious Guild and look them over."

Phil checked them off in his head. Felicia Frump was intelligent, but she had no sense of style. Cathy Calm seemed too much like him. Tessie Talk was too loud and tried too hard to be the center of attention. Somehow the one who appealed to Phil the most was Bob's daughter, Beverly Bossy. She seemed to have life together, could speak up on any subject, and had inherited her father's brand of leadership. Phil could see that she could make decisions that were difficult for him and help him form opinions.

The board loved Pastor Peaceful. He agreed with whatever they wanted, he healed the pains of the past, and he cut the Sunday worship service down to fifty minutes so the men could get home in time for the football games on TV. No one could find fault with Phil.

Meanwhile, Beverly took over the entire women's ministry. She replaced the elderly chairwomen with "young blood with fresh ideas." She read the bylaws, which no one had ever done before, and found them to be woefully outdated and overly spiritual. "Times have changed," she told the women. "We must prepare for the next century." When the former director of the "bandage rolling for the missionaries" committee objected to the new regime, Beverly replied, "Anyone can see that if a cause is dead, it's best to bury it quickly and create something new that works."

In her youth and zeal, Beverly didn't realize that the only problem with burying these dead horses is that they were all created by dear little suffragettes of the faith who, when their personal pet is killed, become martyred saints equaled only by those burned at the stake. Even though Beverly came on too strong and too quickly, the majority of the people liked Phil so much that they shrugged her off with comments like "She is just like her father . . . a chip off the old block."

Pastor Peaceful gave short sermons that praised his people and demanded little from them. He had a pleasing smile and nodded deferentially to all who questioned him. He was so glad that Pastor Powerful had set the people to work. There was little left to do. The walls were freshly painted, the ladies' room tiled pink, the steeple gleaming in gold leaf, the parking lot paved, and the leaks in the baptistery repaired. Finances were stable, making sermons pleading for money unnecessary, and no one seemed to care that the Pew Pillows committee had disbanded.

Pastor Peaceful didn't like the name Power Place for his church, but it was easier to leave it up than to repaint the sign. Besides, he couldn't really think of an appropriate title and no one seemed to care. Beverly liked Power Place and thought his suggestion of Peaceful Pastures made it sound like the group was out wandering the fields of life with no purpose.

Time passed quietly and pleasantly for the folks in Sunny City. Young Phil matured, and the sermons Beverly wrote for him had increasing depth, but one day the people stood around in the parking lot and began to review the easy life. "I know this is good," Steve Silly said, "but I miss the fun we had with Pastor Popular."

"I never liked him much," Sam Serious said. "Too shallow, unprepared, always laughing like a child. Pastor Perfect was the one for me. I liked his sermons; they were really deep."

"But he never got anything done," Bob Bossy stated. I think we didn't appreciate Pastor Powerful enough. He's really what made this church what it is today."

"Pastor Peaceful is so balanced," Floyd Follower added. "He hasn't caused one problem since he's been here. I admire a man who avoids conflict and stays above the fray."

"You're all really right," Betty Bubbles blurted out. "What we need is a combination of all their strengths with none of their weaknesses."

No Weakness Allowed

Isn't that what we're all looking for? All strengths and no weaknesses? No wonder we are so frequently disappointed.

If only search committees could study the personalities before producing the idealistic personality profile for the ideal pastor, seeking a mythological man with the strengths of all and the weaknesses of none. Only the Lord Jesus fit that profile—and they killed Him when He was thirty-three:

- Jesus was the only one who could keep a crowd of ordinary people spellbound on a hot hillside with no pew cushions while He spun parables so fascinating that they never thought of the Golden Arches and were filled with filet-o-fish and baskets of bread.
- Jesus had such depth that even as a young boy He quoted Scripture and confounded the scribes, yet He could convict a sinful woman with a simple "Go and sin no more."
- He had the leadership ability to take a group of ordinary men, none of whom had an M.B.A., and blend together a board that went out to evangelize their world.
- Surely He was the Prince of Peace and the Lord of Lords and was heard to say on the mountain, "Blessed are the peacemakers for they shall be called sons of God."

Did you ever realize before how much we expect of pastors? They're in a no-win situation. Think over the pastors you've had in your lifetime. Make a list of each name, followed by his remembered strengths and weaknesses. What was each one able to deliver? What was his wife like? What did the church expect? What were he and his wife able to deliver? In retrospect, how does your opinion differ now?

We need to understand that we are born with an innate personality, and that with each set of strengths and social skills there is a set of weaknesses that keeps us depending on the Lord for our success. The next time you are on a search committee, have the people read this chapter and mutually decide what your church needs at this point. Whatever your pastor's personality, it is your job to help him work in the area of his strengths and to staff his shortcomings without making him feel inferior or insecure.

The ideal would be a Popular pastor who's organized, a Perfect pastor who's cheerful, a Powerful pastor who's humble, or a Peaceful pastor who's motivated. But you won't find the Popular Perfect Powerful Peaceful Pastor until you walk through the Pearly Gates and see the Lord Jesus face-to-face. Until then, have fun waiting, aim for perfection, stay in control, and keep the peace.

Clergy

Pastoring with Different Leadership Styles

CHUCK ALT

Chuck Alt has been a pastor for nineteen years. He knows firsthand how frustrating ministry can be when the pastor is expected to do the work of ministry alone. Ministry became exciting, fulfilling, and fun when he learned how to place people in ministries that fit their personalities, gifts, and passions. After leading a seventy-year-old traditional congregation into an "equipping everyone for ministry" philosophy, he now helps other churches do the same.

The scenario is all too common. A pastor becomes desperate for help in his ministry. There are only so many days in a week and so many hours in a day, yet many pastors feel the need for a thirty-hour day and an eight-day week. And even that may not allow enough time to accomplish all that is expected. I remember days of feeling overwhelmed by the expectations of the congregation and church board. It seemed that there were people who wanted me to call on the elderly and also relate well to the youth. I was to be able to visit every home in the community and produce well-researched sermons. The hats I wore included that of evangelist, administrator, pastor, youth leader, worship leader, and family man. I was to be active in the community, make hospital calls, keep track

174

of everyone who died, and be on call twenty-four hours a day in case of an emergency. While on vacation I was to leave a phone number just in case someone needed me (sometimes they did call). Was this the kind of ministry God really intended for the pastor?

In Bible college I was taught the Ephesians 4 principle of equipping people for ministry (see Ephesians 4:11–16). I was excited about the potential impact of a local congregation in a community if everyone functioned in a ministry. The professor made it clear that our job was to work ourselves out of our position as pastor. That thought puzzled me. How could I have a job if I kept replacing myself? My Peaceful Phlegmatic/Perfect Melancholy nature could not handle the insecurity of this kind of thinking. My solution was to put the burden on God. Since He had created this system of replacing myself in each ministry, I would just have to trust Him to keep providing churches for me to pastor until I retired.

When I finally entered the real world of ministry, this kind of idealism had a terrible clash with reality. I found out that most congregations are not interested in being involved in ministry like I thought they would be. They let me know that *I* had been hired to "do ministry." What?! Maybe that professor did not know what he was talking about after all. These people believed I had been specially trained to preach, teach, make hospital calls, call on the elderly, lead the worship service and youth program, plus produce a church bulletin and newsletter, as well as turning on and off the lights and heat for all services. I am sure they would have wanted me to work in the nursery during the worship service if I could still do the sermon as well. One elderly lady let me know in no uncertain terms that "the last preacher mowed my yard and it won't hurt you to do it either!" Can you believe that?! My first church equated "busyness in ministry" with "dedicated man of God"—the busier I was the more spiritual I became in their eyes. I was to have a radio program on Sunday mornings plus preach morning and evening and teach a Sunday school class. Every Wednesday night I was to lead a Bible study, and once a month I was expected to lead the worship service for the local nursing home. This was only the tip of the iceberg. Why wasn't ministry working out like my professor said it should?

After five and a half years of trying to do my job (or I should say "keep my job") by pleasing the congregation, I decided to move on. My next church was an exciting situation—at least during the interviewing process. I still believed that what the Bible taught about the equipping ministry was true, and I explained it in great detail during the interview. All thirteen men on the board agreed that this kind of ministry was what the congregation needed. After several weeks in this new location I met reality again. "We hired *you* to do ministry" was the theme song. Where was that professor when I needed him? My frustration level with ministry hit an all-time high. It seemed like it was time to get out. Maybe I wasn't cut out for the ministry after all. Having no trade by which I could support my family, I quickly moved on to another church. This was where everything turned around.

All of the congregations I served saw the value of me receiving more training through seminars. This new church was no exception. The seminar they sent me to was designed for pastors who wanted their church to grow. It pulled together all the lessons I had been taught and all I believed about the equipping ministry. During this particular seminar I was introduced to the book *Personality Plus* by Florence Littauer. Her book helped me tolerate the difficult personalities I met in ministry.

Understanding personalities also improved my relationship with my wife. Now I understood why we had conflict at times. We were opposites in many ways. She was a Powerful Choleric, and I was a Peaceful Phlegmatic. Our strengths and weaknesses were different. Problems in our relationship, we realized, came when we each tried to make the other person conform to our own preferred behavior. She did not have to be like me, and I did not have to be like her.

Suddenly I realized that a large part of my frustration in ministry was because of me. I had strengths that I thought everyone should have. Actually, I thought everyone did have them, but some were too lazy to use them. For example, I can work well on a team. It is very natural for me to come alongside a leader I believe in and support the cause. My secondary nature is that of a Perfect Melancholy, so I love to do research and detail work. Repetitive tasks do not bore me—my real value lies in being analytical.

My weaknesses were the biggest problem. I tend to procrastinate and miss deadlines. My emotions stay pretty well hidden, and people think I am mad at them and never get excited about anything. When researching information for a sermon, I often get so bogged down in gathering details that I lose the big picture and end up giving too much intellectual information. People would rather see more applications to their lives. My preference is to work alone with limited people contact. Therefore, I don't get very excited about going calling. My nat-

Placing People in Ministries

Ministry can become "a mission I am called to" rather than "a job in the church" if you place people in ministries that use their personality strengths. People become frustrated in ministry when they are expected to be strong in an area of weakness (e.g., a Popular Sanguine asked to keep track of financial records). So be certain you aren't placing people in ministries that clash with the weaknesses in their personality type. Spiritual gifts inventories available at your local Christian bookstore will help you determine an individual's role in the body of Christ. These personality squares offer some specific suggestions that will help you find the ministry matches that transform a job into a mission.

Popular Sanguine ***Prefers to Be out in Front*** *Greeters, Ushers, Song Leaders, Hospitality Committee Personnel* • natural strength is friendliness • enjoy interacting with people • work well in a spontaneous and positive environment • prefer a fast pace with few restrictions • allow them freedom to be creative and spontaneous • seek ministries that use their friendliness and relationship-building skills • avoid ministries where they work alone	**Powerful Choleric** ***Prefers to Be out in Front*** *VBS Directors, Sunday School Superintendents, Fund-Raising Chairpersons* • natural strength is getting the job completed • enjoy leading worthwhile projects • work well in getting new projects and ministries started • prefer to lead rather than follow • allow them freedom to make decisions • seek ministries that use their vision, leadership, and problem-solving skills • avoid maintenance-oriented ministries
Peaceful Phlegmatic ***Prefers to Be behind the Scenes*** *Ministry Team Members, Nursery Workers, Nursing Home Volunteers* • natural strength is cooperation and routine • like being a loyal, supportive member of the team • work well following a good leader • prefer a steady and consistent pace • spell out the parameters for them • seek ministries that use their patient, warm, and easygoing style • avoid high-pressure ministries that require frequent change	**Perfect Melancholy** ***Prefers to Be behind the Scenes*** *Secretaries, Treasurers, Ministry Schedule Coordinators* • natural strength is compliance with the rules and guidelines • like tasks that require information gathering and accurate detail • work well alone • prefer to know all the background and specific details before moving ahead • spell out the parameters, allowing them to ask questions as needed • seek ministries that use their organizational and accuracy skills • avoid ministries where they might receive lots of criticism from others

ural shyness and desire to stay in the background hinders me from going into the community and introducing myself to people I don't know. This kind of information about myself helped me realize what needed to change in my ministry.

The challenge was to make sure my strengths were being used rather than expecting perfection where I was weak. The congregation also needed to realize what I did best and where I needed their help. Our problem had been similar to what I realized about my relationship to my wife. I wanted the congregation to behave like me, and the congregation wanted me to behave like them. You can guess how challenging it is to be all four personalities at the same time.

Realizing the congregation was a mixture of all the personalities was a real blessing. Biblical teaching about the different parts of the body of Christ is very clear. Romans 12:4–8; 1 Corinthians 12:4–21; and Ephesians 4:11–16 show that all of the parts do not have the same function. Common sense tells us that different gifts plus different personalities equals unique individuals. It was becoming clear. The body of Christ functions as God intended it to when we help people function in their area of strength!

During the seminar I learned that *everything* I had been taught about the equipping ministry was *true!* I wanted to stand up and shout during the seminar, but I knew that that was not appropriate for a Peaceful Phlegmatic. So I held my tongue. But on the inside there was a celebration going on. I kept saying to myself, *I knew I was right! I knew I was right!* The vision for ministry the professor had started in me was once again ignited.

Hindsight has an amazing way of being accurate. I reflected on the mistakes I had made in ministry by recruiting the wrong personalities for the wrong ministry. For example, it did not make sense to have greeters who did not like to smile. Most of my greeters had been Perfect Melancholies who did not want to turn me down. The best greeters are the Popular Sanguines. They love people and make a better first impression. It was not smart, however, to appoint a Popular Sanguine as an attendance keeper. They are terrible with details and working alone. They want to be with *people!* The Perfect Melancholies are the ones who make excellent record keepers. Asking two Powerful Cholerics to serve on the Vacation Bible School committee is just asking for trouble. They both have a vision of how it should be done—which is usually a different vision, and they both want to lead rather than follow. It would be better to let both head up different committees. The applications of my new insights into personalities were endless!

The more I understood personalities, the more I saw the mistakes I had made. I can remember being in a board meeting and asking for help on a project. Peaceful Phlegmatics would give in to my prodding and never get around to getting it done. One of our board chairmen was a Powerful Choleric. He always seemed so bossy. I resisted him and he resisted me on how ministry was to be done. The quietness of many board members baffled me until I learned that Peaceful Phlegmatics and Perfect Melancholies like to keep information to themselves. A Peaceful Phlegmatic may agree with you on the outside during the meeting but disagree on the inside. Perfect Melancholies fear being criticized and will speak up only when the environment is favorable. Both will clam up if the environment becomes antagonistic. I kept thinking about all the heartache I could have avoided if I had known this information about different personalities sooner. I was glad I knew about it now.

I believe it is important for all pastors and even lay leaders to become familiar with the various personalities. Such a familiarity will not solve all your problems, but it is a tool that will help. Jesus had insight into the behavior of people. He did not need anyone to teach Him what was in people, He already knew (John 2:25). Understanding the personalities gives us insight into people so we can work more effectively with them. Consider some of the possibilities. Powerful Cholerics can make excellent leaders when you need someone to head up a project. They have vision and the ability to solve problems and obstacles that get in the way. If you as the pastor are a Peaceful Phlegmatic, like I am, and need to begin a building project, you should select a well-respected Powerful Choleric to take charge.

Popular Sanguines will work well in any position that puts them in front of people. Recruit them for opportunities where their warmth and friendliness can be used. Have you ever wanted to cry during the worship service, not because of its beauty, but because the worship leader was doing such a terrible job?! A Popular Sanguine who loves the Lord and can sing will always relate better to the congregation than a Perfect Melancholy who worries about the accompanist or the Powerful Choleric who orders people to "smile when you sing!"

The Peaceful Phlegmatic will do well with any job when the parameters are clearly spelled out. Show them where the snow shovel and salt are located and tell them what time you want the walks cleared by for Sunday service, and they will be excellent.

Some people cannot stand the tedious work of record keeping. But *someone* has to keep financial records for the church. What better person than the Perfect Melancholy for such a task? They actually enjoy the detail work, and if the responsibility is important they will do it perfectly. I will never forget the day we asked one of our Popular Sanguines to be in charge of our twenty-four-hour prayer vigil. She had a passion for prayer. Since her secondary personality type was Powerful Choleric, she knew how to organize and get things done—but she especially knew how to have fun. Everyone in the congregation loved her. She is often described as "bubbly." A large number of people signed up for the vigil, and it was a great success. This project worked so well that we asked her to introduce our fund-raising campaign. Once again it went well, and she did an excellent job motivating people to be excited and involved.

Personality behavior is only one facet to consider in recruiting people for a ministry. At the church growth seminar I learned a three-pronged approach and have found it works effectively. The *first* of the three prongs is to help individuals discover their gifts for ministry. There are many tools available today to help people discover their gift for ministry, and I recommend you use one. Help people identify their top three action gifts. There is a difference between an action gift and a support gift. Teaching is an action gift. Faith is a support gift. Giving is an action gift, but mercy is a support gift. Evangelism is an action gift, and compassion is a support gift.

After you find the gifts of individuals, also have them complete a Personality Profile. The Personality Profile is the *second* prong that will help determine if individuals are people-oriented or task-oriented. Are they outgoing or would they rather stay behind the scenes? This knowledge alone will go a long way in avoiding future stress for you and others.

The *third* prong is to find out what individuals love to do. What would they skip a meal or miss sleep to be involved in? What have they enjoyed doing in the past that caused them to lose track of time? The answer to these questions helps you discover their passion. Once you know all three areas about individuals, you are ready to interview them for a ministry that uses their unique combination.

Pastor, don't be surprised if they love the ministry you help them find. It will be extremely close to a custom fit. This is when laypeople begin to enjoy ministry.

One day I told my wife that we needed to begin praying for more Sunday school teachers. Doesn't every congregation have this problem? Our past approach in recruiting teachers involved snatching up the first unsuspecting soul that showed a slight interest. We took "Let me think about it first . . ." to be a definite yes. The length of commitment was "till death do us part." But at this point in our ministry we were more purposeful. Our congregation believed that God had planted us in our town to accomplish a specific mission. No other congregation was going to send a missionary to do what God had placed ours there to do. If we did not reach the unchurched in our community, then who would?

So, I asked my wife and others to pray for more teachers. We were specific that we needed someone who would be willing to teach the junior high class. You already know how challenging that can be. We wanted this teacher to be someone who could teach the young people the biblical view of creation. It seemed that every fall they were brainwashed with evolutionary theories, and the church needed to teach the truth about origins. After several weeks a young man began attending the classes we offered on the gifts and personalities. Believe it or not, his three-pronged profile turned out to be a Perfect Melancholy teacher who loved kids, loved research, and had a keen interest in biblical creation. Can you believe it?!! God had answered our prayer.

As a pastor, you owe it to yourself, to your spouse, and to your congregation to learn as much about the different personality types as you can. It will help you work more effectively with others, but it will also help you understand more about yourself. The discouragement all of us in ministry experience from time to time could well be reduced by knowing the uniqueness with which God has gifted you. There is no one personality that is better than the others. They all have their benefits and liabilities in ministry. The key is to learn to adapt your behavior to the people and environment you are in. For example, if you are a Powerful Choleric pastor, you will naturally be able to show the way when others are wondering what to do. Your vision will inspire others to follow you, but use this skill carefully as the congregation may perceive you as being too bossy. People usually want to be led instead of driven. If you are a Popular Sanguine pastor, people will love you. You will be a good conversationalist, and they will love your story-filled sermons, but they may also see you as someone who doesn't listen or pay attention to important details. If you are a Peaceful Phlegmatic preacher, people will like you and the warm relationships you are able to build, but they may also get impatient waiting for something significant to happen in your ministry. If you are the Perfect Melancholy minister, the people may love the good research you do for your sermons but interpret your "loner style" as a rejection of them.

As you learn the strengths and weaknesses of your personal style, remember to focus on what you do well and learn what parts of your behavior need to be flexible. If you have a weakness where the congregation needs you to be strong, with the power of the Holy Spirit do your best to change or hire a staff person who has that particular personality strength. Rather than trying to be the Lone Ranger pastor who does it all himself, you need to be a team with your congregation and work together.

The call to ministry begins on the inside. You see a need and realize God has equipped you to help meet it. Your motivation grows as you realize the potential impact you can have for God's great cause. The call turns into a passion. It becomes the "one thing I do." Your passion is so strong that even if you were fired from your church, you would still fulfill your call. Someone would have to take your life to keep you from fulfilling this mission. That is what I consider a call to ministry to be. If you know you have been called to ministry, then discover what it is that you do best. What need in the kingdom of God do you see that puts a fire in your soul and reminds you that you were born for such a time as this? God has not made a mistake in allowing you to be where you are at this time in your life. He has a purpose for your life.

My prayer for all the pastors who read this is that God might use what you have learned about the personality types to reignite the excitement of working with people. I hope you will see them as unique individuals with potential rather than as difficult people you wish to avoid. Gain insight into yourself and focus on the strengths you have. Use them for the glory of God. Become the leader God designed you to be!

Spiritual Life
How the Personalities Respond to God

ROSA MARIA FAULKNER

Rosa Maria Faulkner is a Christian speaker with leadership skills honed by her early preparation in the performing arts and a career in teaching. She applies biblical truths to a wide range of topics for women's retreats, conferences, and seminars. Her experiences in addressing more than five hundred groups during the past twenty years provide a rich source of material for her writings on the subject of personalities.

Once in our Bible study class we were asked to go around the room and describe what we thought God was like. A company president said, "God is powerful, decisive, and focused on achieving His purpose." Next, a gentle, grandmotherly type said, "God is loving, kind, and compassionate." At this point, my Perfect Melancholy husband nudged me and whispered, "Do you realize we're all describing ourselves?!" And as we continued around the room, almost everyone proceeded to describe God in terms of their own personality. As a combination Popular Sanguine/Powerful Choleric, my T-shirt says, "Let's do it my way, and do it now, as long as it's fun"—and I too would certainly like to think that my personality is somewhat aligned with God's. I wonder if that's a universal impulse among Christians?

While influenced by upbringing and experience, our basic personality is largely genetic in origin—that is, God-given. Psalm 139:13–14 (NIV) says, "For you created my inmost being; you knit me together in my mother's womb. I praise you because I am fearfully and wonderfully made." It's an incredibly fascinating subject—the different personalities experiencing the same God in very different ways. Or, viewed from another perspective, that same God gifting us with distinct personalities, which by their very nature cause us to see Him differently. It's then just a short reach to the conclusion that God chooses to reveal Himself differently to each of us. I watch people in the church pray diligently and then find themselves 180 degrees apart on an issue. Might that sometimes be true because God doesn't always care as much about the resolution of the issue as He does about His children learning to play out their differences? If we are all preprogrammed to have a unique personal perception of God, it follows that we must have a unique one-on-one relationship with Him. On the one hand, that should make each of us feel very special. On the other hand, it makes us wonder how we can achieve the unity that the Lord Jesus prays for in John 17:23. The Lord Jesus wants that unity so the world will know that He is sent from God. So, in a very real sense, our task on the earth is to become unified in Christ. Given our inherited personality differences, that task is a worthy challenge, not a slam dunk.

Someday, when DNA researchers announce they've discovered the "personality gene" that makes a combination Popular Sanguine/Powerful Choleric very much unlike a Perfect Melancholy/Peaceful Phlegmatic, they will also be announcing that God intended us to have unique personalities so that He can have a unique relationship with each of us.

The Personalities' Search for God

Recently I began to poll my seminar groups to see what personality traits they ascribe to God, and to find out if the various personalities face a different set of conditions as they search for and establish a relationship with Him.

The results have been somewhat similar to the earlier responses in our Bible study class—people tend to see Him as having the best characteristics of their own personality. Or, while they feel that He exhibits

The Holy Spirit Completes and Repairs Personalities

Popular Sanguine	Powerful Choleric
Original Personality: • joyful • enthusiastic • loud • shallow **In the Spirit Can Also Become:** • meditative • sensitive • deep	**Original Personality:** • dynamic • strong-willed • decisive • self-sufficient • quick-tempered **In the Spirit Can Also Become:** • gentle • patient • kind • dependent on God
Peaceful Phlegmatic	Perfect Melancholy
Original Personality: • easygoing • patient • kind • lethargic • indecisive **In the Spirit Can Also Become:** • motivated • energetic	**Original Personality:** • deep • sensitive to others • self-sacrificing • unforgiving • introverted **In the Spirit Can Also Become:** • joyful • outgoing • open

all the known strengths, they focus on only the ones that are characteristic of their own type.

For instance, the Popular Sanguines are the only ones to have specifically mentioned that God has a sense of humor. They often mention that one of the key aspects of the fruit of the Spirit is joy. Powerful Cholerics will emphasize God's power. They see Him as Alpha and Omega, the Beginning and the End. One Powerful Choleric described Him as One who "sees the big picture" (a classic), and another spoke of His "correcting wrongs" and taking vengeance (Acts 5:1–11). I've had Perfect Melancholies point out God's perfection, His inability to look upon our sins and imperfections, His self-sacrifice in sending His only Son, His willingness to hear complaints (Ps. 64:1), His highly detailed and orderly nature, and His love of artistic beauty as shown in the universe He created. Peaceful Phlegmatics will mention how God loves peace, patience, and kindness, the third, fourth, and fifth fruits of the Spirit as revealed in Galatians 5:22. They also like to think of Him as a good listener who turns a sympathetic ear toward His children.

This pattern has repeated itself in so many instances that it seems safe to conclude that Christians in general want to see some of their own positive traits in God, and some of God's traits in themselves. And as I read in Genesis 1:27 that we are made in His image, I find it hard to argue against those views. But in one group, I encountered a woman who seemed somehow more advanced in her thinking. She seemed poised on the brink of a spiritual breakthrough when she pointed out that, rather than claim a comparison or a similarity with God's personality, we would be a lot better off to consider those traits where we are lacking or weak—those areas where there is no similarity—and then pray for God to fill us in and complete us from His supply of the good characteristics our own personality lacks. As Jesus said, "Be perfect, therefore, as your heavenly Father is perfect" (Matt. 5:48 NIV).

Carrying Our Baggage

As I've talked to various groups, no one wanted to say that God in His goodness would show more favor to one personality than to another. Nor would anyone say He might handicap or erect unfair hurdles for certain groups in their striving to get into a close relationship with Him. And before a live audience, I couldn't bring myself to push the point. But I think of the "potter and the clay," where He molds us as He pleases, and I'm going to stick my neck out and say, to the contrary, that some personalities do seem to have an inside track while others may have a harder road to travel on their spiritual journeys. The Peaceful Phlegmatics, for instance, start out with three aspects of the fruit of the Spirit—peace, patience, and kindness—in the bag before they even become Christians.

Christianity is a people business. It's all about love, and sharing, and giving. Aren't the Powerful Cholerics, who may be impatient and manipulative, carrying some particularly heavy baggage in trying to express these qualities? And to the extent a Powerful Choleric is proud of his power and control, he is guilty of the first deadly sin. Also, the Scriptures have some harsh words for the Peaceful Phlegmatic traits of sloth, sluggardness, and lukewarmness. What about "growth" and "maturity" in Christ—do Popular Sanguines want maturity in anything? Will they ever grow up and attain more than a shallow, superficial Christian walk? Then there's the Perfect Melancholy, who is usually wrapped up in "self," is often critical, and may kill the joy for others. My point is that each of the personalities has serious built-in negatives that become glaring faults when held up alongside the standard of Christlikeness—the prize God put us here to attain.

The concept of original sin is that Adam's and Eve's disobedience caused humankind to be expelled from Eden. In our day, we have no specific "tree" to avoid (although we remain disobedient), but we start our lives with these built-in faults, these sins that are natural parts of our personalities. And if we continue to live with these faults, we won't ever progress toward Christlikeness. What this means is that we must repent of a large chunk of our own personalities! Giving up a piece of our original self isn't easy—and depending on our specific personality blend, and the extremity of the personality, some of us have a lot more to repent of than others. Doesn't seem fair? Well, remember the "potter and the clay." There is hope.

The Personalities in Church

It is very obvious from this that different personalities perceive God differently and have vastly different needs and expectations in their spiritual lives. Each personality likewise will experience the same pastor, class, sermon, and program very differently, and will certainly have widely differing desires and expectations about anything the church does or tries to do. This means, of course, that a "one-size-fits-all" church experience isn't going to work.

The truth of this was brought home to me at a recent women's retreat. We had studied the strengths of each personality in the morning. After lunch we started looking at the weaknesses—I always have them study the weaknesses on a full stomach—and when we mentioned "lack of enthusiasm" for the Peaceful Phlegmatic, a lightbulb suddenly seemed to go on over the pastor's wife's head. A combination Popular Sanguine/Powerful Choleric, she excitedly said that she now understood why she hadn't liked a visiting lay ministry team's presentation. It was too laid-back and low-key—a Peaceful Phlegmatic presentation. She had really been quite annoyed that others in the church disagreed with her about it. The Peacefuls in the church hadn't seen anything at all wrong with the presentation.

At a Saturday seminar at a Baptist church in Wilmington, Delaware, we were seated around tables in the social hall completing the

Personality Profile. As usual, the Popular Sanguines had clumped together at one table and were laughing and cutting up. The pastor's wife, a Perfect Melancholy, really wanted to concentrate on doing the test perfectly. She raised her hand and said, "Could we please have it quiet in here?" Unless there is real spiritual unity in the body of Christ, even the noise level becomes a bone of contention. People need to understand and be sensitive to those with different personalities.

We had a disaster in our Sunday school class several years ago. We were discussing the resurrection of Lazarus and the demonstration of Jesus' power over death. Somehow, one of our Popular Sanguines, for whom everything can be a springboard for a one-liner, and one of our Perfect Melancholies, who has a sardonic view of death, got into a side discussion on American funeral customs and how funny it seems when someone states how "good" or "natural" the deceased looks in the coffin. Almost everybody laughed—except the Perfect Melancholy woman who, followed by her husband, got up and left the room. I later went to her home to apologize, taking a little gift, in hopes of getting them to come back. She said, "Rosa, I think Bible study should be serious. There is a time and place for everything, and Bible study is not the place to laugh and have fun. We have too many people in our class who laugh and have too much fun." In all fairness, I must add that at the time her brother was dying of cancer, but neither she nor her husband ever returned. If she had returned she probably wouldn't have seen the humor when my husband later introduced himself as the new deacon for our class and said, "If any of you are going to die, go to the hospital, or have a serious illness, please let me know in advance—as it's terribly embarrassing when the church office finds out about these things before your deacon does." Christians aren't supposed to care too much about death, but some of us don't like to joke about it. In our church, classes are organized by age. I wonder sometimes if they shouldn't be organized by personality instead.

Bob, a combination Perfect Melancholy/Peaceful Phlegmatic, came back from Promise Keepers in May of 1995 totally filled with the Holy Spirit. He was in love not only with God, but with the church and everybody in it, and of course, he wanted everybody else in the church to share the same experience. We know the experience was real because he had the kind of zeal, energy, and strength he just doesn't have on his own. Within weeks he was elected deacon and "small group director," a job that basically involved reorganizing the church. Thinking he could leverage the deacon position, he set about explaining, educating, recruiting, and trying to convince the church how the new non-denominational megachurches use small groups to minister to people, help them grow spiritually, and expand the church at an exponential rate. He quickly found out that most people in the church liked the status quo and weren't interested in making any major structural changes from the way things had always been done in the past. Rather than transforming our church's spiritual life, Bob soon found himself struggling to preserve and maintain his own spiritual "altitude." People need to be in fellowship with others operating on the same spiritual frequency, or it can get very lonely, even in a big, bustling church.

Again at another church, we were preparing to do the Personality Profile when the pastor's wife (who turned out to be Powerful Choleric) raised her hand and asked, "Am I supposed to answer these questions in terms of who I really am on the inside, or as who the people in the church expect me to be?" That made me realize that a pastor's wife, if she's strongly positioned in one of the personalities, is going to be quite different from a high percentage of the congregation, no matter which personality she is. That is true of the rest of us as well, but fortunately for us, unlike the pastor's wife, we aren't expected to try to please everybody.

Spiritual Life of the Personalities

Recently I had the opportunity to ask a group of forty-seven women at a church in York, Pennsylvania, how they felt about their spiritual lives and whether they felt each of the personalities were different in that regard. Asked how they prayed, the Peaceful Phlegmatics said their self-contentment level is so high they may not feel the need to pray for change in their lives. Also they admitted that indecisiveness and procrastination could prevent their making the decision for Christ or delay it until it is too late. Popular Sanguines said they prayed short but emotional prayers scattered throughout the day, with no set time or routine for meeting with the Lord. The Powerful Cholerics admitted that they prayed directive prayers trying to tell God what to do and how to do it. Since I am part Powerful Choleric (my children call me "The Great Choir Director of Life"), I confess I have also prayed that way at times. The Perfect Melancholies, in this case, appear to have the right idea—they are much more likely to have a set prayer time and a specific place for meeting the Lord every day, and to spend relatively more time in caring, intercessory prayers for others.

I was leading a seminar on the Personalities somewhere in New Jersey, and someone raised the question of how the different personalities experience God. I had the women divided into their personality groups, and I, being a Popular Sanguine, said, "Well, I'm a touchy-feely type of person and I want to feel God's presence in my life." A Powerful Choleric went next, stating, "I don't need to feel everything. I want to be able to look around and see God working." A Perfect Melancholy took the position that she didn't so much care about feeling God's presence or observing His work; what she wanted was to spend time studying and analyzing the Scriptures to gain a deeper understanding of how His mind works. A little fiftyish Peaceful Phlegmatic in the front capped off the discussion with "I'm not interested in all of that. I just have a simple, childlike faith in the Lord Jesus Christ."

Frank Dougher, my son-in-law's grandfather, was the most classic specimen of a Popular Sanguine man I ever knew. When he died at age eighty-four, we attended his standing-room-only memorial at a little Methodist church in New Jersey. For the first few minutes the minister, whom I perceived to be Peaceful Phlegmatic, seemed lost, shuffling his notes, somewhat confused, as though he didn't quite know what to do. Then the proceedings started to take on a momentum of their own. One by one, people stood up and began to tell stories from Frank's life—how they liked his smile, his booming laugh, the way he managed to stay a child without ever growing up. They joked about his loud sport coats and ties. He played the best Santa Claus they had ever seen. One woman remembered how he always grabbed the bus microphone when serving as Tour Director for the Pinelands Young at Heart Senior Citizens Club. He would lead them in very loud renditions of old Irish songs. They would yell, "Put down the microphone, Frank!" He even brought a megaphone to church once because the minister had a mike, and Frank couldn't stand for anyone to sing louder than himself.

With tears in his eyes, the chief of the township's rescue squad told how when they needed to raise funds, they simply gave Frank an ambulance with a public-address system, and Frank would drive around and talk people into handing over their contributions. A middle-aged man remembered how Frank had mentored and provided a haven for the neighborhood kids who had played outside his sandwich shop thirty years earlier.

This tribute to Frank went on for an hour and fifteen minutes. The minister was impressed and said that he would like to have the same group together for his funeral some day! And I know many of us in that church secretly hoped that, when our own time comes, we could inspire an outpouring like that.

The minister then went on to say something very appropriate about the difference between "church work" and "the work of the church." The former is the necessary business that takes place within the confines of church walls—the housekeeping, meetings, classes, and sermons—the latter means to take the love of Christ and share it with the world. Frank clearly understood that difference.

Following the service, we walked out into a beautiful, early fall afternoon to a jazzed-up version of "When the Saints Go Marching In." Popular Sanguine Frank would have loved seeing people enjoy his funeral so much. My Perfect Melancholy husband even commented that he's never had so much fun at a funeral! I wish my friend who found our Bible study class too irreverent could have been there. Not all Popular Sanguines will be that popular or that loved. Frank had all the Popular Sanguine strengths but very few of the weaknesses (unless you insist that being loud is a weakness), because the Holy Spirit had over the years repaired and filled in any Popular Sanguine shortcomings.

The Holy Spirit—Our Helper and Our Hope

When we accept Christ as our Savior, we receive as a gift the presence of the Holy Spirit, who is our constant companion, helper, mentor, and guide. The power of the Holy Spirit to change our lives is absolutely awesome.

To become Spirit-filled, we must confess all sins, repent, and submit to God's will. Then we must ask, as Christ tells us in Luke 11:13 (KJV), "How much more shall your heavenly Father give the Holy Spirit to them that ask Him"—and we are Spirit-filled. To stay Spirit-filled we must practice instant confession when confronted with sin, and then immediately pray to be refilled, thus continuing our quest for Christlikeness. With these steps we can truly complete and repair our personalities. So if you run into a Powerful Choleric who is patient and gentle, don't suspect substance abuse, and if your Perfect Melancholy friend suddenly becomes warm, outgoing, and open, don't dial 911—their personalities have just been completed by the Holy Spirit.

It is always heartwarming when one of my students demonstrates that she really "gets it." We were wrapping up a Saturday seminar in a Presbyterian church in Pennsylvania. We had just had communion, and the pastor suggested we form a circle and pray. One woman got a silent, heartfelt A+ from me when she prayed this prayer:

> Dear Lord, please help the Popular Sanguines to buckle down, the Powerful Cholerics to submit to Your will. . . . let the Perfect Melancholies have some joy, and may the Peaceful Phlegmatics be stirred to action. Amen.

The Personality of Jesus

What Personality Is Jesus?

EVELYN DAVISON

Evelyn Davison's personality can be described with one word: Love. *She demonstrates an intense and admirable love for life and knows how to love almost anyone. At her "Love Personality on Parade" seminars, Evelyn teaches others how to be the true love-image of Jesus Christ. Evelyn's life is truly God's love on parade in the fields of speaking, teaching, broadcasting, and writing.*

As Christians most of us have been taught that we should aim to be like Jesus. We know that our goal is to be more like Him, that our lives should exhibit the fruit of the Spirit. Yet, for many this remains an abstract concept. However, when we look at Jesus Christ and His "church"—all of us, in light of the personalities—this principle takes on new clarity.

Being Christlike sounds like an ominous task until we begin to look at the life of Christ as found in the Gospels, and we specifically focus on His personality. Once we understand the basics of personality and then study the life of Christ, we can understand how we can be more like Him and be an example of His life and love.

193

As a Popular Sanguine I like to think of the personality of Jesus as a parade. As we read God's Word, we see an entire parade of Christ's character set before us, much like when the world views Christians, they see a parade of strengths and weaknesses. When people look at us, the parade they see should be as exciting, powerful, pure, and comforting as the life of Christ, which leads us all in the right direction. Romans 8:29 tells us that we are to be conformed to His image, that we may be more like Him. So let's look at the personality parade of Jesus Christ.

The Good News Parade

Popular Sanguine

As we think of Christ through the Personalities, we see that He was a Popular Sanguine! The very first miracle and encounter in His earthly ministry was at a party! There He performed the miracle of turning the water into wine. Without His help the party might have dwindled, and it surely would not have been remembered thousands of years later. We could easily see that Christ was the life of the party.

In fact, everywhere Jesus went, there seemed to be a party. Even the circumstances surrounding His birth became a party, with people coming from far and wide to attend, a heavenly light show, and presents! Popular Sanguines have that same quality; their very presence can turn any event into a party. They do not have to know people to bring them into the group. Their charm and openness attract total strangers, who join in on the activities or eavesdrop from the sidelines, wishing they were bold enough to jump into the action. Popular Sanguines often refer to these people as their "new best friends." Like a parade, everywhere Christ went throngs of people followed Him. With the magnetism of the Popular Sanguine, Jesus called, "Follow me!" and people did. They sat on hillsides and listened to His stories. They stood on the shores and hung on every word. He held His audiences spellbound as He shared with them parables about common things and delighted them with His stories—always leaving them wanting more.

Jesus was an optimist. In Mark 9:23 Jesus says that if we have faith, all things are possible. In Matthew 9:19–24 Jesus spoke of the dead daughter of a synagogue official and said that she was not dead, only sleeping.

While Jesus did not have the vast clothing options we have today, it is clear that, like a Popular Sanguine, He was not afraid to stand

Jesus Christ—Love in Every Personality

Popular Love Leader	Powerful Love Leader
• great storyteller—parables and principles • made friends easily—found the multitudes • had exciting lifestyle—worked miracles • enthusiastic about change—fulfilled the law • highly energetic—love-walked everywhere • inspired others—love-talked with sinners • envied by others—healed hurting hearts • spontaneous seeker—sought out new friends • creative & colorful—served wine at wedding	• active and dynamic—brought change • goal oriented—driven to the cross • knew His identity—Immanuel, God with us • independent of man—faced His Father's will • moved quickly to action—upset money tables • delegated responsibility—fed bread/fishes • thrived on opposition—met and defeated the enemy • focused leader—trained and trusted His disciples • persistent worker—counted time and cost
Jesus Love-Talked	*Jesus Love-Walked*
Peaceful Love Servant	**Perfect Love Servant**
• patient and well balanced—loved to the end • quietly endured—wore His crown of thorns • good listener—woman at well • cautious under pressure—endured trials to end • competent teacher—sought Father's wisdom • pleasant and enjoyable—delivered joy and peace • compassionate and considerate—John the Baptist • thoughtful mediator—intercedes for His own • good servant—washed disciples' feet	• appreciated nature—valued vine and branches • sensitive to everyone—loved everyone • ideal pacesetter—love-touched outcasts • set high standards—royal Law of Love • faithful and devoted—gave His all for all • saw real needs—woman caught in adultery • found creative provisions—caught fish for taxes
Jesus Loved Much	*Jesus Love-Touched*

out in the crowd. Much of His ministry took place on mountaintops and rooftops, in synagogues, and on the streets. In John 18:20 Jesus acknowledges that He has spoken openly, and in John 18:8 He steps to the front, acknowledging who He is.

Physically, Popular Sanguines seem to have an unlimited supply of energy, which they can call into service as needed. As we look at the life of Christ, and especially study a map of Bible lands, we see that He had amazing strength. The vast territory covered by Christ in His three short years of ministry shows He could outlast all the others.

Yes, Jesus was definitely a Popular Sanguine.

Powerful Choleric

Yet Jesus also shows many strengths of the Powerful Choleric. Certainly He was a born leader. No other world leader has had such an

impact as to have all of time marked by his presence! He was goal oriented and purposeful. Christ knew why He had come to earth and
everything He did was to meet that end. In John 8:14 (NIV) He says,
"I know where I came from and where I am going." Such purpose and
confidence positioned Him to preach in the synagogue at a young age.
Satan tried to tempt Him with many exciting possibilities during His
stay in the wilderness—all of which fit His personhood, yet none of
which fit His purpose or goals. He turned them all down, staying
focused on the plan He was called to fulfill.

Like a Powerful Choleric, Christ was a man of action, not just an
observer on the sidelines. He boldly went into the temple and turned
over the tables of the money changers. He turned water into wine.
He prepared a meal for thousands. The list could go on and on. Even
John could not catalog all of Christ's activities. At the conclusion of
his written record of Christ's life, John said there was no way to capture all of the things Jesus did—to do so would require more books
than the entire world could hold (John 21:25). As a man of action,
Jesus did not often stop to rest. In John 5:17 (NASB) He said, "My
Father is working . . . I myself am working."

Christ was not afraid of a good fight. He thrived on opposition. In
Matthew 10:34 He reminded the Twelve that He did not come to
bring peace to the world, but rather a sword.

Powerful Cholerics also like to get right to the point. They do not
want to hear all the details or all the excuses. They are interested in
the facts. So was Christ. When the Pharisees came asking for advice
on which of the laws was the most important, Jesus got right to the
point and said, "You shall love the Lord your God with all your heart,
and with all your soul, and with all your mind. . . . You shall love your
neighbor as yourself." In two brief sentences He captured the bottom
line of all the laws (Matt. 22:37 NASB).

The Gospels are full of incidences where Christ delegated authority. In the feeding of the five thousand, His disciples came to Him
with what they saw as an insurmountable need. Jesus quickly assessed
the situation, as it didn't allow for planning or committee meetings,
and told the men how to take care of the need. Under His authority,
He sent the disciples out to heal the sick. To each of us He delegated
the responsibility of bringing in the harvest when He said in Matthew
9:37 (NASB), "The harvest is plentiful, but the workers are few."

Yes, Jesus was a Powerful Choleric.

Perfect Melancholy

Certainly anyone who knows anything about Jesus Christ would not deny that He was a Perfect Melancholy. After all, He was "perfect"! Not only was Christ perfect Himself, He encouraged the same qualities in us (Matt. 5:48). He was clearly a planner and organizer. When Jesus commissioned His disciples He didn't just send them out. He gave them full, detailed instructions including what type of cities to visit, what kind of money to carry, and what specific clothing to wear (Matt. 10:1–23). Christ had a plan, the Father's plan, that He was to fulfill. He frequently spoke of things as being part of that plan, including His death.

Jesus also appreciated time alone. He often recharged His batteries with the solitude of the garden, the desert, or the mountaintop. After a very busy day, Jesus liked to spend time alone in prayer on a mountaintop (Matt. 14:23). In Mark 1:35 Jesus was in a "solitary place" when Peter and the others were anxiously looking for Him. As Christ's popularity increased and great multitudes flocked to Him, He often withdrew to talk to His Father (Luke 5:15–16). We know that when the soldiers found Him to arrest Him, He was alone in the inner garden as His followers slept (Matt. 26:36). He was also alone in the wilderness for forty days and nights when Satan tempted Him (Matt. 4:1–3). Imagine a Popular Sanguine spending forty days and nights alone!

Like the Perfect Melancholy, Christ was caring, sensitive, and emotional. He looked out for the social outcasts and the untouchables—the lepers, the Gentiles, the sinners—and He cared for them. In Mark 1:40–41 we see that Jesus took pity on a leper. He blessed the prostitute and forgave her sins. He instructs us that not even one little sheep should perish as all are important. He cared for the little children. He "took the children into his arms and placed his hands on their heads and he blessed them" (Mark 10:16 TLB). The Bible verse all children love to memorize because it is the easiest, John 11:35, simply says, "Jesus wept." He was not afraid of tears or emotion.

The Perfect Melancholy is genius prone. At only twelve years old, Jesus was wise beyond His years and spent time teaching in the synagogues.

Truly, Jesus reflected the qualities of the Perfect Melancholy.

Peaceful Phlegmatic

As we look at the strengths and personhood of Christ, we see many skills the world applauds. He was popular. He was a great leader. He was organized. But a thorough search of Christ's character reveals an abundance of traits that few people strive to achieve. Within these traits lies the true essence of Christlike behavior. He was a man of service. He had compassion. He was willing to do the lowly task. He wasn't so busy with accomplishment that He forgot to "smell the roses." He played with the children. He held the hand of a little girl. He grieved with a family. He was fair. He took time to look people in the eye and love them. He was humble. He took time to notice the lilies swaying in the wind—and He admonished us to do the same: "Consider the lilies." He told us to treat everyone we meet with value, as though they are the children of God. What personality has all of those attributes? None other than the Peaceful Phlegmatic. Now you know why Jesus was known as the Prince of Peace!

Christ took the time to serve even the lowly through the task of washing the feet of the disciples. In doing so, He used His own clothing to dry their feet and instructed us to follow His example. He tells us the first shall be last and the last shall be first.

Jesus was fair to all. He came to set the captives free, He came as the Messiah for the Jews. Yet He reached out to everyone, the healthy and the sick, the Jews and the Gentiles, the men and the women. We have already seen how Christ touched the untouchables. We know that He conversed with the rich (Matt. 19:16–23; Mark 10:22) and the educated (Matt. 8:5–6; Matt. 12:9–10; Luke 2:46–47). Interestingly, both the first and the last to take a leadership role in the life of Christ are women. Of course, it was Mary who brought Him into the world. The angel of the Lord spoke directly to Mary, telling her to "be not afraid." After Christ's resurrection, it was the women who were the first to recognize Jesus. They were instructed to go and tell the others (Matt. 28:1–10). Jesus was certainly fair to everyone!

In the story of the rich young man in Mark 10, we see that Jesus took time to look people in the eye. Not just a quick passing by, but long enough to be moved by them and their needs. Verse 21 tells us that Christ *looked* at him and *felt* a love for him.

When we look at the life of Christ, we must agree that He was a mighty man. He did many wonderful things, and He was a great person. Jesus knew who He was—a king to be worshiped—yet He did lowly things, He served, and He was humble! In John 14:12 Christ tells us that while He does great things, anyone who believes in Him can do them also—and even greater things.

Clearly Christ was and is a Peaceful Phlegmatic, the Prince of Peace.

Jesus had all the personality strengths and none of the weaknesses. He had a perfectly blended personality that reflected His Father's image. He said, "Anyone who has seen me has seen the Father" (John 14:9 NIV). He came to be an example for us, that we might be like Him and please the Father.

Becoming like Christ

As we understand the personalities and the personality of Jesus, we can more easily see how we can become more like Him. If we are supposed to be like Christ, having some of all of the personalities, why did He make us each with such a distinct personality? I believe there are two specific reasons for our own defined personalities, or our own unique approaches to becoming more like Christ.

First, as we grow and mature, we learn and allow the Holy Spirit to shape us to be more like Christ (2 Cor. 3:15–18). As the Holy Spirit shapes us, we hopefully begin to lose those rough edges of our personality—the weaknesses—and we begin to recognize the spiritual gifts we need to complete the work the Lord has called us to. We develop some of the skills and strengths of the other personalities as we become more Christlike.

Second, I believe that when we look at the church as a whole, with all of the various personalities, we do have all of the strengths present already—like Christ! As humans we also have the weaknesses, but when the Christian community comes together as one, we should have all of the strengths as well. One parade with many floats to make it all interesting. One body with many parts. One vine with many branches.

The Work of the Spirit

When we accept Jesus Christ as our Savior, we take on a new life. Ephesians 4:20–24 (KJV) tells us to "put off former conduct, the old man . . . and be renewed in the spirit of your mind." Colossians 3:10 tells us that we are renewed in His image. I view this renewal process as receiving a new heart, a heart with three parts made up of the soul, body, and spirit.

The soul is composed of the mind, will, and emotions. When we are functioning in our natural personality, we see the Popular Sanguine operating in the emotion, the Powerful Choleric functioning in the will, the Perfect Melancholy operating in the mind, and the Peaceful

Phlegmatic functioning as a blend of all three—balanced. Before we are made new as Christians, our personalities operate in the soul only. But with new life in Christ the Holy Spirit begins to work in our lives and we begin to function in both the soul and the spirit.

As we learn to live in the spirit, our life becomes energized. We are given spiritual gifts that add to our basic personality strengths. He gives us special gifts needed to perform His ministry. The ultimate result of Jesus in control of our lives is that He brings forth fruit—fruit of the Spirit: love, joy, peace, patience, kindness, goodness, faithfulness, gentleness, and self-control (Gal. 5:22–23). When we look at the specific qualities of the fruit of the Spirit, we see that it contains aspects of each personality type. The Popular Sanguine—joy; the Powerful Choleric—self-control and faithfulness; the Perfect Melancholy—gentleness and love; the Peaceful Phlegmatic—peace, patience, and kindness. Notice which personality includes the highest number of the characteristics of the fruit of the Spirit—the often misunderstood Peaceful Phlegmatic.

As the soul and the spirit come together in our lives, they do not compete—they complete our personalities. It is not that our personalities change or that we lose whom God originally created us to be, but rather that we become complete in Him—the abundant life He promised, full and overflowing. When we are complete, the world notices something different in us. We are on parade for them to see the love and truth of Jesus Christ in our lives. "If we are living now by the Holy Spirit's power, let us follow the Holy Spirit's leading in every part of our lives. Then we won't need to look for honors and popularity, which lead to jealousy and hard feelings" (Gal. 5:25–26 TLB).

The Work of the Body of Christ

When we are all living Spirit-filled lives and we come together in our strengths, as a group we become more like Christ. I find that this is how we as Christians are intended to function. No one has every skill or strength. But as we come together we make a whole, complete in Him. Whether the group we are referring to is the entire Christian community, a specific church body, or a group of Christians banding together in a cause, we are always more effective together. Some of us are activists, some are lovers, some are encouragers, some are students of the Word, some are intercessors, some are healers, some are compassionate, some are leaders. Wherever our individual personalities fit, there is a place for each and every one of us to serve!

This concept was made very clear to me when we had a major flood in our small, two-hundred-person community. It was Christmastime. Both my husband and I share a portion of the Powerful Choleric personality. We had the usual family and work activities planned for the holidays and did not have time for a flood. I was looking forward to our now traditional interview with my dear friend Florence Littauer on my radio program, "Love Talk." For ten years now she has reserved the last Saturday before Christmas to share good news and encouraging words with my listeners in Austin, Texas.

But we had extra worthy causes planned as well. My husband, Van, and I were smoking turkeys for the Salvation Army Christmas dinner. Not just one or two turkeys, but forty turkeys were smoking on our driveway and patio!

When I awoke on this memorable morning, it was not to the "brrrrring" of an alarm clock. It was to the sounds of thunder and steady rain. I knew we were in trouble. I got up and looked out from our front porch to check the lake level. "Yikes!" I shrieked as I ran to wake up Van. "Our turkeys are floating down Lake Travis!"

Van is a combination Perfect Melancholy/Powerful Choleric. He is not as excitable as I am, but he can make quick decisions and move into action. He waded into the waist-deep water and began to haul the borrowed smoking trailers to higher ground, while I was in the kitchen making coffee and a hearty breakfast. I could see we would need plenty of both! Breakfast renewed our strength, and we felt better-equipped to face the day. While we were eating, the TV weatherman assured us that "the lake will rise very little after 10:00 this morning."

Thankfully we had moved our vehicles up to the local police department the night before as a precaution against the continuing storm. So, armed with the encouraging weather report, I headed off to the radio station for my live program, knowing that Van had the turkeys under control. After the show I called home to check on him and the turkeys.

It turned out that the weather report was wrong. Van was exhausted. He was worried about the turkeys! He told me that the U.S. Army Corps of Engineers had come by around 10:00 and warned that the garage would be under water by noon. Our son David and some of his friends had come to help move everything from the garage to the first floor. But now the report was that it too was going to flood!

My impulsive reaction was to jump in the car and rush out there to help, not thinking that I could not even get there! Van told me not to come, but he did need some advice as to what to do with the turkeys. My cohost, Joan, and I put our heads together and remembered a mutual friend who owns a helicopter service. We envisioned a great "Turkey Lift" being covered by all the local news stations. Maybe we'd even make the national news! We got very excited. We called our friend Ron and got everything lined up. I called Van to report on our exciting plans. "Guess what?" I asked Van. "We are coming to get the turkeys in a helicopter, and the reporters will be there to capture it for the evening news!"

With desperation in his Perfect Melancholy voice, Van told me that it was too late. There was no more flat ground where the helicopter could land. Hearing the hopelessness, I declared, "I am coming home!"

As I drove toward our little town, I prayed, "Lord, what do we do now?" His response was immediate and direct as He spoke to my heart, "Lean not to your own understanding" (Prov. 3:5). I heard the words, but I was not sure what they meant to me at the moment. After parking nearby, I trudged over the mountain to discover a lake of raging water. Hiking those last few feet to what was exposed of our home, I prayed and gave God permission to use this experience to honor Himself.

Van and I walked through the house, talking about our home and making hard choices. "What can we not live without?" "What family treasures will the boys want that we can carry out on our backs?" Evening came quickly and in the dark we prepared to say good-bye to a storehouse of memories and family treasures. Together Van and I huddled in the living area and came face-to-face with the reality of the sovereignty of God. Holding on to each other we prayed, "Lord, Your Word says You can turn the heart of a king like You turn a waterfall (Prov. 21:1). That tells us that You send the rain and You can stop it. This home is Yours and we belong to You. Thank You for all the good times we have enjoyed here. We give it to You. We ask that You turn our hearts to joy and give us Your strength to weather this storm of life." We walked away together up the mountain, leaving our home behind.

After crawling into my grandson's bed at our son Danny's home, I prayed myself to sleep. "Come, Lord, and show me your mercy, for I am helpless, overwhelmed, in deep distress" (Ps. 25:16 TLB).

Sunday morning I woke up slowly after a night of little rest and lots of rain. However, an early call from our Powerful Choleric son

David brought us to attention and action. He barked orders, commanding us: "Start toward the lake! Pick up a U-Haul on the way! Call your church and get some help! We are moving you by pontoon boat today! The water will be to the fourth and top level by the middle of the afternoon. Hurry!" We were an hour away, which made the hurry part of his instructions difficult. But we followed his orders despite torrential rain.

During the drive, Van kept praying out loud, "Lord, just stop the rain." I was singing and praising, "God is so good," and "Speak to my heart, Lord Jesus." After what felt like an eternity, we arrived at the end of our street. We were preparing to back the truck toward the raging lake when an amazing thing happened—after three months of seemingly nonstop rain, it stopped raining!

Under the clouds and rolling thunder, we boarded the waiting boat, and the men began navigating through the treetops to our house. Knowing how God works, I couldn't wait to see what He would do with this day. As the boat sloshed against the walls of the upper floor of our home, we struggled through the doorway into the home we never expected to see again. Inside were fifty people working on packing up our possessions! Our Powerful Choleric son David had organized them into work teams.

Van and I each had different reactions. Perfect Melancholy/Powerful Choleric Van said, "What a job!" My Popular Sanguine/Powerful Choleric self shrieked, "Oh! What a blessing! Oh! What fun!" Our Powerful Choleric personalities love a good crisis, and we all kicked into high gear. David and Van began directing the sorting and packaging of treasures in some very unusual containers and in some very strange ways. Everyone seemed to gravitate to a job that fit their personality. A couple of Powerful Choleric engineers removed the heating and air conditioner units. Perfect Melancholies carefully packed crystal and china into garbage cans. Two young Popular Sanguine college guys from my discipleship group, with their eyes half closed, were throwing my intimate apparel into plastic trash bags. As I scanned the room, I smiled at the parade of personalities that had filled my home!

One Perfect Melancholy stopped her packing for a moment and looked at me in amazement. She whispered in my ear, "I can't believe you. If this were my house, I would be in a corner kicking and screaming. But you, you . . . are here in the center of it all, lively as a bee in a honeycomb."

The Lord sent lots of help—we moved in two ski boats and a large pontoon boat! The man with the pontoon boat asked our son David, "How is it that your parents have so many different and delightful friends? If I were to need this kind of help, I don't know of five people who would or could help me."

We spent the next eighteen months gutting what was left of our home and putting everything back into place after thirty feet of flood-water devastated it. One of the things that helped me through this trying time was the beautiful picture of the parade of personalities that came together as one body with all the help I could need during that crisis moment. God has richly blessed our lives with friends who seek to serve Him and others, people who have grown and matured, whose lives exemplify the qualities of Christ.

As you gain a greater understanding of Jesus Christ through knowing His power and love, I hope that you, too, will grow and mature, and that your life will bear the fruit of the Spirit so that your personality will be a parade of the life and love of Christ!

Women's Ministry

Reaching All the Personalities

SHIRLEY LINDSAY

Shirley Lindsay has a passion for sharing the Lord with other women. As a wife, mother, and grandmother, she believes "living life without the Lord isn't really living at all." Shirley is a women's ministry consultant and loves to help women become "all that they can be" according to God's design. As she disciples leaders, teaches Bible studies, and speaks at retreats, she shares the Word and helps women identify their unique personalities and understand how they affect relationships in all aspects of life.

omen's ministries" is a relatively new term. When our grandmothers were involved in church activities, they met together for quilting bees where they sat in a circle, sewed, and talked. The older women gave counsel to the younger ones in an informal way, and no one was in a hurry to go somewhere. Sometimes they got together to prepare a meal for everyone in the church: the Harvest Dinner, the Lenten Luncheon, the Strawberry Festival. They had recipe and cookie exchanges. Some women's groups rolled bandages for the missionaries and took turns feeding them when they came home on furlough. The women had servants' hearts and seemingly endless hours to give to the church.

When the feminist movement hit America and women were told to go to work, the old-fashioned ladies' sewing circles began to unravel. Suddenly no one had any spare time, and the former activities were left to the elderly. The powerful, aggressive women were out taking on the world. The family as we knew it changed, the dinners around the table were replaced, and everyone was in a hurry to get somewhere. Marriage problems rose up in good church people, teens got in trouble, and emotions were dripping from overextended women.

As the women looked for help and for hope, they began turning to the church because of a renewed interest in spiritual food. Canning plums gave way to preserving sanity. Religion was replaced by relationships. "How can I get along with all these people, and how can I hold my family together in these trying times?"

I never planned on being a leader of women, especially women with problems, but as a visible woman in church and as one of the "older women" set, I found the younger ones coming to me for advice. They needed someone who seemed stable and who had answers. These young women were Christians, but they knew little about Scripture or the power of the Lord to change lives. I began ministering hope to individuals and then brought them together in groups and ultimately retreats where we could get away together and call upon the Lord for help. The success of these weekends away spread to other churches, and now I serve as a consultant to those groups wishing to start women's ministries that will literally be ministering to, serving, and caring for the women of the community and bringing them into a personal relationship with Jesus Christ.

At first I had difficulties with women who didn't see things my way, who fought what I told them to do, who didn't seem to get on with the program. It was so easy for me to see what they needed. Why didn't they all move on at the same speed? The answers came as I began to study *Personality Plus* and saw the basic differences in people. Because I am the Powerful Choleric type, I functioned with a "problem/solution" mentality. Here's what's wrong; now let's correct it! This method worked well with other Powerful Cholerics, but I began to realize that my plans were no fun for the Popular Sanguines, too overwhelming for the Peaceful Phlegmatics, and too cut-and-dried for the Perfect Melancholies who needed to think it all over. I had to soften my approach, pull up some of my Popular Sanguine humor, and love each individual whether or not she was like me.

Women today have similar needs but different personalities. As a leader, I must be aware of both. They have need for fellowship; they feel so isolated and lonely. They need to share their hurts where they won't be judged for expressing an opinion. They need to see a light

The Effect of Personalities in Women's Ministry

Popular Sanguine
"Ms. Personality"

Motto: "Let me entertain you."
Basic Desire: social
Desires Involvement: to have fun
Major Strength: creativity
Major Weakness:
- rather talk than work

Natural Strengths as a Leader:
- loves people
- outgoing, exciting
- creative
- encourages and uplifts others

Weaknesses as a Leader:
- takes off on tangents
- undisciplined
- unscheduled
- unpredictable

Spiritual Conflict:
- being a Christian demands discipline

Group Need: fun and excitement

Powerful Choleric
"Ms. Bossy"

Motto: "I'll take charge."
Basic Desire: control
Desires Involvement: to lead
Major Strength: leadership
Major Weakness:
- rather give than take orders

Natural Strengths as a Leader:
- born leader
- decisive, productive
- knowledgeable
- motivates people to action

Weaknesses as a Leader:
- not open to others' ideas
- result rather than people oriented
- intimidates less-confident people
- bossy and intolerant

Spiritual Conflict:
- can't give up self-control for God control

Group Need: productivity, direction

Peaceful Phlegmatic
"Ms. Agreeable"

Motto: "I'd rather not be seen or heard."
Basic Desire: peace
Desires Involvement: only by invitation
Major Strength: support
Major Weakness:
- rather be indifferent than offer advice

Natural Strengths as a Leader:
- calm and gentle spirit
- brings peace where chaos exists
- offers comfort to others
- provides balance

Weaknesses as a Leader:
- spirit of indifference
- indecisive
- lacks motivation
- fear of criticism

Spiritual Conflict:
- too much work to change

Group Need: comfort and quiet

Perfect Melancholy
"Ms. Perfect"

Motto: "Don't deviate from the plan."
Basic Desire: detail and depth
Desires Involvement: to keep order
Major Strength: detail
Major Weakness:
- rather achieve perfection than completion

Natural Strengths as a Leader:
- very detailed
- sensitive to others' needs
- scheduled and orderly
- intellectually astute

Weaknesses as a Leader:
- demands perfection
- overanalyzes issues
- easily distracted
- critical spirit

Spiritual Conflict:
- must be perfect to accept Christ

Group Need: order and detail

at the end of the tunnel, hope in a world that offers only momentary satisfaction through going and doing.

Ministering out of Your Personality

Women's ministries can provide the caring warmth women so desperately need today. Are you willing to take on the mantle of leadership? I found that a willing spirit, a heart for God's Word, and a knowledge of the personalities was the foundation for women's ministries. In training others to be leaders, I show them the Christlike attributes of each personality. (See chapter 16 on the personality of Jesus.)

The Popular Sanguine personality has a bubbling enthusiasm for life that is contagious, but that could appear insincere to those who are depressed. Use your humor as a magnet to draw women in, but allow the love of the Lord to shine through. Become the trusting friend the women don't have. Use your eagerness to reach out and touch those in need, to put an arm around the slumping shoulders, to pat the hand of a discouraged soul, to be the Lord Jesus in human form. Work personally to overcome your weaknesses instead of depending on your wit and charm. Spend time in preparing your lessons instead of rushing in with stories of what happened on the way. Don't exaggerate to the point where women whisper, "You can't believe a word she says." Be careful not to focus unduly on yourself or make people feel they must become like you. Popular Sanguines so easily build a following of adoring fans who become dependent on them and not on the Lord. Look over your personality weaknesses, discuss them with a friend who has observed you, and prayerfully ask the Lord to use your personality strengths to shed His light in this hurting world.

You that are the Powerful Cholerics are made to be leaders as long as you can learn to love those who aren't like you and who don't get enthusiastic over your ideas. Realize that your strong personality may overwhelm others and make them pull away from you. While your skills of organizing a women's ministry and motivating others to action are much needed, you should pray for a gentle spirit and a humble heart. Listen to what others have to say, and don't interrupt with pat answers. Ask others for suggestions even when you know how to do it. Tone down your approach so you won't appear bossy and domineering to those who already feel of little worth. Remember the leadership Jesus gave His disciples was exhibited without raising His voice, by showing love and not authority, and by having the attitude of a servant.

The Perfect Melancholy leader has so many Christlike qualities that you start out ahead of the others. You have a sweet and gentle nature, compassion for the hurting, and no need to be the center of attention as the Popular Sanguines and Powerful Cholerics do. You think deeply, speak truthfully, and see beneath the surface. You prepare well, and people trust you. You will need to become more flexible and realize that people with problems don't always react positively or show up on time. They aren't sensitive to your schedule or needs and are self-focused much of the time. Don't get discouraged when they don't do what you've assigned, and don't take it personally when they feel like giving up. Realize the Popular Sanguines need a loving arm and a light touch, the Powerful Cholerics want to feel appreciated for their efforts, and the Peaceful Phlegmatics want to know you recognize their worth even if they don't participate with enthusiasm. Let them all see the caring character of Jesus when they look into your eyes.

Sometimes Peaceful Phlegmatics don't volunteer to be leaders because it seems like too much work. Let all those loud and bossy women do it. They love to be up front. You who are Peaceful Phleg-matics, please listen. You are the only ones who by nature have the peace of Jesus in your hearts. You calm the troubled waters, bring balance to the emotional ups and downs, and have the patience of Job. You don't need your own way, you are inoffensive like the Lord Him-self, and you aren't easily swayed by others' opinions. People see the meekness and the love of the Lord in you and in your willingness to care for others. You do need to be careful, though, that you don't let people abuse your good nature or usurp your time in such a way that it keeps you from your family. You may need to say no more than you would like to and set some boundaries for those you help. You may wonder at times if the effort you put into preparation and comfort-ing is worth it, especially when you don't see improvement or hear praises, but all that you do should be done cheerfully as unto the Lord. What He sees you do quietly, He will reward you for openly. Keep yourself motivated to good deeds, don't get weary in well doing, and the peace of the Lord will fall upon you and those around you.

No matter what personality you have, you can be used of the Lord to lead and give hope to those women exhausted from seeking answers in the world. You can communicate God's love to the lost.

What are some of the possible ministries that we could bring into our churches? Aside from what we may create ourselves, there are some available that we can tap into. These programs might include: MOPS (Mothers of Pre-Schoolers); Heart to Heart (older women mentoring younger women); Woman to Woman; Moms in Touch (moms pray-ing for the schools, students, and teachers); Mom's Fellowship (moms and children sharing and playing together); Hearts on the Mend (min-istry to widows); Weigh Down or First Place (weight loss and Bible study programs); Women in the Workplace; and many others. We can start recovery or support groups, service committees, missions groups, prayer gatherings, and the list goes on. These ministries may vary in character from church to church, but they are all serving to help women grow in the knowledge of Jesus Christ, to become mature in their relationships with Him, and to encourage one another in the body of Christ by being united in our faith. Did you notice that most of the groups have a relational focus in contrast to a task focus? This is why the need for understanding the personalities and how they affect the dynamics of these groups is more important than ever before. In a society where people are seeking instant gratification and instant success, we unconsciously ignore the real needs within a group, attempting to meet the goals at hand rather than the relational needs of the people.

At a conference on women's ministry, Jean Milliken, church trainer and consultant for the Northwest United States, shared this statement: "The primary goal and purpose of Women's Ministries is to communicate a true understanding of Jesus Christ and God's Word in an atmosphere of love so the others will respond to it and lives will be changed." As women involved in any aspect of women's ministry, we are expected to model and communicate an atmosphere of love in which other women can see by our words and actions that in Christ their lives will be changed.

Personalities and Leadership in Women's Ministries

Those of us who are in positions of leadership also must understand ourselves, so we can understand others. As it says in Psalm 139:23–24 (paraphrased slightly), "Search me, O God, and know my heart—what is way inside the real me—try me, test me and know my ways—how I behave and get along with others. If there be any offensive way in me— actions and moods that offend or hurt other people—please help me to change." We examine ourselves, as we read in Galatians 6:4 (NIV), "Each one should test his own actions," so we can get along with other women.

How do we accomplish this? Through experiencing the Holy Spirit at work in us as we actively participate in the various components of ministry. We accomplish this through desiring to love others as God designed them and by learning how they function in everyday situations. We accomplish this by understanding ourselves, so we can understand others.

Whether in leadership or in attendance at a women's group, understanding the strengths and weaknesses of each personality helps us accept others. Each of us is a unique individual as God designed us to be, according to Psalm 139:14 (NIV), "I am fearfully and wonderfully made; your works are wonderful, I know that full well."

When I became a leader aware of the personalities, I reviewed the assets of those I had worked with and saw that the very annoying qualities became positives as I saw them through this new understanding.

Suddenly Frances became the Peaceful Phlegmatic in my eyes. I had previously been frustrated by her lack of creativity and enthusiasm. Now I am in awe of her beautiful spirit, wealth of Bible knowledge, and concern for people. I now see why people are so comfortable with her.

Mary Lou drove me crazy with all her charts, her changes, her expectations, and her need for control. When I realized she was a Powerful Choleric, I attempted to do things faster, her way.

When Gwen was president everything was perfect, but she was so quiet I was never sure she liked anything we were doing. As a Perfect Melancholy, she was able to handle any job and do it right.

Popular Sanguine Diane upset the group as she continually implemented new creative ideas, bubbling with excitement at the prospect of drawing in more people for each event. I saw that everyone loved her, and God helped me to see her spontaneous spirit as a positive quality.

I prayed, "God, give me the peace Frances has, the drive of Mary Lou, the perfection of Gwen, and the enthusiasm of Diane." I prayed that I would continue to see other women through Jesus' eyes and help them minister to the best of their abilities, enhancing and encouraging their strengths and working around their weaknesses.

Personalities and Successful Women's Ministries

As we serve the Lord in the capacity of leader or attendee in women's ministries, I see four components necessary for each woman to grow in her personal relationship with Jesus Christ. They are prayer, fellowship, spiritual content, and guidelines.

Prayer

Without prayer we are depending too much on our own wits to keep our group growing to maturity, and yet not every woman wants to pray. Florence tells of the group she taught in the Women's Club. They came faithfully and loved the Bible stories. After teaching the class for years, Florence decided to divide the women in small groups and teach them to pray for each other. She announced the plan the week ahead, and when the day came only half the usual number arrived. When she questioned those who were there, they said the others didn't want to pray out loud because they might not do it right. They had been happy to come and listen, but they didn't want to pray.

Prayer is difficult for many who think it has to be full of lofty thoughts and Thees and Thous. We as leaders need to show our people that prayer is like a phone call to a friend, not a speech to a congregation. Given the necessity for prayer in our spiritual growth, we should teach some simple ways to pray and then serve as models and practice praying with women until they are comfortable praying themselves. Popular Sanguines may want to monopolize the prayer time, and Powerful Cholerics will tend to preach. The Perfect Melancholies will prefer to do it silently until they've built up confidence and then come out with deep and impressive words of praise. The Peaceful Phlegmatics will want to keep their thoughts to themselves, but as they lose their fear of judgment, they will take pleasure in talking with God.

Fellowship

I became very uncomfortable recently when I witnessed the interaction between two women cochairing a meeting, a Powerful Choleric and a Perfect Melancholy. The Powerful Choleric was pressing on with the agenda, not allowing time for the expression of people's feelings and detailed stories, while the Perfect Melancholy became depressed because the Powerful Choleric seemed insensitive to people, and because people's feelings were being hurt in an attempt to keep things moving. Tension built between the two, and they eventually were unable to function as a team. I was asked to share with these women my knowledge of the personalities so they could relate their specific problems to their inability to understand each other.

The dynamics of fellowship help create a safe, secure environment where each person feels accepted by the others in the group. This acceptance can, then, become the foundation for working together as a team rather than feeling constantly challenged or at odds with others in the group.

Fellowship is always an integral part of the agenda when women meet together, but it can, too often, preempt the true purpose of the group. Delegating properly, taking into account the personalities, can benefit everyone. The Popular Sanguines make wonderful hostesses

and greeters, but the details of the agenda are better left to the organized Powerful Choleric. The attendance records would be best in the
hands of the fact-minded Perfect Melancholy. The Peaceful Phlegmatic would be a wonderful quiet person to hand out the materials and
read a devotion if she is given enough time to prepare. I strongly believe
that the personalities normally establish the course of fellowship. Popular Sanguines believe they invented the word *fellowship*, and come to
a group ready to entertain, have fun, and talk. They lead the way in
making sure refreshments and conversation are a part of the group
dynamic. However, fellowship often overrides the purpose of the group.

Powerful Cholerics will not generally recognize fellowship as part
of the meeting agenda. Being result oriented, in contrast to Popular
Sanguines who are people oriented, they see little need for fellowship and are impatient with those who do. They come ready to take
charge, with the intent of being productive, making decisions, and
motivating people to action. Fellowship is generally not included in
their agenda, unless it is programmed in prior to the meeting—and
they can come late and miss it. It is important for Powerful Choleric
leaders to include fellowship as part of the group activity, since fellowship can provide a foundation for working in unity.

Perfect Melancholies may also tend to neglect the fellowship factor. They come with a specific plan in mind, and deviation from the
plan means failure. The Perfect Melancholy is sensitive to the needs
of others but will not often initiate or participate in group fellowship.
They prefer one-on-one conversation and find group participation
somewhat uncomfortable, since they prefer to be silent rather than
interrupt any conversations.

The Peaceful Phlegmatic often sits in the last row or behind the
other people, hoping no one will directly include her in the conversation. She can be led into fellowship but will not become involved vol-
untarily. Her desire is to be neither seen nor heard if at all possible.

Just as the body of Christ is made up of many parts, a group is made
up of unique personalities. Understanding personalities helps us work
together as a team.

Spiritual Content

The third component is the spiritual focus and should be a part of
every group. Spiritual content helps us remember why we're here and
keeps us focused on God, not on the agenda. If we are actively involved

with women's ministry in any capacity, we should be witnessing and modeling the ways of Jesus Christ. If we do not acknowledge or focus on the Lord, we are simply a group and not a ministry. Our personalities can affect how we stay focused on spiritual content.

I led a Bible study where it became clear that some of the attendees' expectations were not being met. A Perfect Melancholy came to Bible study perfectly dressed without a wrinkle, carrying her Bible, notebook, and pen in hand. Her expectations were to study the Bible. After attending two sessions, I noticed she was absent for two consecutive weeks. When I called her to inquire about her absence, she told me there was too much time spent in fellowship and prayer, and not enough time spent in study. She wanted to study the Bible and didn't want to spend her time talking and socializing. Understanding this up front, I was able to match her with another group in the church with more focus on spiritual content.

Cathy was a Powerful Choleric who came to Bible study demanding a support group environment. After dominating the first two studies with her own agenda, I called Cathy and asked appropriate questions that helped me guide her to a support group as well as a Bible study. Sally, the Popular Sanguine, loved prayer time and asked that we spend less time studying the Word and more time in prayer. This allowed her to pray minisermons without interruption. Having established at the onset that this was a Bible study and content was the focus, I could, then, direct her to a prayer-focused group, which she attended in addition to the Bible study.

Perfect Melancholy Mary came to study the Word, nothing more and nothing less. Yet, as I encouraged her participation in the study, she became more comfortable with the other women, eventually becoming one of the teaching leaders. The Peaceful Phlegmatic, Phyllis, was a treasure waiting to be found. Although she chose to sit in the back of the room and not participate, I watched her with interest as she seemed to emotionally participate with her gentle spirit and pleasant smile. One day after study I asked her permission to address certain questions to her during the session. She not only agreed, but thanked me for being so aware of what she might have to offer the group. She eventually became a Bible study facilitator. Discipling, encouraging, nurturing, and training are the ways in which we build on people's strengths and help them overcome their weaknesses.

Remember: Women's ministry without spiritual content is not ministry!

Guidelines

I often teach women's Bible studies where I see personalities come to life. I recently asked Kristy to substitute for me as Bible study leader for one session, although I did attend the study. We had been using the same Bible study format for over six months; however, I gave Kristy, a Powerful Choleric/Popular Sanguine leader, permission to lead as the Holy Spirit led her.

At the outset of the study, Kristy told the group that she would be deviating from the normal format and asked everyone to close their study guides. She continued by saying, "Today we will be answering questions about the study that I have personally prepared." As I observed the various personalities react to this, I had to control the smile on my face. The Popular Sanguines were very excited about a new format—and were showing more excitement than usual because it definitely sounded like fun. The grimaces on the faces of the Powerful Cholerics clearly showed decisions pending on whether this new implemented plan was logical and worth following. The Perfect Melancholy was so distraught that she risked interrupting and said, "You mean I can't use my book? You're not going to go question by question like we always do? I don't think I can do it this way. Please, may I keep my book open? I'm too confused!" Meanwhile, the Peaceful Phlegmatics didn't show any emotion toward the new format of the day. They probably weren't aware that a change was being made.

Guidelines are necessary for women's groups, or any group for that matter, to stay focused; however, they are received differently by the four personalities. Popular Sanguines, who are undisciplined, unscheduled, and unpredictable, find guidelines too restricting. Rather than follow the guidelines, they will ignore them or simply forget any guidelines exist. Out of sight, out of mind! Powerful Cholerics usually write the guidelines and will ignore or rewrite, without reservation, any guidelines with which they disagree. As one Powerful Choleric said, "After all, I know what the intent is supposed to achieve." Guidelines must also be logical, or there is no need to follow them. Perfect Melancholies love guidelines. They thrive on knowing what to expect, how to do it, and learning any details that help create a scheduled and orderly group. The Peaceful Phlegmatic will not purposely ignore the guidelines but will choose to follow the flow of the group dynamics. Have you ever seen a Peaceful Phlegmatic read a set of instructions? Reading is too much work, uses too much energy, and may require a change in their life.

Remember: Guidelines give guidance to "well-intentioned" groups.

Whether you work with women in the church or women in secular organizations, an understanding of the personalities will allow you to offer Popular Sanguines more fun, give Powerful Cholerics more control, provide Perfect Melancholies the necessary details, and provide comfort to the Peaceful Phlegmatics—all while avoiding undue conflict and becoming the woman God designed you to be!

Personalities impact people. People impact each other. The question that looms before us is, What impact are we having on other people? Psalm 139:23–24 (NIV) says, "Search me, O God, and know my heart; test me and know my anxious thoughts. See if there is any offensive way in me, and lead me in the way everlasting." When I asked the Lord to search me and show me the offensive ways in me, I saw how my inability to understand myself affected my relationship with God, my husband, my children, and my friends. As the Lord continues to show me my offensive ways, He also reveals my uniqueness: "For you created my inmost being; you knit me together in my mother's womb. I praise you because I am fearfully and wonderfully made" (Ps. 139:13–14 NIV). He created me; He gave me my personality; He wants to work His purpose out in me. Paul tells us in Romans 8:28 (NIV) that "in all things God works for the good of those who love him, who have been called according to his purpose." God has called each of us into a love relationship with Him. When we accept Jesus Christ as our Savior, we are responding to God's love for us. The remainder of our lives are to be spent in obedience to our loving God as He works His purpose out in our lives and in the lives of others.

Accepting who I am, accepting how God made me, accepting and understanding the personality that He has entrusted to me, I can now accept the personalities of my husband, my family, and all the women for whom God has given me a passion. Women's ministry gives me the opportunity "to communicate a true understanding of Jesus Christ and God's Word in an atmosphere of love so the others will respond to it and lives will be changed." I challenge each of you who read this book to ask God to search your heart and "see if there is any offensive way" in you that needs your acknowledgment and God's healing touch. May God receive all the glory as we seek to minister, woman to woman.

18

Youth Ministry
From Stumbling Blocks to Stepping Stones

CAROL MILLER

From secretary to supervisor, military wife to mom, Carol Miller tried for years to map her own course. In her travels, she careened around the corners and finally plunged into a pit of a pothole. Carol now uses her own life examples and experiences as she speaks to audiences around the country. She challenges and encourages her listeners to step up with confidence, stride forward with courage, and stay close to Jesus.

Nobody leaves this room!!! You will stay here, listen, and be polite to our speaker. She has traveled over an hour to get here; don't make her regret her trip!"

So ended the introduction the youth leader gave me that evening. I was there to speak about the personalities. Even as I approached the podium, before I uttered a single word, I knew the barriers were there. As I eyed, and was eyed by, this roomful of teenagers, I felt chosen, I felt challenged, I felt . . . like a Christian in the lion's den!

As I began introducing personalities to the group, the Lord was introducing new perspectives to me. He impressed on me that I was witnessing to a roomful of teens who knew religion but didn't know Jesus. They thought they knew all the rules to live by, but each personality had its own fears about seeking a relationship with the One who lives in them. I was here to help them understand that Jesus

217

knows them inside and out. He knows about their fears, and He is the answer for all of them.

"It's not cool to be Christian. You can't laugh anymore. You have to be serious and spiritual all the time. Anyway, I don't want to change and lose all my friends!"

"I don't need the Lord. I can make it on my own. I know what's best for me. Besides that, after all I've been through, and have gotten myself out of, why should I trust anyone else with my life?"

"I can't ever be a true Christian. I've made too many mistakes. God is perfect, and I'm so far from it, it's not even funny! Even God can't forgive me for all I've done wrong."

"Hey, I'm basically a good person. I follow the rules, I do good things, and I don't make any trouble. My life is okay as it is. I don't need the Lord."

Can you hear them? Can you hear the barriers go up within these teenagers, all with different personalities, as they respond to the invitation to accept Jesus as their Savior? Though we can't actually see these barriers, Jesus does. With His help and our understanding of the four basic personalities, we can witness to each one in a way that will ease fears and encourage faith in the One who knows us so well. Using the building blocks of the personalities, we can begin to break down the walls of witnessing and restore relationships. When we understand each personality and the gifts within each one, we can better accept and love one another as He loves us. When we truly understand that Jesus loves us for who we are, not for what we do, we are free indeed! Free from condemnation from Him and from people around us. Jesus was the only man who ever walked the earth who was all four personalities, with the strengths of all and the weaknesses of none. So if anyone understands and loves us unconditionally, it's Him.

Sanguine Sandy

Sandy, a Popular Sanguine, has great gifts in the personality that God gave to her. She is the motivator. She is friendly, hopeful, compassionate, and full of fun and laughter. She loves to talk, and you can usually find her in the hallway entertaining her friends with funny stories and wild gestures. She loves to be with a crowd, and she draws kids to her without even trying. She is cool to be around

From Stumbling Blocks to Stepping Stones

Popular Sanguine	**Powerful Choleric**
Fear in Accepting Christ • no more fun in life • will be too serious	**Fear in Accepting Christ** • loss of control • will have to follow
Reality to Convey • joy of Jesus • freedom in Christ	**Reality to Convey** • strength of the Holy Spirit • working for Christ
Ways to Witness • express joy • give approval	**Ways to Witness** • express appreciation • give merit for work
In Christ, the Sanguine will receive JOY.	*In Christ, the Choleric will find LEADERSHIP.*
Peaceful Phlegmatic	**Perfect Melancholy**
Fear in Accepting Christ • hasn't sinned that badly • change will disrupt	**Fear in Accepting Christ** • isn't perfect or worthy • too many mistakes
Reality to Convey • all have fallen short • peace of the Holy Spirit	**Reality to Convey** • sensitivity of Jesus • Christ's total forgiveness
Ways to Witness • express peace • give gentleness	**Ways to Witness** • express sensitivity • give comfort
In Christ, the Phlegmatic will find PEACE.	*In Christ, the Melancholy will find PERFECTION.*

and always makes those around her smile. She is eager, spirited, and imaginative.

Sandy doesn't know the Lord. Without His leading, her great personality strengths are now her greatest weaknesses. Her stories aren't so funny, because she is exaggerating to the point of telling tales about other people, including her friends. Rather than using her gift of talking to brighten people up, she's using it to cut them down. Somehow, she feels that doing this will boost her up. Her friends are turning away because they know she's been spreading rumors about everybody. In her effort to be more popular than anyone else, she's become the "party person," at all the wrong parties and with the wrong crowd. She's headed for a bad fall. She desperately needs the Lord in her life, but she is afraid that being a Christian will be dull and boring.

Sandy needs to know that Jesus was like her in many ways. Far from dull, He was a joy to be with! He loved to talk with people. He talked to anyone and everyone—even those to whom others wouldn't even give the time of day. Jesus could talk to anyone about anything, to one person or to a crowd. He told stories, too—except back then they called them parables. And He liked parties! We know this because His first miracle was performed at a big party—a party that lasted all week—the wedding at Cana.

With Jesus in her heart, Sandy will have delight she can't even imagine! The joy of the Lord will become her strength. She will have love and laughter in her life—as she fulfills His plans for her. Sandy will be able to purely love and relate to others with compassion and hope. With the Lord's leading, when she speaks her words will bring glory to Him and joy to her listeners. She can now begin to understand the love that Jesus has for her. He knows her so well because He made her the way she is. Through Him, she is loved and lovable.

Choleric Connie

Connie, a Powerful Choleric, has many personality gifts. She is outgoing, and she is a mover. She is strong, dynamic, confident, and a born leader. In whatever club she joins, she rises to leadership in record time, and people are more than happy to follow. She can organize any group or activity with great vigor and with great results. She is wonderful in a crisis, and her friends depend on her to help them. She will very quickly study a situation, decide what needs to be done, and do it! When her friends tell her their problems, Connie sees the solution. Connie is a hard worker and is willing to do whatever it takes to get something done. When she fails, she tries all the harder next time to make it right. But Connie doesn't have the Lord in her life. Connie is headed for trouble.

Connie's strengths have become weaknesses and are bringing her down. Connie has become very bossy and rude. Rather than being a leader, she's trying to grab control of everyone and everything! She's no longer cool; now she's crass. The gang she controls is really tough, and is even dangerous sometimes. She seems to always be in crises, and her life is really out of control! Nobody wants her in charge anymore, they want her out of here. She wants to be the master of her own life, so she's trying to make a name for herself. She's heard of Jesus, but she says she doesn't need Him. What can we say to that?

If Connie only knew how strong Jesus is and how He can use all the gifts that she has! He was a born leader, confident, and He was stronger than anyone Connie has ever met! He knew the way to go, without hesitation, and He led people to it. He didn't have to stand up and announce that He was in charge—His leadership showed in all He said and everything He did. When He saw a couple of guys whom He wanted as friends, all He said was, "Come, follow me," and they did! He proved that He was strong enough to handle anything— even Satan himself! He was so powerful, He could settle the sea! When Connie gives Jesus control of her life, He will lead her in all that she does. Not only that, through the power of the Holy Spirit, He will enable her to serve Him with a confidence and strength that she doesn't even have yet. Jesus always knows that Connie needs hugs; sometimes even her friends forget that. Jesus knows Connie, her great talents, and her innermost needs. He knows because He made her that way.

Melancholy Melanie

Melanie, the Perfect Melancholy, is a deep thinker and a very sensitive person. She is a meditator. While others seem to talk without thinking, Melanie thinks without talking. If you want someone who can quietly and systematically analyze and figure out all the details, long-term and short-term, Melanie is the one to look to. Her gift for accuracy will often find her in the library doing research to pursue avenues that others haven't even thought of. She keeps track of everything, from research to receipts. A loner, she reflects a great deal on the meaning of life and how she can fulfill it. She admires and loves her small circle of friends, and is always ready to listen in love as they pour out their hearts to her. Melanie has a great appreciation for the arts, an appreciation that other personalities may not understand. Rather than just listening to a great piece of classical music, she *feels* it. As intense as others may be on the outside, Melanie is intense on the inside. This intensity is beginning to get to her.

Melanie is on the verge of depression and needs help! Keeping all her troubles and thoughts deep inside, she often retreats to quietly ponder the intricacies and problems of her life now and in the future. The feelings of her friends are of utmost importance to Melanie; she feels their pain as much as they do. Perfection in all things is Melanie's ultimate goal. To her, "do your best" means "do it perfectly," and she feels guilt and shame when she falls short of the high expectations she has for herself. She feels such pain and anger for the mistakes she has made that she's getting depressed. She's into the "paralysis of analysis" and is beginning to isolate herself from everyone who may be able to help her.

Nothing her friends can do will cheer her up, and she is crying more often than not. She's carrying the weight of so many burdens. Every mistake she has made adds to her feeling of being unloved and unlovable. Without Jesus, she feels lonely, uncared for, and sad. How can we witness to her and help her understand the grace and mercy of our Lord?

Melanie needs to know Jesus' unconditional love for her. Through His walk in this world, He proved He knew everyone's innermost thoughts, even before anyone told Him. He had such deep love and compassion for everyone, even those of whom others were afraid. He felt the pain of His children so deeply that He cried. He loved us so deeply, absolutely unconditionally, that He gave His life so that all our mistakes would be forgiven. He went to the cross and took all our pain and all our mistakes on Himself. When He needed to think and pray, He retreated to be with the Father. He understands Melanie well. He knows Melanie's worth; He has made her worthy. He will prove to her that she is never alone; He will never leave her nor forsake her. He gave her a personality to bless and be blessed. What gifts!

Phlegmatic Phylicia

Phylicia, a Peaceful Phlegmatic, is easygoing with a great sense of humor. She gets along with everyone, blends into any situation, is patient, and is a great listener. When all others around her are getting upset and in a panic, there is Phylicia—cool, calm, and collected. She is the mediator. She can see all sides of any situation and can bring harmony just by her demeanor and her respect for those around her. Determined, with a will of iron that cannot be bent, she will avoid conflict if at all possible! She doesn't say much, but when she does, it's worth listening to. Everyone knows that Phylicia can make the whole school break up laughing with her one-liners. Not a lover of crowds, she is most comfortable with her small group of friends. Her personality has a gift of *being* rather than *doing*. To see her, you would never know that Phylicia has challenges, but she does.

Because Phylicia has no clear goals for the future, her grades are dropping. Nothing really excites her or motivates her, nor does she care. Since she doesn't have clear direction in her life, she's following a crowd that is really taking advantage of her. She's in trouble, but she can't seem to stand up to them. Upstaged by "up-front" folks, Phylicia feels lost in the shuffle. People think that if she's not *doing* anything flashy and cool, she's not *worth* anything. They judge her to be lazy rather than laid-back. That hurts. She needs direction. She needs drive. She needs Jesus as her Savior and as her Leader. She thinks, "If I accept Jesus, I'll just have to *do* stuff. I have enough pressure on me; I don't want any more!" How can we minister to the fears of the Peaceful Phlegmatic?

Phylicia will be comforted in knowing that Jesus is the Prince of Peace. When He walked the earth, He was never showy, but He never got lost in the shuffle. When He spoke, people listened. He didn't seek conflict but handled stressful situations peacefully. People just couldn't understand it! Even when He cast out demons, He didn't say a whole sermon, He just uttered one sentence. He had a will of iron, bent purely to the will of the Father. When Phylicia accepts Jesus as her Savior, He will replace her fear with faith and her worry with His peace. No longer lost in the shuffle, she will know she is in the hands of God. He will give her clear direction and motivation. God created Phylicia to have a quiet heart—in Him. Even in the hustle and bustle of this world, she will hear His still, small voice above all others.

When we understand that others may be different and that *everyone is special,* wonderful things begin to happen. Hearts are opened! The Holy Spirit moves! The light of our living Lord shines through. Lives are gloriously changed! Barriers of conflict are broken, and bridges of communication are built—block by block! As we experience the joy in loving each other and our merciful Father, stumbling blocks become stepping stones.

Part 4

Life Issues

Money

Financial Challenges
for Different Personalities

VIVIAN BANIAK

Vivian Baniak has enjoyed debt-free living for the past twenty years by applying biblical principles of finance in her personal money management. She currently teaches on the emotional, relational, personal, and spiritual aspects of money in Money Mentors, a personal financial workshop conducted with her husband, Andy, who teaches the practical aspects of budgeting. Andy is Manager of Finance for U.S. Field Operations for World Vision. Vivian attended West Virginia University and Asian Theological Seminary.

If it's true that we're approaching a moneyless society, then some of us are ahead of our time!

aving shopped around the world, I was more than a little excited when I read something recently that confirmed scientifically what I've always suspected. Shopping is in the genes! A *New York Times* journalist, in a recent newspaper article entitled "Gene Linked to Extrovert Behavior Trait," wrote that scientists reportedly found evidence that human personality is inborn. The article states:

Two teams of researchers have reported detecting a partial genetic explanation for a personality trait called "novelty seeking."

People high in a novelty-seeking quotient tend to be extroverted, impulsive [as in impulse buying], extravagant [as in not living within their means], quick-tempered, excitable and exploratory—your flamboyant Uncle Milton who shows up with an armload of presents [just put on his credit card], bellows his hellos, pretends to pull coins from your ear and then sits around after the family dinner looking faintly bored.

Those who score lower than average on novelty seeking "tend to be reflective, rigid, loyal, stoic, slow-tempered and [here's my point] frugal." (emphasis added)

Now, at last, a genetic explanation of why some people tend to be overspenders while others seem to be able to hold on to their money. Inborn personality characteristics seem to predispose some to be extravagant spenders and others to be more frugal. The gene described in the article fits the description of the Popular Sanguine personality! Those without the novelty-seeking gene have traits of the Perfect Melancholy personality.

While I have been teaching Money Mentors financial planning workshops and the personalities for many years, I continue to be amazed that when people begin to understand how they were uniquely designed to function, with their particular strengths and weaknesses, they are freed to apply that knowledge of themselves to the area of personal finances. A financial plan that is designed for a detail-oriented Perfect Melancholy will never work for a fun-loving, nonstructured Popular Sanguine. Therefore, in order to gain financial success in budgeting, your basic personality must be taken into consideration.

Hank and Christel were struggling in their marriage, which they tried to keep together for the sake of their two small boys as well as their commitment to Christ. Financial problems began early in their marriage and got progressively worse. Christel, feeling hopeless and overwhelmed, sought legal help and filed for divorce. Hank was devastated and asked Christel for one more try. They began Christian marriage counseling, and the counselor referred them to our Tacoma-based Money Mentors Workshop for help with their finances.

After completing the Personality Profile, they realized how some of the bad financial patterns had been set early in their marriage, and they learned who should be handling the finances. Christel says that communication in their marriage has improved dramatically. They now

Understanding
Your Financial Personality

Popular Sanguine	Powerful Choleric
Wants: items for fun	**Wants:** items for work
Debt Trap:	**Debt Trap:**
• parties and vacations	• starting own business
• clothes and jewelry	• seminars
• sports equipment	• home office
• cars, boats, and motor homes	• finance the next vision—takes chances with money
Making Your Finances Work:	**Making Your Finances Work:**
• plan fun into your finances	• obtain input from others
• hire help	• communicate with spouse
• seek source of spending needs	• involve spouse in your financial plans to give some control to spouse
• discipline yourself	
Peaceful Phlegmatic	**Perfect Melancholy**
Wants: items for others or for ease	**Wants:** items for organization
Debt Trap:	**Debt Trap:**
• co-signs on loans for family members	• computers
• picks up checks in restaurants	• office supplies
• does anything to keep peace and avoid confrontation	• books
	• best of everything
	• fine china, sterling, and crystal
Making Your Finances Work:	**Making Your Finances Work:**
• learn to say no	• choose to have the best of some things until you can have the best of everything
• learn to confront overspending spouse	

not only incorporate what they learned into their personal finances, but into their real estate rental business as well. This story has a happy ending. Today Hank and Christel are working on their marriage together with a better understanding of each other's personalities.

There are currently seven to nine credit cards for every adult in America! Most of us with even a decent credit rating are offered several preapproved credit cards a week, making it very easy for every type of personality to get into trouble. One of the problems with these preapproved credit cards is the low interest rate they tout. The rate may be true—at least for the first couple of months—then, as the fine print states, it jumps up without additional notice to 18 or 19 percent. We all need to watch out for such come-ons, but some personality types seem more susceptible than others—particularly the Popular Sanguine!

Through the Money Mentors workshops I teach with my husband, Andy, I've learned that Christians of every personality type find themselves in financial straits. At a recent CLASSeminar (Christian Leaders, Authors, & Speakers Seminar) attended by ninety-four Christian leaders, a survey was given. The purpose of the survey was to demonstrate the extent of potentially devastating life circumstances that those in Christian leadership or their immediate family members had experienced. Of the thirty-seven categories listed, ranging from Alcoholism to Suicide, the highest-ranking problem was Financial Loss, with seventy-four of those responding experiencing some type of financial trouble for themselves or their family members.

Andy and I have been married over twenty-five years, and throughout our marriage we have always worked to understand each other and to keep communication about money open. We have read books on marriage, attended marriage enrichment seminars, and watched videos on improving our marriage. Gaining an understanding of the personalities has been the best tool in helping us objectively look at how we each handle finances without tearing one another down. It has saved us a lot of hot arguments over cold cash! Knowledge of how the personalities handle money has taught us to draw on each other's strengths and complement each other in the areas of our individual weaknesses. Our personal experience has provided our passion for passing this helpful tool on to others.

Personality Mottoes for Money Management

As with all areas, financially each different personality type has strengths and weaknesses. In the discussion of money, we have found that most people know what their strengths are—it is the weaknesses we need to face and correct or improve on! Based on what I teach about the personalities in Money Mentors, I call these areas potential debt traps. Therefore, as we look at each personality type in relation to money, I have chosen to begin with the areas that need the most prompt attention—those potential debt traps.

The Popular Sanguine's Motto:
Only one more shopping day until tomorrow!

FINANCIAL WEAKNESSES

The fun-loving Popular Sanguine will most likely get into financial trouble spending money on fun-related items: vacations, parties, sports equipment, clothes, motor homes, fun automobiles. I find Popular Sanguine males notorious for buying the big-ticket items that take longer to pay off, such as the big-screen TV, a new set of golf clubs, or a motorcycle.

An impulsive Popular Sanguine can easily fall for the preapproved credit card applications that come in the mail to most of us on a weekly basis. Since shopping is a stress reliever for the Popular Sanguine personality, if all other cards are maxed out, it may be too difficult to resist applying for just one more card.

Popular Sanguine Renee naturally used shopping for stress reduction. Her combination Melancholy/Phlegmatic husband, Edward, saw her shopping trips as irresponsible and frivolous. Taking the Personality Profile during the Money Mentors Workshop showed them the root of their conflicts over finances. They were a perfect example of what Florence Littauer said in *Your Personality Tree,* "When the Sanguine gets depressed, she goes shopping. When the Melancholy gets the bills, he gets depressed!" Now Edward realizes Renee's need for shopping, and Renee understands her need to curb the major debt she has incurred. She is cutting up credit cards and working toward paying off her accounts.

FINANCIAL STRENGTHS

Of all the personalities, Popular Sanguines certainly have the most fun shopping. If they could make a business out of shopping, they'd certainly enjoy their job. For financial strength, however, they must look outside themselves. Since opposites attract, either their spouse, close friend, or roommate is probably a Perfect Melancholy who is known for their frugal nature. Having a Perfect Melancholy on their team and being open and receptive to their suggestions and help in handling the budget would be a real asset. For many Popular Sanguines, their best financial strength may be hiring a bookkeeper to pay the bills and balance the checking account.

The Powerful Choleric's Motto: We'll spend our money my way

FINANCIAL WEAKNESSES

One of the basic needs of the Powerful Choleric is to be in control. If the controlling Powerful Choleric partner in a marriage has control of the checkbook and credit cards, the less aggressive spouse may never feel that his or her financial needs are being met. Because they crave control, Powerful Cholerics are the type of people who will start their own businesses and can easily overextend themselves and their marriages financing the next vision. Often married to low-key Phlegmatics, Cholerics seldom consider the fact that their spouses may not speak up about their reckless spending. They forget that "in an abundance of counselors there is victory and safety" (Prov. 24:6 AMP).

FINANCIAL STRENGTHS

If the Powerful Choleric personalities can unleash their inborn strength for organizing well on their finances, they are well on their way to financial freedom. Also, once Powerful Cholerics realize that they will get a lot further financially if they control their money rather than letting their money control them, their inborn desire for control is met, and they can surge ahead financially. Because Powerful Cholerics are goal oriented and usually accomplish their goal, they can apply this strength to the area of finances by setting realistic, attainable, and measurable financial goals, and succeeding financially.

The Perfect Melancholy's Motto: You get what you pay for

FINANCIAL WEAKNESSES

The Perfect Melancholy personality is normally the most frugal of all the personalities. However, because perfection is the byword of the Perfect Melancholies, they closely examine the quality of the item purchased. In America, quality always comes with a price tag—typically a high price tag. The Perfect Melancholy's desire for the best runs credit card debt up quickly.

Another area of trouble for the Perfect Melancholies is their love of organization. They can easily overspend on items to get themselves organized. Their spouses may point out that the kids need back-to-school clothes, but Perfect Melancholies want to buy the three-hundred-dollar closet organizer instead.

The quiet, artistic, reflective nature of the Perfect Melancholies compels them to spend time alone. Reading, listening to or playing music, painting, and spending time at the computer may be their favorite pastimes. These areas can cause financial problems when the budget will not allow for buying the best of everything. And the Perfect Melancholies do want quality items like the most expensive computer system, the highest quality sound equipment, or the musical instrument their perfection-driven personalities covet.

FINANCIAL STRENGTHS

Of all the personalities, the Perfect Melancholy is the best at handling money. They are naturally frugal and waste little money. Because they buy quality items, what they do buy will last and not need to be replaced often.

Since Perfect Melancholies are naturally attracted to details, charts, and graphs, they also like meticulously kept financial records, budget books, and checkbooks. They may stay up half the night trying to get the bank statement to reconcile to the penny each month.

However, one Perfect Melancholy's quest for *the* perfect budgeting system almost led to financial disaster. When the automatic teller machine told her "No funds in this account," she could hardly believe it! Life was no longer perfect, and she knew she needed help. Perfect Melancholy Lucy and her Peaceful Phlegmatic husband, Richard, took the Personality Profile at our workshop. Lucy had tried every budget book and system imaginable in their eighteen years of marriage, and none of them worked for very long. Being an artist, she already knew she loved detail and had been the one to handle the family bookkeeping. Richard was always laid-back and not as deeply concerned as she was about handling the money. She found that the way our system was broken down into categories suited her "more perfectly" and she has adopted it with great success. "I love this system," says Lucy. "It's the perfect one for me."

The Peaceful Phlegmatic's Motto: Peace at any price

FINANCIAL WEAKNESSES

The Peaceful Phlegmatic personality, who will do anything to avoid conflict, can easily overspend, picking up the tab at restaurants when out with friends simply because they hate the scuffle that will ensue over who's going to pay. Another debt trap for the Peaceful Phlegmatic is not their own spending, but that of others. When a friend or relative calls and asks them to co-sign on a loan, the Peaceful Phlegmatic's mind may tell them, "Just say no," while their mouth is saying, "Yes." The wisdom of Proverbs 22:26 (NIV) clearly warns: "Do not be a man who strikes hands in pledge or puts up security for debts." If you are a Peaceful Phlegmatic who has struggled with this area in the past, you may want to place this verse where you will see it often.

Peaceful Phlegmatics' penchant for peace will cause them to avoid confrontation at any cost. If their spouse is overspending, they will bury their heads in the sand rather than confront the overspending spouse. Peaceful Phlegmatics will seldom deny a request from their spouse or children because they want to keep peace at all costs.

The Peaceful Phlegmatic personalities usually will not spend money on themselves, but rather use it for others. Because they are happily reconciled to life, it usually takes very little materially to make them content. The best gift I ever bought my Peaceful Phlegmatic husband, Andy, was a big, overstuffed La-Z-Boy recliner. He enjoys it tremendously but never would have gone out and bought it for himself.

Another Peaceful Phlegmatic strength is that they are conservative, low-risk takers. This means they will not buy into extremely high-risk investments, bringing much needed balance to the less cautious Powerful Choleric spouse—if the Powerful Choleric will only listen!

Overcoming Your Personal Debt Trap

Because each personality has specific areas in which it tends to get into trouble, each needs a personalized financial plan that will overcome weaknesses and escape the debt trap.

The Popular Sanguine Personality Needs Fun

Your financial plan needs to be a personal plan, one based on your own personality needs. If it's not, it will work for a month, or two months, or six months, but it will ultimately fail because the basic need of your personality has not been taken into consideration. Since the basic need of the Popular Sanguine personality is to have fun, a financial plan or budget that does not include fun is doomed to failure. Therefore, a Popular Sanguine must include some fun and social categories in the budget. Categories such as Vacation, Entertainment, Gifts, Christmas, and Eating Out are a must in a Popular Sanguine's budget.

The Powerful Choleric Personality Needs Control

One of the most difficult things for Powerful Choleric personalities to do is to take advice, even from their spouses. They often interpret taking advice as giving over control to another person. The strong personality of Powerful Cholerics makes them great leaders. In areas such as financial planning in a marriage, where cooperation and input from their spouse is critical to success, Powerful Cholerics must learn to listen to and accommodate their spouse's needs.

The Perfect Melancholy Personality Needs Perfection

Since an underlying basic need for the Perfect Melancholy is perfection, and they want high-quality items, in order for their budget to work, they must learn to compromise in some areas. For example, if a Perfect Melancholy cannot afford the very best of everything, they must learn to be satisfied for a time with the best of some things. In order to accommodate the needs of their spouse, or in order to get out of debt, they may decide that for a specified period of time they will meet their need for quality by buying the best clothing, or the best automobile, or the best computer, but not the best of everything at once. They must realize that compromise in quality may be necessary for a time, but there is the hope that as their budget becomes more workable, they will gradually be able to add back more areas where they are able to upgrade items.

The Peaceful Phlegmatic Personality Needs Peace

The "peace at any price" mindset of the Peaceful Phlegmatics will ultimately set them up for a major financial confrontation. The Peaceful Phlegmatic must learn to say no—no to relatives and friends who ask them to co-sign on loans; no to a spouse who is running up credit card debt; no to children who badger Mom or Dad for the latest hot item advertised on TV; no to picking up the check when with a group in a restaurant simply because they hate the squabble over who's going to pay for it.

Personality and Your Beliefs about Money

In light of your unique personality, I encourage you to carefully consider the underlying motivations that govern your attitudes toward money. Some may be false, some true. Are you the Popular Sanguine personality who believes money buys fun: "If I just had *(fill in the blank)* I would be happy"? Are you the Powerful Choleric personality who believes money gives you control—after all "He who has the gold makes the rules"? How about the Perfect Melancholy personality who believes money makes life perfect: "If I have enough money, I will have no stress and won't have to worry anymore"? Or are you the Peaceful Phlegmatic who believes, "Money buys peace—this will make everyone happy"?

Examine your belief system about money in light of the truth of God's Word. Ask yourself, "Am I operating on the basis of truth or fallacy in my financial life?"

Masking and Money

When someone is not operating within their God-given birth personality for one reason or another, they are said to be masking, or wearing a mask that is not their true personality. Any number of traumatic events in our family of origin or along the road of life can cause us to put on a mask to hide the pain we experience. Due to a molestation in a movie theater at the age of nine, my life took a sharp turn. I put on a Popular Sanguine mask to deal with my pain. After the molestation, the man handed me two dollars. I sat in the dark of the movie theater filled with shame over what had happened. Feeling shame over the two dollars in my small hands, I ran back to the candy counter to get rid of the money before going home.

As I grew up, my Popular Sanguine mask was so firmly in place that I even employed the Popular Sanguine personality's stress reliever and became a shopaholic, shopping in twenty-seven countries on four continents! The mask, coupled with the shameful memories of the molestation that money evoked, was inevitably a formula for financial disaster. Shopping was a stress reliever because it helped me get rid of the money, which I subconsciously thought was dirty.

If in completing the Personality Profile you find you are wearing the Popular Sanguine mask, ask the Lord to show you the root of the stress that you are trying to relieve by shopping. Examine the spending patterns in your family of origin as well as the spending patterns you follow in your adult years. Determine if you have an underlying false life message about money that may be rooted in a trauma you have experienced. This might cause you to mask your true inborn personality. For further reading on masking, I recommend *Your Personality Tree* by Florence Littauer and *Freeing Your Mind from Memories That Bind* by Fred and Florence Littauer. Another excellent book that deals with emotion-motivated spending is *A Woman's Place Is in the Mall (and other lies!)* by Karen O'Connor (Thomas Nelson, 1992). (These books are available from CLASS, 1-800-433-6633).

As you can see, our personality can greatly influence how we look at money and how we spend or save it. By understanding your own personality's strengths and weaknesses, you can get out of your own personal debt trap!

Organization

Making Time Work for You

SANDI LUCAS

As a wife and mother of three, including toddler twins, Sandi Lucas understands the demands of the breakneck speed of living in the nineties. She is the founder and president of DayMaster, Inc., and conducts workshops and seminars nationally on the DayMaster day planner system, as well as on time management and organization based on personalities. For more information on the DayMaster organizer, call 1-800-644-7929 or see the web site at www.daymaster.com.

o you feel like life is on fast forward and you're on pause? Have you ever felt like running away from home? The adage "God first, family second, and everything else is underneath," is being crushed in the epidemic "breakneck speed" of living in this age, the eve of the millennium.

And if the pace isn't bad enough, there's the guilt we shoulder for not being the epitome of success in all areas of life—perfect homes, perfect bodies, perfect careers, perfect children, and on and on it goes, right? Part of the problem is our own misconception that everyone but "me" has it all together! In addition, many times we equate success with *performance* rather than *purpose*. We pour our talents and time into *task accomplishment* rather than *balance* and *building relationships*.

Just like our VCRs, we must learn to pause and play, erase the bad tapes and plug in new ones, adjust the tracking, and then record the most precious moments of our lives.

In order to accomplish this, however, we must first take a good look at who we are and how God made us. I have learned that some people are naturally organized, and some people are not. I fall into the "are not" category. I would attend time management and organizational seminars, and I would get so excited! I would rush out and buy lots of boxes and index cards and file folders, and as Marita Littauer puts it, go home for a "brief organizational binge." Like being on an organizational yo-yo diet, after a few weeks I would be right back in the same clutter, piles, and debris as before, and many times worse than before! As the years passed, I became more and more hopeless and frustrated that I would never be able to erase the "bad tape" of disorganization.

I just couldn't figure out how my friend Susan had her makeup on by 6 A.M., her children's breakfast dishes set at the table the night before, and sparkling floors and counters at all times—seemingly all with the greatest of ease! While her refrigerator shone with Jubilee kitchen wax, I was cleaning my vegetable drawer out with a garden hoe! (That's a true story!)

I reached an all-time low point, however, when my daughter Stephanie was eight years old. She had attended a Brownie meeting after school, and I was to pick her up at 5 P.M. It was not the norm for me to pick her up—most of the time my husband did it. However, this day I simply forgot about her. When I arrived home at 7 P.M., my husband asked, "Where's Punkie?" "Oh no," I gasped, "She's still at Brownies!" (To complicate matters, our phone had been out of order for nearly twenty-four hours due to a bad storm the night before.)

I raced to my soon-to-be ex-friend's home (unless God intervened) only to discover that it was Ms. Brownie Leader's birthday! Her in-laws were fuming in the living room. Her birthday "dinner out" was ruined, and she said words to me that I will never forget. She said (in front of my little girl), "What kind of mother doesn't care where her child is?" I was shattered. The words stung. Why was I so unorganized? Why didn't I remember? Why didn't I think?! How could I be top in sales for a multibillion-dollar electronics company and forget my baby?

I knew that something had to change, but I feared secretly that I would never *really* be able to change. I had tried before and failed. I knew that those bad tapes were still in there. *Maybe I didn't have to completely become a different person,* I thought to myself. *Maybe I just needed to "adjust the tracking" in my life.* I felt I had enough desire. I felt I had the talent. What I lacked was the *tool.*

Time Management and the Personalities

Popular Sanguine

Basic Desire: Have Fun

Time Management Challenges
- tends to be late
- unorganized by nature
- forgetful

Tips and Tools
- make organization fun!
- use some type of planner/organizer
- find someone to hold you accountable

Powerful Choleric

Basic Desire: Have Control

Time Management Challenges
- not detail oriented
- killer "to do" lists
- no time for rest and relaxation

Tips and Tools
- learn to delegate
- seek advice from experts on details
- plan exercise and relationship building into your busy schedule

Peaceful Phlegmatic

Basic Desire: Have Peace

Time Management Challenges
- procrastination
- lack of energy
- not goal oriented

Tips and Tools
- exercise to increase energy level
- use a planner to keep everything in one easy place
- set one goal at a time

Perfect Melancholy

Basic Desire: Have Perfection

Time Management Challenges
- overplanning
- perfectionism that leads to procrastination
- cannot function in chaos

Tips and Tools
- look at the big picture
- remember: the blessing is in the doing!
- be understanding of those around you

I met Florence Littauer in Denver, Colorado. What I have learned from her has changed my life forever. Florence taught me about the personalities and how we are all so different! She taught me that no one personality is better than the others, although each has strengths and weaknesses. We are just different! This applies especially in the area of organization and time management.

Some of us can't go to sleep if there are dishes in the sink, while others of us only dare to open our garage doors under the shroud of night-fall! For the clutter-ridden, unorganized person, even the grocery store carryout boy can be a threat. "No thanks, I'll get it myself," we say. In reality, we would love the help, but we fear the judgment when he eyes the trail of paper, soda cans, and Nachos Bell Grande that fill the back-seat. The trunk is unthinkable! That's where we tossed the last several loads of backseat junk just before we had to make an emergency cleanup to let someone ride in our car!

There are those who wouldn't ever allow food in their cars. "Once your car smells like french fries, it *always* smells like french fries," one friend quipped. I've often wondered if they would ever come out with a car freshener that could take care of that smell. "Road-trip-be-gone" could be the name! Or maybe "Kid-goo-shoo!" The same clutter challenges can be seen in the workplace, in our cupboards, and in our closets. Chances are that even if we are naturally organized, we either work with, are married to, or have children who are our organizational opposites!

I hear frequently from neat-as-a-pin men who have married bubbly, fun-loving wives who were ready to drop everything to go to a party (looking positively gorgeous, of course) when they were dating. But now that they are married and are sharing a bathroom, a closet, and a kitchen sink, these men feel betrayed that "she doesn't have the courtesy to even pick up her shoes," as one husband told me. "I feel like I'm married to a child," he griped. "I've pleaded with her time and time again. I guess she just doesn't care." There was such resignation in his voice, and I could see big relationship problems ahead for this couple. "Ken," I told him, "she doesn't even *see* the shoes!"

I empathize with these newlyweds. Many times we marry our opposites, and it doesn't stop in the area of organization. I have come to the conclusion that for the most part, it is not the big tragedies in a marriage that blow them apart, it is the daily inconsiderations. It is our inattentiveness, our unforgiveness, and our unrealistic expectations that drive us apart over time. Christian marriages are breaking up at the same rate as non-Christian marriages. Many times what seems to be the "ideal couple" on the outside is the very one that will shock a congregation when a divorce occurs. Our fear of judgment keeps us from sharing our frustrations, especially at church.

Time Management Tips for the Personalities

We often live in hopeless isolation, thinking that we are the only ones facing difficulties in our relationships. The truth is that everyone has trials, frustrations, and irritations with mates, children, coworkers, and friends. This holds true *especially* in the area of time management and organization.

So what is the solution? Let's first begin by examining the time management and organizational challenges of each personality.

Popular Sanguines

The Popular Sanguines are fun-loving and spontaneous, are drawn to people and parties, need attention and approval, and hate drudgery and routine. These people tend to be the most unorganized by nature.

It is no fun to have to do never-ending piles of laundry, keep track of paper, clean the refrigerator, closets, and on and on it goes. Because of their need for approval, they are motivated to clean house only when someone is coming over. Popular Sanguines tend to be late because of their basic lack of the concept of time. Even if they realize what time it is, they can't find the directions to where they are going, or their shoes, or their keys. This can be very devastating for them because it may cause those around them to be frustrated, angry, and even bitter about their seemingly flighty attitude. In reality, Popular Sanguines have to put much more effort than many other personalities into the area of organization, so much so that the tasks become too difficult to handle. Some Popular Sanguines even go into depression because of their lack of organization. They believe they will never change. If you are this type of personality, I want you to know that not only is there hope for you, but you can become more organized permanently, just the way God wired you!

My first suggestion to you is to get an organizer or daily planner to help you begin to get control. I recommend our DayMaster—The Personality Planner—which is designed to help every personality. The DayMaster will help you as a Popular Sanguine to be on time, remember commitments, and follow through on your great ideas! Many Popular Sanguines tell me that they have tried to carry an organizer, but they stopped after a while because it just became "too much." However, we have included a lot of "fun" sections in the DayMaster, including holiday planning, party planning, wardrobe needs, shopping (now that's really fun!), as well as a personality tip for each day! One Popular Sanguine mother of triplets told me, "This is the first organizer that I have ever used that I have been able to stick with! It helps me have fun and get things done!"

In addition, Popular Sanguines tend to be *visual* people. When I have attended other time management seminars, I have been told to put all papers in a file drawer because "it takes a certain amount of energy *not* to look at something; therefore, get it out of sight to increase your productivity." I have found that for most Sanguines, out of sight is out of mind, possibly never to be found again. One idea that works for me is to get pretty stacking trays for the desk or tabletop and use colored folders. I have four trays. The top one is "new material," or "in basket." The next one is my "hot basket." These are tasks that need immediate attention. Next is my "important, but not-life-threatening-if-I-don't-get-them-done-today" tray. Last but not least is my bottom tray, in which I keep new magazines and other material that I would like to attend to, but if I *never* get to it, it will be okay. If you really want to be risky, you can use different colored folders in each tray to separate projects and groups of things, but the idea is to keep the important working projects *out* where you can see them.

If you are really struggling and do not even know where to begin, let me suggest a tip that I learned from Emilie Barnes. It is called the "Three Bag Clutter Buster." Just take three trash bags (that you cannot see through) and label the first one "give away." Label the next one "throw away," and the last one "put away." Take just fifteen minutes in an area that is causing you the most stress, whether that be a hall closet, your car, the living-room floor, your desk, or wherever. The task may seem overwhelming at first, which is why Emilie recommends just fifteen-minute bites of time. In just a short time you will have that area under control. For further fifteen-minute tips, I highly recommend Emilie's book called *The 15-Minute Organizer* (Harvest House, 1991). This will prove to be an invaluable reference tool to help keep you organized.

Finally, I want to encourage Popular Sanguines to find someone (probably *not* another Popular Sanguine) to encourage you and hold you accountable. Sometimes we Popular Sanguines simply forget what we set out to do, and it helps to find someone to encourage us to stay on course! We call these people our "Encouragement Partners." These are people who can help us "unwind and rewind" our commitment tapes and, if need be, help us "adjust the tracking" in our lives. In no way should there be any more guilt heaped on us. By contrast, with gentle, loving encouragement these mentors can help keep us focused on tasks that will matter forever.

Powerful Cholerics

The Powerful Choleric loves for life to be under control. This personality is somewhat naturally organized, but only as it relates to *task accomplishment*. You may see them dressed in their business suits, carrying leather organizers at all times, but if you were to look at their cars, or their kitchen drawers, you might find tons of clutter and disorganization, especially in areas the Powerful Cholerics feel don't need to be organized for productivity. Many time management seminars are taught by Powerful Cholerics. They exude confidence and expertise in this area. In reality, they too tend to be late, not due to disorganization, but due to their need to feel productive. They create impossible to-do lists for themselves and strive to accomplish everything in superhuman fashion. One Powerful Choleric friend of mine rides her exercise bike while listening to the Bible on tape and cracks pecans at the same time! Now that's productive! While the Powerful Cholerics tend to be highly organized in work, clubs, and organizations, their time management skills can become very unbalanced when it comes to recreation, relationships, and family.

Because the Powerful Choleric is not detail oriented, proper attention may not be given to things like balancing a checkbook, building relationships with children, and home organization. If they are not careful, they can have a tendency to place projects ahead of people.

Again, using the DayMaster organizer, the Powerful Choleric can keep track of accomplishments, schedule personal time and family activities, and keep life under control. Because the Powerful Choleric is very goal oriented, we have included an entire section on goals, with an emphasis on balancing the physical, the emotional/mental, and the spiritual life. Remember, for the Powerful Choleric personality in the area of goals, be specific but flexible! As it says in Proverbs 16:3 (NIV), "Commit to the LORD whatever you do, and your plans will succeed."

In addition, I recommend that Powerful Cholerics schedule time for exercise into their daily routine. Exercise can be a great stress reliever. Exercise is good for everyone, but it is essential for this personality, who tends to have angry outbursts when under too much pressure.

Another time management challenge for the Powerful Choleric can be the tendency to try to control things and to do things "my way." While they are extremely capable, sometimes they try to do everything themselves. This personality needs to delegate tasks, even if it means giving up a little control. The children can be recruited to help with sorting laundry, setting the table, vacuuming, and preparing meals in the home. This principle applies as well in the workforce. Since Powerful Cholerics do not tend to be detail-oriented people, they often procrastinate doing certain tasks like filling out forms, filing, or returning phone calls that are "nuisance" calls in their opinion. These sorts of tasks are the kind that can be examined for the possibility of delegating them to others who are more administrative and detail oriented.

Finally, Powerful Cholerics can greatly benefit by realizing that those around them may not necessarily be as task oriented as they are. Powerful Cholerics need to allow others to move at a *reasonable* pace and not expect the people closest to them to be as goal oriented as they are. Particularly at home, this personality can project impatience, anger, and frustration when those around them are "caught" relaxing! By learning to lighten up, they can find much more harmony in their dealings with friends, family, and even business associates. If you think that you may be at least partially this personality style, I applaud your diligence and leadership. We need you to keep us moving at reasonable speed, even though your comfort zone may be *fast forward!*

Perfect Melancholies

The Perfect Melancholies are the most naturally organized of all the personalities. They have an innate need for order and perfection. Their natural strengths in the area of charts and graphs can be most useful in their quest for the perfect system for living. Perfect Melancholies are almost always on time! They can actually set a schedule and stick to it. This is mostly due to the amount of time this personality spends on thinking and planning their life. Their time management challenge is that they can get so caught up in the planning phase of a thing, that they never get around to actually doing it.

One Perfect Melancholy friend of mine has been planning to start her own business for five years. She's not sure what type of business it will be, because she wants to make sure that it will be the *perfect* thing for her. In the meantime, life and opportunity are slipping away while she pores over the decision. If she ever actually decides what she will do, it will probably be another five years before she actually begins her business, while in the meantime she plans exactly how she will organize every aspect. Not that planning is all bad, in fact, I highly recommend it. But the real blessing is in the doing!

Perfect Melancholies tend to function best when there is not much commotion going on around them. This can be a real problem for the Perfect Melancholy mother of toddlers. Not only are their lives a series of constant interruptions, but their little terrors can destroy a room in the blink of an eye. My twin toddlers, Samantha and Shannon, are commonly referred to as the "Twin Tornadoes." I know that for now, they are not allowed to go to my Perfect Melancholy friends' homes because I understand what a tremendous upheaval that could cause. I also understand that this is just a season in my life, and "this too, shall pass"—all too quickly I'm afraid. If you are this Perfect Melancholy personality, understand that you need silence and space, but these moments can be infrequent at times, especially during a busy season of life.

We tend to work with, marry, or choose as friends our organizational opposites. If you think you are a Perfect Melancholy, understand that the rest of us desperately need your natural skills. I bought one of those tiny organizer purses that hold your checkbook, sunglasses, keys, lipstick, and not much else! Inside, on the checkbook holder, there was a clear plastic window that held one of those ID cards, which should be filled in with name and address. I always end up throwing away my wallet without ever having filled in the pertinent information, simply because it is a detail I don't want to be bothered with and it's no fun! One day I was enlightened when my Perfect Melancholy coworker pulled out her tiny purse to write me a check. In her "window" she had neatly placed her driver's license. What a concept! I'm sure most of you reading this would have automatically assumed that is what that plastic window was for, but I kid you not, I have spent countless frenzied minutes at the checkout counter searching frantically for my driver's license. Seeing her license in a secure place made me want to follow her around to see what other nifty secrets she had been keeping from me!

I want to encourage you Perfect Melancholies to speak up to the rest of us with your helpful suggestions. We desperately need you. But we also need you to understand that organization and time management doesn't come as easily for the rest of us. Marita and Florence Littauer had a story in their wonderful book *Personality Puzzle* that I keep in the forefront of my mind when I have a schedule that is completely out of control. A Perfect Melancholy named Gayle had summed up her attitude toward other less perfect personalities in a sign she kept on her desk that read: "Poor planning on your part does not constitute an emergency on my part."

The DayMaster organizer will also help you keep the many areas of your life in one neat place, as well as help you to schedule quiet time. There is plenty of room for charts, graphs, and for planning and perfecting your life! Furthermore, it will help you to understand those around you and to begin to reach out and build those relationships that matter most.

Peaceful Phlegmatics

This wonderful all-purpose personality can be very gifted in the area of administration. I have often thought that the CPI, or Continuous Process Improvement, teams that are now in many corporations in America ought to be lead *not* by Powerful Cholerics, but by Peaceful Phlegmatics. They have an innate ability to be able to find the easiest and most timesaving way to accomplish tasks. My husband, Luke, is a master at this. In fact, we recruited him to set up our assembly line at DayMaster because we knew that he would find the most efficient way to put the product together without unnecessary back-and-forth motions. And sure enough, from beginning to end, a DayMaster Deluxe Edition will move down the manufacturing line with one continuous simple flow.

Recently my mother asked Luke to cut down a tree in her backyard. Now this may seem like an enormous task to some, but Luke tied a rope around the tree, and while I pulled in the forward direction, he felled the tree with a chain saw with the greatest of ease. While I was busy basking in our conquering of the tree, my mother was planning how to remove the obstruction from the view from her kitchen window. "Well," she said, "we can just cut the tree up and load the limbs and logs in the truck and haul it off!" That sounded like a great plan to me. About that time, I looked out the window and noticed that the whole felled tree was moving! My Peaceful Phlegmatic husband had tied a rope around the trunk, tied the other end to his tractor, and let the tractor do all the work! Many of us who are Powerful Cholerics pride ourselves in the amount of work we produce, but you've got to ask yourself, who is the smart one here? I have learned much about saving time and energy from low-key Peaceful Phlegmatics.

The Peaceful Phlegmatics' biggest time management challenge is without a doubt procrastination. If the task requires the expenditure of too much energy and time, they will simply put it off. The frustrating part for those around them is that when Peaceful Phlegmatics are asked to do something, they will often agree just to avoid a conflict. They don't tell you no, they just don't do it! My Peaceful Phlegmatic daughter cheerfully agrees when asked to clean her room. My frustration comes when I go in her room the next day and find she hasn't touched it. It is lucky for her that we live in Texas where the term "I'm fixing to . . ." can preface any task or project. It is a perfect Peaceful Phlegmatic phrase because there is no commitment to any sort of time frame. You are allowed to be "fixing to . . ." *forever* in Texas!

Peaceful Phlegmatics tend to avoid organizers like the plague. The idea of goal setting, the possibility of failure, and the general overwhelming appearance of most time management systems can be too much for them. However, this personality really needs an organizer the most. It is wonderful for Peaceful Phlegmatics to be able to look at their calendars and say no to a commitment when something else is scheduled, even if it is time that they have scheduled for themselves for R&R! In addition, a Peaceful Phlegmatic needs to feel respected, and even just carrying an organizer makes you look confident. In the goal-setting area, I encourage Peaceful Phlegmatics to begin by setting just one goal at a time and to be willing to take a risk!

As with the Powerful Cholerics, Peaceful Phlegmatics can greatly benefit from exercising. It is well-known that exercise will help you increase your energy level, and therefore the lure of the living-room couch, complete with remote, can be held at bay for just a little longer!

As with any time management system, we all have to find what works best *for us*. My advice to everyone is that no organizer will help you if you have too much to do. Even good things can be the enemy of the best. As Hebrews 12:1 (NIV) says, "Let us throw off everything that hinders . . . and let us run with perseverance the race marked out for us."

We must learn to pause and play, to lead balanced lives, and to focus our attention on people and not projects. We *can* erase those bad tapes, and with God's help plug in new ones. As I learned to get organized myself and then started showing others how to do so, I began to teach using the personalities. People could see that we aren't all the same, and that we need to organize according to our own abilities. From this revelation came the need for a planner based on our differences, with daily suggestions for each personality. Now that I use the Day-Master myself, I've not forgotten a child, the cleaning, or the groceries. As you work with your God-given strengths, you will become wise in using your time and talents.

This is not a dress rehearsal. It is the *time of your life!*

Trouble

How the Personalities Cope

GEORGIA SHAFFER

Georgia Shaffer's struggle with cancer and her master's degree in psychology qualify her to speak out about dealing with hardships in life. We all face difficult times and our personalities impact our approach to adversity, what others can do to help us, and how we attempt to offer help to others. Georgia explains how to use your personality as you cope with trouble in life.

I refuse to sit around feeling sorry for myself. I need to be strong. Get on with my life," Sam told a close friend after discovering he had a serious form of leukemia.

Allison delivered a stillborn baby boy. "I wanted to be left alone—to sort things out. But my friends, neighbors, and family kept calling or stopping by unexpectedly."

"It's been a month since my husband left me," Whitney said. "Now, I feel so alone. I think people have forgotten about me. If only someone would call or invite me out to eat. It would help if I could be around people."

Jack lost his job after twenty-six years with the same company. "Sure it hurts. But these things have a way of working out. Lately, I spend most of my time fishing."

Each of these people encountered a difficult loss. But their responses were quite different. Allison wanted to be left alone. Whitney wanted lots of company. Sam wanted to take charge of his problem, while Jack preferred to ignore his loss.

Since our basic personality type influences and colors how we approach most everything in life, it also impacts our individual response to adversity. As caregivers or friends attempting to support those who are suffering, we need to understand how the personalities impact our ability to cope. Otherwise our actions may hinder the healing rather than help.

Reminiscent of the old "Golden Rule," in a time of need each of us has the tendency to do for others what we would want them to do for us. In 1988 I was diagnosed with breast cancer. Six months later, because of a recurrence, I began aggressive treatments that included a bone marrow transplant. During my treatments, my close friend Meg attempted to schedule visits and telephone calls from my friends in an effort to keep up my spirits. While it was good to have my mind off my problems occasionally, I didn't want to be entertained constantly. Her personality, a combination Popular Sanguine/Powerful Choleric, was more outgoing than my Perfect Melancholy/Powerful Choleric personality could handle.

The treatments left me low on energy. I wanted to be by myself more than ever. I needed time to withdraw and process what was happening. As a Perfect Melancholy, I needed the time alone to recharge my batteries. Although I understood her desire to help, I resented fighting for the solitude I needed. Why didn't she hear me when I said, "I need more time to be by myself"?

Thinking of how she would feel in my situation, Meg thought this time of isolation was unhealthy for me. Without an understanding of the personalities, she failed to see how draining interactions with people were for my Perfect Melancholy personality.

After weeks of her trying to help and me struggling with it, we finally sat down to discuss this issue. Misunderstanding the problem, Meg said, "Well, if I'm such a problem, maybe I should just get out of your life!"

"I need my best friend now more than ever," I told her. "But, I also need stretches of time to rest and be alone." In a tone of dejection, she said, "I'm sorry. I just assumed lots of company would be good for you. It's what I want when I am sick."

Meg, like most of us at one time or another, assumed incorrectly. We need to realize that only those with personalities similar to ours will have the same desires as we have.

Different Personalities/Different Needs

Each personality, like different flowers, has distinctive needs. I enjoy the beauty and diversity the many flowers in my garden provide. But as a gardener it is my job to understand what conditions each flower wants in order to thrive. My roses require that I plant them in full sunlight and prune them once a year. During the growing season, I fertilize and spray them about every ten days. My daffodils, once they are planted, require little attention except to cut off their dead stalks in the summer. I could say to my roses, "Why can't you be more like my daffodils?" We all accept and understand the foolishness of that statement. If I don't give the roses what they need, they won't flourish. Likewise, the daffodils are best left almost on their own. Yet how many of us are taught what each personality needs emotionally during stressful times?

Popular Sanguines

Popular Sanguines can get depressed when life is not fun. Emotionally they need attention and approval.

Minor illnesses can be a positive for Popular Sanguines, for illness brings with it what they long for: attention, visitors, flowers, presents, and pity. "Poor little me!" But if the problem is full of pain or wipes out their beauty, they can sink into depression. If you have Popular Sanguines in your life who are having problems, be sure to tell them how much you love them—how important they are to you. Accept them as the fun-loving people they are and cheer them on. Because of their spontaneous nature, Sanguines need some freedom in their schedule. Rather than structure each hour of the day, allow them time to do whatever looks exciting to them.

Don't tell friends not to bring flowers to a recovering Popular Sanguine because "she's got too many already." In her mind the number of bouquets represents the level of her popularity. For Popular Sanguines, "too many flowers are never enough!" What specific things can we do to lighten the load during difficult times? Take the time to visit the Sanguines in your life or call them on the phone. Their extroverted personality means their emotional batteries are recharged around people and they get depressed when left alone: "Nobody loves me." They will appreciate the chance to interact with people and share their latest experiences. They like to talk through everything, often sharing more than they should and describing in detail parts of their anatomy best left to the imagination.

Understanding Our Differences during Adversity

Popular Sanguine	Powerful Choleric
Basic Desire: Fun	**Basic Desire: Control**
Emotional Needs: • attention • affection • approval	**Emotional Needs:** • loyalty • achievement • appreciation
Cause of Depression: • life no longer fun	**Cause of Depression:** • life out of control
Stress Relief: • moments of fun in the midst of their difficult experience • freedom in their schedule	**Stress Relief:** • detach from uncontrollable situation • exercise more • start new project • be proactive in other areas of life
How to Help: • visit and give flowers • eating out and/or shopping	**How to Help:** • recognize their efforts and hard work • provide them with choices even if small
Peaceful Phlegmatic	**Perfect Melancholy**
Basic Desire: Peace	**Basic Desire: Perfection**
Emotional Needs: • respect and a feeling of worth • peace and quiet	**Emotional Needs:** • order and sensitivity • silence and space
Cause of Depression: • life filled with problems they must solve	**Cause of Depression:** • life not perfect, little hope for improvement
Stress Relief: • turn on TV • time alone to relax	**Stress Relief:** • keeping personal space organized • long stretches of silence and space
How to Help: • keep conflict, pressure, and arguments to a minimum • allow them to ignore all but the most important issues	**How to Help:** • support with cards, letters, and well-spaced visits • listen carefully to their problems and show concern with a sense of warmth

Any little deed that makes them feel special and gives them attention will be appreciated. You may decide to take them a present, go out to eat, or take them to the movies. They will want to go shopping even when they can barely walk. A wheelchair with bells would be fun! Becky, a Popular Sanguine who had a bone marrow transplant several months before mine, brightly told me of all the company and gifts she received when she arrived home from the hospital. Her voice dropped as she looked down at the floor. "That was three months ago. Now I think everyone has forgotten about me." She no longer received the attention, affection, and approval she so desperately needed. Adding to her sense of abandonment, she and her husband had borrowed more than sixty thousand dollars to pay for their portion of the transplant not covered by insurance. Their tight budget allowed only for the necessities. Becky couldn't go shopping for new clothes or out to eat, two activities that had brightened her days in the past. Fortunately, a group of caring friends recognized Becky's predicament and took her to lunch twice a month at different restaurants in town. Becky looked forward to these exciting afternoons out, which, better than pills, added to her recovery and provided emotional therapy.

What if it is the caregiver who has the Popular Sanguine personality? Of the four personalities, the Popular Sanguine often has the toughest time visiting someone in the hospital, going to a funeral, or caring for someone over an extended period of time, as these experiences aren't anything close to fun. For my bone marrow transplant, I went to the Dana Farber Cancer Institute in Boston, Massachusetts, about nine hours from my home. Betsy, a Popular Sanguine friend, said, "I'm so glad you went to Boston. I don't think I could have visited you in the hospital." While I was in Boston, Betsy had a party at her house in my honor. She videotaped my friends cheering for me and sending me their love. Watching that tape in my isolated hospital room helped to brighten my day and let me know Betsy cared. And she had a great time doing it!

What if you are a Sanguine and don't have the support of any close friends? Begin by writing down a list of activities that you enjoy. If you haven't had fun for a long time, this may be a difficult assignment. Give yourself time to think. If you have a photo album, or even a box of snapshots, look through them for preproblem photos. Which pictures bring a smile to your face? Maybe you'll enjoy seeing yourself riding a horse, eating an ice-cream cone, or going to a movie. Next, make a conscious effort to make space for moments of fun in the midst of your difficulties, and include those activities that have brought you joy in the past. Each day try to do something to put a hint of fun into your life. Call a friend, but don't hold them on the phone telling them your traumas too long, or they won't return your call.

Perfect Melancholies

Perfect Melancholies becomes depressed when life is not perfect and there appears to be no way to organize it or straighten things out. The Perfect Melancholy emotionally longs for sensitivity to his or her feelings and also needs periods of silence and space to think.

What can you do to help Perfect Melancholies? Listen carefully as they share their problems. A sense of warmth and caring is very important for their sensitive spirit. Don't tell them to lighten up! Melancholies take life seriously and are the most prone to depression. They know the depths of despair.

Silence and space are also treasured by the Melancholy personality. Allison's husband was recently killed in an automobile accident, leaving her to raise their three teenage daughters. She desperately needed time to be alone and work through her feelings of anger and sadness. However, legal concerns and responsibilities for the house and family left Allison feeling overwhelmed. Allison confided to a friend, "I desperately want some silence. Time to think! But it doesn't exist at this house. The girls either have the TV on, the music blaring, or are fighting about the telephone." Allison was able to articulate her needs, and her friend offered to stay with the girls for a weekend. This gave Allison the much needed opportunity to get away by herself.

Perfect Melancholies love organization and perfection. Any little deed or action that will help them move in that direction will be appreciated. My cancer treatments lasted for a year and a half. My desk and drawers were no longer organized. Finding simple things like the stapler became next to impossible. Just because I didn't have the strength to rearrange things didn't mean my desire for order had disappeared. As the months went on, I got more and more depressed searching for things in the midst of the accumulating clutter. A close friend volunteered to help me get the house back in order. About once a week we spent an hour or two cleaning a closet or a few drawers. She took everything off the shelf and dusted it. I decided which items needed to be thrown out and which ones to keep. She then placed the articles back on the shelf. It was a slow process, but I felt better knowing that some progress was being made. Gradually my house was cleaned and reorganized, and I could relax. That simple task helped to relieve my growing frustration and therefore allowed me to focus my energies on getting better.

Humor or a lighthearted approach to life is not a strength of the Perfect Melancholy. If you can provide opportunity for some laughter when helping a Perfect Melancholy in time of adversity, it may help to relieve the stress. Bill, a Peaceful Phlegmatic friend from high school, telephoned me in Boston at a time during my transplant when I was quite ill with a high fever. At the end of his call he said, "I wanted to ask you—do you need my shirt size?"

"Your shirt size? Why would I need your shirt size?"

"Well, I thought you might need it for the gifts you are bringing home from Boston for your friends."

I laughed. There I was fighting for my life and wondering if I would ever get home. The last thing on my mind was shopping. How many people would have had the nerve to pose such a question at such a tense time? But I enjoyed his dry sense of humor at a moment when I was so focused on my condition that I didn't even feel like smiling.

As a Perfect Melancholy what can you do for yourself? Whether you are the caregiver or the person needing the help, realize you need solitude to recharge your batteries. Be willing to create or schedule time to be alone. Not just a few minutes, but stretches of time to read, write, and go deep within without feeling guilty. Maybe, like Allison, you can get the chance to go away for a few days. Quite often, when we are able to get away physically, we get a fresh perspective on our situation as well as a chance to rest and renew.

Powerful Cholerics

Powerful Cholerics get depressed when life is out of control with little hope of getting on top of the situation. Of the four personalities, when dealing with a major tragedy, the Cholerics will have the most difficulty. They want to be powerful, not weak and helpless.

A Powerful Choleric friend who was recently diagnosed with cancer said to me, "I felt fine. I didn't think anything was wrong with me. I went for a routine Pap smear and found out I had cancer. I feel like my body betrayed me." She was angry, which can be one of the easiest emotions for Powerful Cholerics to express and is often the first response during a time of difficulty.

Shortly after John lost his business, he said, "I'm a stable, logical person—not crazy. Why do I feel like I'm losing it—falling apart?" Maybe because he is losing it—"it" being control. Powerful Cholerics hate that feeling. Emotionally, Powerful Cholerics need achievement, appreciation, and a sense of loyalty from their friends and family. They appreciate when others recognize their hard work or efforts with statements like, "I don't know how you manage to keep going considering all you are facing."

Unfortunately, in tough times Powerful Cholerics may not have the ability to "do something." For a week during my bone marrow transplant I had an infection with a 104° fever. My main accomplishment of the day was a walk around my tiny hospital room supporting myself on an IV pole filled with bags of drugs. I felt worthless. What a horrible feeling for me—I had always prided myself on my accomplishments.

One day when I felt especially useless, I received a letter from my college roommate's daughter. Kiera was thirteen years old when she wrote this:

> Dear Georgia,
> How are you doing, and most importantly, how are you feeling? I'm writing this letter to let you know about a speech I did in school. It was to be about the person we admire most. I picked you as that person. While I was giving my speech I had everyone's direct attention. When I finished there was a silence in the room. It was a silence of admiration. After class my classmates came up to me and told me how brave and determined they thought you are. Everyone feels this way, my friends, my teacher, and especially me. I admire your sense of will and strength. You're an astounding woman and I give you my very best. Keep fighting, we'll all be here for you.
>
> Kiera

Stunned, I thought she must have the wrong person! The idea that I could be valued just for who I was, rather than for what I had accomplished, was totally foreign to me. It also was a valuable lesson.

Providing Powerful Cholerics with choices, even if it is only what they will eat for dinner or which movie to rent, will help to restore some sense of control. Chuck had a serious heart condition. His wife encouraged him to use his limited resources in activities he enjoyed. Chuck had always wanted to take a trip to Washington, D.C., to see the cherry blossoms in April. In the past, his hectic schedule had never permitted the time. Although his wife didn't particularly care about seeing the blossoms, she understood he needed a sense of control over some facet of his life. He planned the trip, and they went. She later said, "The trip was very empowering to Chuck. To see something he had always wanted to see was just what he needed."

If Powerful Cholerics have the physical ability, working harder, exercising longer, or starting a new project will help to lift their depression. Powerful Cholerics like to get their difficulties behind them. Wallowing in despair is not their style.

If the caregiver is a Powerful Choleric, be aware of how difficult it can be for them to face an uncontrollable situation. Cholerics like to remove themselves from situations they can do little about. Nicole was terminally ill. Her Choleric husband worked long hours, spending less and less time with her. He had tried to reverse her condition by providing the best medical care possible. But he now realized he could not control his wife's deteriorating health. Unable to face the pain, he stayed away from home. One morning Nicole commented to her nurse, "I guess work is more important than me. He doesn't seem to care that I won't be here much longer." He cared. He was struggling with his feelings of loss. No matter how painful, Powerful Cholerics must remember to balance work and exercise with time to be with the loved ones who need them most in times of adversity.

Peaceful Phlegmatics

Peaceful Phlegmatics can be depressed when life is filled with problems and conflicts that can't be ignored. Emotionally they need peace and quiet.

For weeks after the death of Michael's wife, several women in his church provided meals, cleaned his house, and fussed over his every need. "They wore me out just listening to them," Michael said. While their intentions were good and he appreciated the help they provided, Michael would have preferred that their generous gestures took place while he was at work! As a Peaceful Phlegmatic he was unable to tell the women what he really desired—some peace and quiet. Instead, he spaced out in front of the TV set and took frequent naps.

Peaceful Phlegmatics tend to share very little and often stuff their emotions inside them. Unfortunately, they expend tremendous amounts of energy when they internalize their feelings. This only adds to their already depressed level of available strength. Frank and Jenny's son had been in a coma for months as the result of a hunting accident. Every time a decision needed to be made, Peaceful Phlegmatic Jenny said, "I can't handle it right now." Frank, her Powerful Choleric husband, grew frustrated with her inability to confront the issues related to their son's accident. One evening Jenny asked Frank, "Would you mind dealing with these problems and making all but the most critical decisions without me?"

"No, I don't mind." Frank felt that it would probably make things easier for both of them. The relief of this stress allowed Jenny to begin to face the situation in a way that was comfortable for her without overwhelming her with recurring decisions.

When trying to help the Peaceful Phlegmatic, avoid conflict as much as possible. Conflict only adds to their level of stress. Rather than attacking Peaceful Phlegmatics about why they refuse to deal with a problem, appeal to their gentle nature. A Peaceful Phlegmatic understands that the best results come through cooperation. Frank cooperated with Jenny. But if he had responded, "It's about time you face the facts. Our son's problems aren't going to disappear. We need to make some decisions," he probably would have run into a brick wall. Though easygoing, Peaceful Phlegmatics can be strong willed and quickly build a strong defensive wall around themselves. However, a spirit of cooperation will do wonders to avoid this stubborn streak.

It is also important to validate the Peaceful Phlegmatic. As caregivers, they are so good at quietly working in the background that people often take them for granted. For months Barb had tirelessly helped her sister, Amy, as she recovered from a series of medical complications. One day, after Amy's strength returned, she asked Barb to set a day aside to do something special. Amy said, "Everything I planned that day was something I knew Barb liked. I took her to her favorite Chinese restaurant and to a museum she had always wanted to visit. I wanted her to feel as special as I had during the months she cared for me and my children."

As a Peaceful Phlegmatic, what can you do for yourself? Allow yourself a chance to rest and do something you enjoy. Maybe that's fishing, golfing, hiking, reading, or watching TV. Remember, being around people twenty-four hours a day is draining.

Understanding that each personality copes with loss differently can avoid many misunderstandings. Much tension can be alleviated when we allow the people in our lives to grieve or cope in their own way.

Just as a carpenter doesn't build an entire house with only a screwdriver, the personalities cannot explain all our responses during a life-disrupting event. We as human beings are far too complex. But understanding the responses of the personalities to adversity is an invaluable tool in both your own recovery and your ability to help others.

If you are ever confused or at a total loss as to how to best support someone, simply ask them what would be most helpful. If they aren't able to give you a clear answer, ask if there was ever a time recently when they felt a bit better. If so, what were they doing? This question may trigger a suggestion. If they state that they need to be alone for a while, don't take it personally. That may be exactly what they require.

One thing that seldom helps those who are suffering is to share stories of similar disasters that happened to others. One day a friend from college brought me lunch. Good food was something I especially appreciated. However, during her visit she shared one tragic cancer story after another. Not what I wanted to hear. When there appeared to be no end to her sagas, I finally said, "Can we talk about something else besides cancer?"

Peaceful Phlegmatic Katie had phlebitis. She was in bed with her leg propped up when a Popular Sanguine friend came to cheer her up. The friend asked what she had eaten, and Katie told her what she had had for lunch. The guest gasped and explained, "My friend Jean had the same thing as you and she ate the same thing for lunch. The blood clot broke loose, traveled up her leg to her heart, and in minutes she was a goner!" The friend smiled with the satisfaction of a good story—and Katie spent the rest of the day waiting for the clot to start its journey.

Common Ground

Whatever your personality or the personality of your friend in need, cards with handwritten notes are usually a safe way to let others know you care. You will want to personalize your message with the recipient's personality in mind. The following suggestions may give you some ideas about what would be appreciated by each personality:

- for a Sanguine—"Hoping your strength returns quickly. Looking forward to taking you to lunch at the new French restaurant."
- for a Melancholy—"You are in our prayers. Somehow you will get through this—we believe in you! May God's comfort and love surround you during this difficult time."
- for a Choleric—"Only someone with your remarkable determination could handle what life has brought your way. Keep fighting—we're cheering for you!"
- for a Phlegmatic—"Take care of yourself. Get lots of rest and know we love you and miss your quiet spirit."

There is a saying, "The grass is always greener on the other side of the fence." As a gardener, I have found the grass is usually greener where it is given what it needs—be it sunlight, water, lime, or nitrogen.

What do the people in your life desire? An opportunity for excitement in the midst of pain? A chance to withdraw and sort things out? Time to work or exercise harder? Or moments to pull away from the realities of life to rest?

Be willing to reach out and help those facing difficult times. It may be just what they need to move beyond simply existing toward the anticipation of a new life.

22

Humor

Our Funny Bones Are Different Too

PATSY DOOLEY

Patsy Dooley has conducted many personality workshops. She has a background in administration that gives her insight into worksite relationships, potential conflicts, and how to use Personality Plus *with staff and employees! She has been a part of church leadership and has taught others how to bring volunteer leadership together for its greatest impact while loving through weaknesses. She is a mother and grandmother, able to give real-life situations in* Personality Plus *for family workshops. And every workshop includes humor—that God-given gift that oils the whole process. She is a motivational humorist and is available to speak on many other topics in addition to* Personality Plus. *Give her a call to speak at your retreat, workshop, or banquet!*

I s there anyone who does not believe that God has a sense of humor? Take a tour of any zoo and look at the long nose and wrinkled skin of the elephant, the tall neck and legs of the giraffe, and the colorful rear end of the orangutan. Put yourself in Adam's shoes. Can't you just imagine the conversation between Adam and God when Adam was told to name the animals? "Lord, it would have been nice if I had been included on the initial planning so that I could have had some input here!" While God expressed His sense of humor with animals, He certainly did not skip us. We come with big ears, large noses, bald heads, and freckles. We come short, tall, thin, and "fluffy"!

Jesus, who kept the crowds spellbound for hours, must have caused His audiences to laugh and chuckle when He talked about struggling over a splinter in someone else's eye when you have a large plank in your own. Created in His image, we are blessed with the ability to laugh!

Norman Cousins, in his book *Anatomy of an Illness*, tells how he faced incredible odds of survival in his fight against cancer. During that fight, laughter played an important part in his miraculous healing process. With friends he played funny videos, and as he and his friends laughed, he healed. For every ten minutes of laughter, he got two hours of pain-free sleep. He lived, and he shared with the world the secret healing power of laughter.

Four Funny Personalities

God breathed into each of us a sense of humor because He knew that we would need one. God knew we would hurt. God knew we would have times of stress. We need to know ourselves well enough to know what it is that triggers our own unique God-given sense of humor so we can laugh when we are in crisis and allow our laughter to help others. Laughter is vitally important to our health, to our relationships, and to our own self-esteem. So join me as we look at the sense of humor of the Popular Sanguines, the Powerful Cholerics, the Perfect Melancholies, and the Peaceful Phlegmatics! In order to establish my credibility, I am often referred to as "an expert on humor." Let me put this in perspective for you. I come in a "fluffy" size and am also a former expert on losing weight! Having put things in focus, let's laugh and learn. . . . Jest for the fun of it!

Popular Sanguines:
"A funny thing happened to me on the way to . . ."

Popular Sanguines are by nature storytellers and can find humor in almost any situation. They enjoy a variety of types of humor and are quick to share anything funny. They are very social and cannot resist telling the whole world the events of their day. Even when feeling dry within they can find and give laughter to others, only to discover that after they have made others laugh, they no longer feel dry inside. It usually starts with some normal event that gets out of control.

One night I was dressed in my red nightgown and sitting in front of the TV. I was watching a show about a boy who was divorcing his family. At the critical point, when the judge was going to deliver his verdict, the movie broke for a commercial. Dashing outside to the patio to grab a Diet Coke from the pantry, I suddenly had this sensation of "oh no!" I turned, reached for the door, and found my "oh no" was "oh yes!" I had locked the door. There I stood on my patio, in my floor-length, extra-large, red silk nightgown. Desperate, I began to rattle every door to my house—all locked. My first instinct was to think, *Who can I call?* Then I realized I couldn't call anyone. My phone was in the house! *Where could I go?* The closest person was Pastor Bob two blocks away. Not even thinking about how I must have looked storming down the middle of the asphalt road barefoot with my size 3X red nightgown flowing in the wind, I made my way to his house. I knocked. I pounded on the door. No one was home. I banged some more. Maybe the dog would let me in! The dog didn't cooperate, so I wandered to the wrought-iron fence and sort of hung on the gate, trying to decide what to do. The police station was another two blocks away, but I was not sure what kind of a reception I would get at that hour of night with no ID, dressed for bed in my red nightgown and slightly on the edge of hysteria. Suddenly a car came around the corner, slowed down, then started to go right on by. The driver changed his mind and pulled to the curb. It was Pastor Bob. He shouted, "I couldn't imagine who was draped on my fence so I thought I'd pretend I don't live here!" Now, until this point, I must admit I had not seen anything too humorous about this situation until his wife, Darlena, began to laugh. Pastor Bob began to laugh. I began to laugh. Laughter lifted their tired spirits. Their laughter fed my sense of humor and I immediately had a story I couldn't wait to share about how "a funny thing happened to me on my way to the patio!"

The Popular Sanguine can take normal, everyday occurrences (this was normal, wasn't it?) and find the ability not only to laugh at themselves, but to tell it in such a way that others feel like they were right there in their own red nightgowns.

Popular Sanguines like to poke fun at themselves, but they also like to tease others. My daddy, a Popular Sanguine/Peaceful Phlegmatic, is a big tease, much to the dismay of my Perfect Melancholy mother. When someone calls and asks to speak to his wife, he responds, "Which one?"

When a Popular Sanguine/Powerful Choleric uses humor, it is a joking, teasing type of humor that says, "There's work to be done, but

Personality of Humor

Popular Sanguine	Powerful Choleric
"A Funny Thing Happened on the Way to . . ."	**"Just Joking! Just Joking!"**
• situational sense of humor • storyteller • "ribs" others • uses a variety of types of humor that allow exaggeration • hearty belly laughter	• joke teller • uses occupational humor • uses a variety of types of humor as long as it can be delivered quickly and has a point • smiler
Peaceful Phlegmatic	**Perfect Melancholy**
"Now That's Funny!"	**"Humph!"**
• quick, original wit • uses one-liners, absurdity, puns, irony • excellent ability to use humor to defuse tense situations • can be tinged with sarcasm • chuckler	• best kept secret! • rarely delivers humor except with close friends and family • internalizes humor • values all varieties of humor, but especially analytical, thinking humor • stoic expression

let's have fun while we do it!" This type of personality will tease people unmercifully, and most of the time the teasing is received in the spirit given. This meets this personality type's emotional needs and makes them and others laugh.

Popular Sanguines feel comfortable laughing even when others aren't. They are keen observers of human nature, have the ability to see things from others' points of view, and defuse stress by seeing the humor in serious situations, sharing it, and lightening up the spirits of those around them. Powerful Cholerics enjoy the Popular Sanguine's fun nature and tolerate their lengthy stories. The Perfect Melancholies, who keep their laughter inside, envy the freedom of laughter that emanates from the Sanguine. The Peaceful Phlegmatic is the perfect audience for the Popular Sanguine because they appreciate the storytelling and respond with hearty laughter.

Powerful Cholerics: "Just joking! Just joking!"

Powerful Cholerics are task focused, fast moving, and do not have time to tell stories. Nor are they necessarily the deliverers of a lot of humor. They are often so caught up in getting the job done that laughter is seen as "joking around" and a definite waste of time. Powerful Cholerics have what I call "a sense of occupational humor"! It is seldom appreciated or understood by those outside particular occupations,

and contains humor unique to the medical field, the funeral home industry, or law enforcement teams, for example. Those who do understand
it find it creates a bond of friendship among peers. Cholerics appreciate the humor of "The Far Side" because of its offbeat humor. Powerful Cholerics can take credit for making the Three Stooges with their
occupational humor successful. This meets their emotional need for
laughter because by their very nature they often choose to work in critical work fields that require instant decision making. In one emergency
room, the number one game they play on Friday nights is guessing the
blood alcohol content of all drunks. Betty, a nurse, shared that a totally
passed-out drunk man was brought in. The entire emergency room
staff began putting their dollars into the kitty and placing their bets as
to this man's blood alcohol content, when suddenly the man sat right
up, shouted "1.7," and then passed out again. This brought the house
down and made the Friday-night ER tolerable. Powerful Cholerics
reduce the stress level by inserting occupational humor.

The Powerful Cholerics' frustration level at the incompetence of
others is relieved by comments directed at others in a humorous way,
but still making a point. It can be in a teasing manner and can have
quite a barb to it. While they claim the right to use this type of humor,
they get a little touchy if it is directed back at them or at the way they
handle things. Being a Popular Sanguine, I arrived fashionably late
one morning, and my boss greeted me with, "Don't kill yourself getting here too early!" Though put in a joking way, I knew there was a
message for me—a stinger!

Powerful Cholerics are "joke tellers." It's quick—it gets a response
and they can get going on task again. They use sarcasm in their delivery that can backfire on them when the recipient of the humor takes
it personally. The Powerful Choleric tries spontaneous humor using
dry wit, only to find that others sometimes can't tell whether or not
they are joking. A very common expression of the Powerful Choleric
is, "Joking . . . just joking!" or "Can't you take a joke?" They hate to
hear people complain and will be the ones that pantomime holding
a violin and playing it with a bow, silently giving the message "My
heart bleeds for you—now quit complaining!"

The Powerful Choleric plays funny pranks on others. Eva, a pastor's
wife who is a combination Popular Sanguine/Powerful Choleric, shared
that she and her friend Grace were driving past a walnut grove. Grace
noticed that there were a lot of walnuts on the ground, probably going

to waste. Grace was sure the owners of the grove would not object if she and Eva got a sackful. A Powerful Choleric member of their church drove by as they were collecting the walnuts and couldn't resist joking with them about getting arrested for "lifting" walnuts. Later that week, that same member ran an ad in the local newspaper, "Help wanted: Walnut pickers" and gave Eva's phone number. She began to get a lot of calls from people looking for work. While embarrassed to have to explain that it was a practical joke, Eva reported that she met a lot of interesting people through that ad. She was honored with a homemade "nut broach" several months later, and nut pranks continued for almost six months to the enjoyment of the whole congregation. The Powerful Cholerics have a tenacity that is carried over into their jokes and pranks.

Emily, a participant in one of my workshops, shared how her mother hates fruit. A Powerful Choleric, Emily designed a fake "Fruit of the Month Club" certificate and presented it to her mother on her birthday. Her mother thought it was a real certificate and was trying to show her appreciation while the whole family was trying to hold back bursts of laughter as they watched her squirm.

The Powerful Choleric does have a sense of humor and takes the time to liven things up with these types of pranks. Recognizing the value of diffusing tense situations with humor that is quick and to the point is the strong suit of the Powerful Choleric.

Popular Sanguines enjoy the ability of the Powerful Choleric to focus on and joke about something that is in the process of happening. Perfect Melancholies enjoy the Powerful Choleric's sense of humor because while joking they never lose their high energy, focus, or drive. Peaceful Phlegmatics like the fast, off-the-cuff irony and sarcasm that is so much a part of the Powerful Choleric sense of humor.

Perfect Melancholies: "Humph!"

The best-kept secret is that Perfect Melancholies do have a sense of humor. By their very personality, Perfect Melancholies are the hardest to read about what is funny to them because they are so private in what they share. Even in the area of their humor, they rarely give you a glimpse of what generates laughter within them. And it is within them! In response to one of my questionnaires, Perfect Melancholies reported that they enjoy analytical, intelligent humor. They all reported that they look for humor found in books or watching others but rarely try to be humorous. Perfect Melancholies want to be sure that any humor they share is funny and delivered with perfection. They fear that what they see as humorous will not be funny to others or that they will not deliver it correctly. On one questionnaire, a Perfect Melancholy responded, "I check my computer for a list of something funny." In a discussion about having a humor file, one Perfect Melancholy lifted her hand and said, "I have one of those. The only trouble is—it's empty!"

One woman shared that if she got a "humph" out of her Perfect Melancholy sister, that was equal to a belly laugh from the rest of the family. Perfect Melancholies especially find sophisticated or analytical humor the funniest. They enjoy puns, plays on words, malapropisms, and incongruities. They like stories that have a double meaning, letting others draw their own conclusions. They enjoy the storytelling of the Popular Sanguine (the first time they hear it), the one-on-one wit of the Peaceful Phlegmatic, and the teaching humor of the Powerful Choleric—but their response rarely reaches the facial muscles. My mentor and friend in humor, John Kinde, is a Perfect Melancholy. Yes, he is a humorist and a very good one, and yes, he is a Perfect Melancholy. Wonders never cease! We often joke that I need less zip and he needs more zing! When he is in my audience, I know I've scored a good one if his eyes twinkle and his head nods! The laughter of others lifts and reenergizes Melancholy spirits.

In so many ways the Perfect Melancholy has a deep capacity for feelings, which they rarely let people see. This carries over to their sense of humor. Jackie had watched a movie that had caused her to laugh hysterically. She kept trying to get her Perfect Melancholy mother to see the movie. She talked about it constantly until finally her mother agreed. Jackie called her mother, expectantly waiting for her mother's reaction to the movie. Her mother said, "Jackie, you were right. It was so funny, I almost laughed!"

In my audiences there are always some people sitting there without an expression on their faces. I feel I am bombing as a humorist—that they don't like me. I've shared this with others, and invariably, someone will say, "That's my husband. He will look bored to death, and when I ask him how he enjoyed the program, he'll say, 'It was good.'" That's about as good as it gets for the Perfect Melancholy who is processing the humor on the inside.

I share a home with a woman who is a combination Perfect Melancholy/Peaceful Phlegmatic. She has lived through many hard times and keeps things to herself until she feels she can trust you. I felt the need to "mother" this new friend and would jump to do things for her. One day she told me, "I have lived to a ripe old age taking care of myself. I think I can still do it," which was the humor of her Perfect Melancholy personality telling me to "bug off," she did not need mothering! I am so glad. I'm not very good at mothering at this stage of my life anyway.

One day when we were in the produce department I caught a glimpse of the "dubious, suspicious" thinking of the Perfect Melancholy. Shopping for fruit, we found some apples on a shelf. Some of the apples had been put in sacks to form a support wall around the edge of the shelf. Then individual apples had been piled high in the middle for customers to bag. These apples were three pounds for a dollar, a good price, which was important to my Perfect Melancholy friend. I spied the bagged apples thinking, *Isn't this nice, they even bagged some for us!* Betty, with her analytical mind, immediately saw that if I removed the bag I reached for, apples would soon be falling all over the floor. She quietly told me that she didn't think I was supposed to take the sacks. Too late! I had already pulled the sack of apples off the shelf and was placing it in the grocery cart when I looked back. Poor Betty was trying to keep this whole display of apples from falling through the gap I had created by throwing her entire body against the hole. I quickly tried to put the bag back into the dike when I heard her muttering, "She just wants to see me pick up all these apples." That she would give a Popular Sanguine that much credit for analytical thinking struck me so funny, I began to giggle and then laugh hysterically. The more I thought about her thinking that I had planned this, instead of realizing that without even trying we Popular Sanguines can create our own catastrophes, struck me so funny that the more we tried to plug the hole the harder I laughed. Suddenly she began to giggle. For the first time I saw my Perfect Melancholy friend let go and let laughter escape from inside her. Fortunately for me, her skills got us out of that mess. We were able to restore the display for its intended purpose. However, when I need a good laugh, I remember her words, "She just wants to see me pick up all these apples!"

Perfect Melancholies need to know that it is dangerous to hold back laughter. It goes back down and spreads out in their hips!

Peaceful Phlegmatics: "Now that's funny!"

Unlike the Popular Sanguines, the Peaceful Phlegmatics normally are not storytellers, but they have a quick wit that comes out in one-liners that pick up on the absurdity of a situation, surprising every-one and generating laughter. Peaceful Phlegmatics love a play on words and puns. They get intense enjoyment when the receiver of their humor is caught off guard. The humor of the Peaceful Phleg-matic slips up on you. At a MOPS (Mothers of Pre-Schoolers) meet-ing, one Peaceful Phlegmatic mother was demonstrating how to make good chocolate chip cookies. She had a flip chart with the recipe explaining what she was doing. As she put the flour in the bowl to demonstrate the procedure, we could follow it on the flip chart. When the recipe called for eggs, she got the eggs to add to the batter, only to discover that the eggs she had brought had been boiled. She told us to pretend she had added the eggs, finished her demonstration, and flipped her chart to the last page, which said, "Got Milk?" Every-one laughed. She gave all of us cookies she had baked earlier. Then a Peaceful Phlegmatic in the audience quickly grabbed a piece of paper, wrote something in large letters, and held it up for all to read. It said, "Got Eggs?" The quick wit of the Peaceful Phlegmatics!

Because they generally keep a very low profile, their sense of humor is enjoyed by those who find themselves one-on-one with the Peace-ful Phlegmatic. A normal conversation can be taking place when all of a sudden, the absurdity of something said is picked up by the Peace-ful Phlegmatic, and in the way only a Peaceful Phlegmatic can deliver, they point out the absurdity, and others think: "Now *that's* funny!" Their wit is original in its delivery and very refreshing, not only because of the appropriateness, but because of the surprise. . . . who would have thought that Peaceful Phlegmatics could be so funny!

Many seniors over fifty-five take advantage of vacationing in the college systems through a program called the Elderhostel. Their vaca-tion not only includes interesting places and economical accommo-dations, but also provides opportunities to attend many interesting classes. At a recent Elderhostel where I was teaching a class on how to develop your sense of humor, I began a mixer by defining the fol-lowing categories on the blackboard: "Stars," "Directors," "Stage Helpers," and "Audience." People who know us well can often pick out our personality much more quickly than we can ourselves, so I asked each person to come up and put their spouse's name under the category that best described their spouse's personality. One attractive woman wrote her husband's name under Director. She then turned to the group and said, "He told me to write his name there and my name here," whereupon she wrote her name under the category of Audience. Obviously a Peaceful Phlegmatic wife married to a Powerful Choleric husband! Everyone laughed as the Peaceful Phlegmatics came forward with their one-liners setting the tone for the whole class.

One Peaceful Phlegmatic said that her husband was always pushing her to tell him what she wanted. He asked her if she wanted to drive. She thought she would please him with the response, "Yes, I'll drive today." She got behind the wheel and began driving. Her Powerful Choleric husband immediately began telling her exactly how to drive and which direction to turn. She turned to him and said, "I'm sure glad we're driving today!" While Peaceful Phlegmatics are peacemakers, their humor can take on a sarcastic twist.

Peaceful Phlegmatics are the chucklers while Popular Sanguines are the belly laughers! While the Popular Sanguines are great at exaggeration and painting funny pictures with their words and their body language, the Peaceful Phlegmatics have the art of delivering a well-worded, one-line response, something the talkative Popular Sanguines envy. Since Powerful Cholerics thrive in areas of tension, the insertion of unexpected humor brings a brief release, giving them an appreciation for the subtle humor of the Peaceful Phlegmatic. Perfect Melancholies also appreciate the humor of the Peaceful Phlegmatic because it is often an intellectual type of humor that is clever and thought-provoking. The result: Everyone feels the God-given gift of the lighter touch.

Laughter—Given to Us Because We Need It

Each of us has a sense of humor because we *need* to laugh. There is medical documentation that a couple of good belly laughs a day equal a mile of jogging. Now that's my kind of exercise! Each of the personalities has a different way of seeing humor and sharing humor because each has different emotional needs. It is in this vast variety of laughter that our own needs are met and our humor is shared with others, whether we are Popular Sanguine, Powerful Choleric, Perfect Melancholy, or Peaceful Phlegmatic. Remember, God gave us this gift of laughter for our well-being. If you can't find something to laugh about, borrow something, laugh on credit!

Keeping humor in mind, always remember that any day aboveground is a great day!

Part 5

Women's Matters

23

Fitness

Change Your Body, Not Your Personality

DANNA DEMETRE

Danna Demetre understands the challenge and frustration of trying to achieve and maintain a lean, healthy body. She has successfully battled her own struggles with bulimia, body image, and weight management issues. As a lifestyle coach and president of LifeStyle Dimensions, she teaches others how to make permanent lifestyle changes using innovative tools and techniques including the personalities.

Ask ten women what they would change first about themselves. Eight would change their bodies, most specifically their size and shape. Ask ten men the same question. Most would change their incomes first. What would you answer? Whether first or last on your priority list, your health and fitness will dramatically impact the quality of your life.

Think of your body as a car. Really! What car would best describe your ideal body? Use your imagination to see that vehicle right now, the one you would choose to drive if practicality and money were no issue. Maybe it's a sleek, shiny sports car or a luxury sedan. Or perhaps your dream car is a powerful and fully decked out Jeep Grand Cherokee.

Now, be honest. What vehicle best describes your body right now? Is it that dream car you just pictured in your imagination? Perhaps it's closer to a 1962 Volkswagen Bug rusting and worse for wear with failing spark plugs and deflated tires? How can we possibly fulfill God's purpose for life if our body needs a complete overhaul?

In Romans 12:1 (NIV) Paul admonishes us with these words: "I urge you, brothers, in view of God's mercy, to offer your bodies as living sacrifices, holy and pleasing to God." I once heard Charles Swindoll say, "The only problem with living sacrifices is they keep crawling off the altar!" Living a healthy lifestyle takes work.

Lifestyle, Habits, Fitness, and Diet

What kind of emotions do those words create in you? The condition of our body, our health and vitality, is directly linked to genetic and lifestyle patterns. Genes are simply our God-given *physical* blueprint. We cannot change it. Personality is our God-given *emotional* blueprint. We cannot change it either. But we can influence both blueprints dramatically and make positive changes by recognizing our strengths and weaknesses and living accordingly.

As a lifestyle coach, fitness professional, nutritionist, and registered nurse I have seen people struggle seriously with the dilemmas of changing their habits and ultimately their bodies. While many factors influence making permanent and healthy lifestyle changes, the most ignored factor is the importance of our unique, God-given personality.

In all my experience, the most desperate and frustrated clients have been the ones trying to make changes according to someone else's formula or standard that is completely contrary to their unique personalities. To understand this reality better, let's take an intimate look into the lives of four individuals with four distinctively different personalities. Perhaps one or more will sound uncomfortably familiar. These life snapshots will reveal how the four basic personalities—the Popular Sanguine, Powerful Choleric, Perfect Melancholy, and Peaceful Phlegmatic—can develop unhealthy and potentially devastating lifestyle habits.

Don't let their stories get you too depressed. At the end of this chapter the four will meet one another at a "Personality Power and Lifestyle Change Workshop," where I will offer constructive and appropriate suggestions for each personality!

The Peaceful Phlegmatic "Fallout"

Janet had grown increasingly frustrated over the years as she struggled to lose weight after the birth of each new baby. Now, at thirty-

Your Personality Lifestyle Guide

Popular Sanguine
Basic Desire: Fun

Do: *Gain fundamental knowledge about nutrition and exercise*

- choose a fun book or fast-paced program to get started
- find an accountability partner to help keep you on track

Don't: *Don't go on a diet!*

- don't try quick fix, short-term solutions
- don't buy every new piece of exercise equipment

Exercise

- find a variety of activities you enjoy
- turn exercise into a social event—walks with friends or an aerobics class
- schedule time to exercise each week and stick to it
- give yourself lots of variety

Powerful Choleric
Basic Desire: Control

Do: *Gain fundamental knowledge about nutrition and exercise*

- be patient with yourself and your progress
- give yourself adequate time for results

Don't: *Don't go on a diet!*

- don't have unrealistic expectations
- don't go overboard with exercise; balance is the key
- don't forget to warm up and stretch to prevent injuries

Exercise

- choose simple exercises that are time efficient
- create a realistic exercise schedule and alternate activities for best results
- early morning exercise may be best (you only have to shower once)
- find a class, trainer, or coach who will provide the challenge you need

Peaceful Phlegmatic
Basic Desire: Peace

Do: *Gain fundamental knowledge about nutrition and exercise*

- find a class or book that will instruct you step-by-step
- take one step at a time—it's okay
- keep your plans simple
- take small steps each and every day

Don't: *Don't go on a diet!*

- don't wait until Monday or the first of the month to begin your new habits
- don't get overwhelmed with too many details
- don't become apathetic about your health

Exercise

- find a workout partner or trainer to keep you accountable
- make appointments with yourself to work out and keep them
- find creative ways to move more each day—you don't have to sweat
- maintain your own pace and don't succumb to others' pressures or programs

Perfect Melancholy
Basic Desire: Perfection

Do: *Gain fundamental knowledge about nutrition and exercise*

- find a comprehensive, detailed program or book as a resource
- begin taking action BEFORE you have all the answers
- schedule your new lifestyle changes into your calendar
- accept that others may choose to do things differently

Don't: *Don't go on a diet!*

- don't expect perfection or procrastinate until you have the perfect solution
- don't go overboard with your new lifestyle
- don't expect others to readily participate in your "new program"

Exercise

- create a realistic schedule and pace yourself
- choose a variety of activities
- select a club or gym that offers a comprehensive orientation
- consider a personal trainer to fine-tune your fitness
- use an activity monitor to help you track your progress
- take a break now and then

continued on next page

(cont.)

Popular Sanguine
Basic Desire: Fun

Nutrition: *Follow the Energy Formula*
- breakfast, water, fiber, protein, limited caffeine and sugar
- keep it simple with a solid nutritional base
- find creative ways that you can live with to cut calories
- plan for "fun foods" and stick with your plan

Stress
- avoid overcommitment
- learn to have realistic expectations
- slow down and purposely relax
- enjoy some time alone

Motivation: *"As a man thinks, so is he"*
- specifically visualize your goals and write them down—read them daily
- ask for feedback from your accountability partner
- turn off any negative self-talk
- use positive self-talk tapes specific to your personality

Powerful Choleric
Basic Desire: Control

Nutrition: *Follow the Energy Formula*
- breakfast, water, fiber, protein, limited caffeine and sugar
- make some simple, basic changes in your overall nutrition to meet goals
- eat breakfast every day no matter how busy you are
- stop eating lunch while you work and enjoy your meals
- avoid heavy, late evening dinners

Stress
- slow down and take the time to experience the "small stuff"
- schedule "downtime" into your life
- use proactive stress busters like walks, journaling, massage, and fun!
- get adequate sleep and avoid caffeine

Motivation: *"As a man thinks, so is he"*
- determine your physical objectives and weigh the cost
- create a realistic action plan and schedule it into your life
- use positive self-talk tapes specific to your personality
- your greatest motivation will be results, so . . . **Just Do It!**

Peaceful Phlegmatic
Basic Desire: Peace

Nutrition: *Follow the Energy Formula*
- breakfast, water, fiber, protein, limited caffeine and sugar
- watch out for grazing with sedentary activities like TV
- choose one or two dietary changes at a time
- shop with a list and a plan
- think about what you are going to eat beforehand

Motivation: *"As a man thinks, so is he"*
- ask your workout partner or trainer to help you evaluate your progress
- celebrate even small successes
- believe in your ability to "stick with it"
- listen to "healthy talk" audiotapes at least twice each day
- remember: "Garbage in . . . garbage out; good stuff in . . . good stuff out!"

Perfect Melancholy
Basic Desire: Perfection

Nutrition: *Follow the Energy Formula*
- breakfast, water, fiber, protein, limited caffeine and sugar
- start with the basics first and modify your diet as you learn the facts
- use organizational skills to create healthful meal plans and shopping lists
- keep a log of your new habits and chart daily
- relax your standards occasionally to enjoy life's little pleasures

Motivation: *"As a man thinks, so is he"*
- examine your beliefs and learn to let go of the lies
- celebrate small victories and keep records of your small steps
- listen to "healthy talk" audiotapes specific to your personality

six with three children, she was at an all-time low both physically and emotionally. The original ten pounds she added after Nicole, her first child, became twenty after Jonathan, her second. Though she had tried desperately to exercise and diet, she ultimately added another ten pounds before she was surprised with her last pregnancy. She had felt so hopeless and defeated that she had not even tried to minimize the weight gain during this last pregnancy. When baby Laurel entered the world, Janet was so overweight and depressed that she had a hard time bonding with her newest daughter.

At her six-week checkup, Janet cringed as the nurse recorded her weight at a whopping 205 pounds. Dr. Kaplan admonished her with a warning when her blood pressure registered at an all-time high as well. "Janet, it's important to get this under control. Now, your health is at risk with this kind of blood pressure."

"Dr. Kaplan, I don't know what to do. I've tried every diet out there and failed," she sighed.

"Janet, you have to lose at least fifty pounds. Stop at the reception desk on the way out and I'll have the nurse give you a one-thousand-calorie diet. Oh, and you should get some exercise too."

Janet cringed at the thought of another cycle of deprivation and frustration. She'd been down that road many times. A wave of anxiety began to sweep over her just thinking about the enormous task of shedding all this weight. Driving home, she determined that Thursday was not a good day to start this new endeavor. *Monday is always a great day for a new beginning,* she reasoned as she pulled toward the Burger King drive-through window and rationalized her last Whopper with cheese.

As a Peaceful Phlegmatic, Janet had always been well liked with a wide variety of friends. Her "go with the flow" personality never ruffled any feathers, and she had sailed through childhood and adolescence with minimal stress. Of course, that is exactly the kind of life a Peaceful Phlegmatic prefers—smooth, carefree, and peaceful. As a new wife, Janet had discovered that her Perfect Melancholy husband, Jim, was more of a challenge than she had realized. His desire for perfection and his self-disciplined nature left him little patience with Janet's expanding waistline and apparent lack of self-control.

She remembered the "program" Jim had designed for her to shed her excess weight after the first baby. He presented it to her complete with charts and graphs and a detailed menu plan he had sent away for. Janet became easily overwhelmed and gave up after two weeks.

Jim had persisted through the next five years, criticizing her adamantly with each new pound. She had withdrawn to the television and sleeping late to avoid Jim's obvious distaste for her enlarging body.

While the kids were at school and Jim was at work, Janet buried her frustration with bingeing. At dinner she would pick at her food and pretend to be dieting. This had become the vicious cycle of her life, and the thought of starting one more futile diet was more than she could bear.

What Janet had not realized through the years was the influence her Peaceful Phlegmatic personality had had on her ability to change lifestyle habits. She had been unsuccessful using her husband's Perfect Melancholy approach. Janet needed a fresh, new approach—one that suited her Peaceful nature.

She almost missed the ad while thumbing through the newspaper, but one word caught her attention and she read on . . .

The Powerful Choleric "Complex"

Frank could feel the tension rising up his neck as he slammed down the receiver and pushed the intercom button on his phone. "Martha! Send Mr. Gibson the Donnelly proposal, yesterday! What is *wrong* with this company? The mail room loses everything. And we may end up losing our largest account!"

"No problem, Frank. Just relax, I'll express mail it. He'll have it by tomorrow," Martha assured her boss. She'd been Frank's secretary for ten years and had watched him age before her eyes. "Frank?" She buzzed the intercom into his office, "How about a sandwich or something? I'm going out to get a bite when I mail this proposal."

"Nah, don't have time," he grumbled back, "just a cup of coffee if it's not too much trouble." Frank noticed a burning sensation in his gut as he washed down the last swig of cold, black coffee. In his busyness and concentration, he consciously ignored the little flutter-and-squeeze sensation deep in his chest. He'd been ignoring a lot of things lately, like his wife, Susan's, gentle suggestions to get a little exercise or to cut back on the caffeine. She just didn't seem to understand all the pressures he had and how much his company depended on him. He was sick and tired of her sweet, yet persistent admonishments for him to slow down.

"Frank, darling, I just worry about you," she had whispered to him last Friday night as he lay dozing on the couch, the newspaper in a heap on his lap. "You're just so exhausted at the end of each day. You can't keep up this pace forever!"

She hadn't realized how prophetic that statement would be. Martha had returned with Frank's coffee that afternoon only to find him pacing the office clutching his chest. "Aaah, I've got some killer heartburn, Martha. Have any Tums or something?" he asked as he rubbed his left arm. "Frank, you don't look good. I'm calling Susan. I think you need to see a doctor!" "Naah!" he retorted and stopped abruptly, gasping for air as he collapsed in a heap on the floor.

Susan met Frank in the emergency room. His pale, clammy skin frightened her, and she held back tears knowing he would appreciate a strong front. She sent up a silent prayer, "God, I sure hope this will get his attention!"

Frank had become a good example of how our strengths can become our weaknesses. His Powerful Choleric personality had always driven him toward success, especially in the business world. Unfortunately, his health had paid the price at the risk of his very life. He was going to have to make a choice. But what would motivate this driven Powerful Choleric man to change? He needed a lifestyle approach that would give him a sense of control, purpose, and accomplishment. Recovering from his mild heart attack gave Frank some time to think about the changes he needed to make.

Susan came rushing into his room bright-faced and glowing. Tossing a folded newspaper onto his bed, she quipped, "You need this, Frank. And this time I won't take no for an answer; you are too important to me. Read this and get dressed . . ."

The Perfect Melancholy "Method"

Karen sat staring at her computer monitor. She was exhausted. It felt like she'd been working on her thesis for an eternity. This machine had become her constant companion and Friday-night date. Her back and neck ached from hunching over at her desk for hours on end.

"I've got to get some exercise," she thought. But she knew she wouldn't take the time unless she could really dedicate herself to a complete routine. In her mind, nothing was worth doing unless you did it completely right. So for now her routine was work, study, work, study. At least she would be sure she received the perfect A on this paper.

The sad truth was, once she finished her thesis, her life wouldn't get any more active. She had been offered an advanced research position at the university. "Now that's a high energy job!" she mused. She could imagine herself twenty years from now as a hunched-over, weak, and pale old maid.

"Maybe I should get a life," she laughed to herself. The ring of the phone interrupted her thoughts. It was her college friend Elise inviting her to an old-fashioned picnic complete with three-legged races, volleyball, and croquet. "Okay, okay, Elise," she was succumbing to her friend's gentle pressure to emerge from her "high-tech" cave. It would be good for her to see sunlight once in a while.

Perfect Melancholy Karen checked one more item off her Saturday morning to-do list before leaving for the picnic. If she hadn't promised Elise she would show, she would have stayed home and completed every item. She could almost hear her computer audibly calling her from the doorway, "Get back here, you're not done yet!"

She had jumped into all the day's activities with total enthusiasm, figuring she could make up for five years of inactivity in a single afternoon. Her lungs ached as they sucked for more oxygen; they were unused to this level of demand. She pushed herself to the limit, her competitive spirit pushing her to win at every event. She finally pushed beyond her body's current ability to respond. Leaping for the volleyball to make the game point, she heard a loud "pop." And down she went.

"Ouch! No, I can't step on it; I think I've ruptured my Achilles tendon!" Karen screamed as Elise and two of the stronger guys helped her off the field. Recovering from her injury, Karen realized how out of shape she had become. Not only that, her nutritional habits were atrocious. She had shelved any of the healthy habits she once followed and had become "tunnel-visioned" on getting through school. At twenty-eight, she realized she was more out of shape than some of her active forty-year-old friends.

"Okay, that's it!" she decided. "But where do I start?" She glanced down at the local paper sitting on her desk, and a key word caught her eye. "Hmm, that sounds like me; maybe I'll check this one out!"

The Popular Sanguine "Solution"

"Oh, my gosh! It's too small, my favorite dress is too small! What happened?" Sharon squealed as she stood gawking in the full-length mirror. Her husband, Dan, came running, thinking something was terribly wrong, only to find Sharon huffing and puffing around the bedroom with seemingly dozens of outfits thrown onto the bed.

"Sharon, we have to leave for the party in ten minutes! What are you doing?" Dan questioned, the irritation seeping into his voice.

Frustrated, Sharon responded, "I'm trying to find something to wear! Everything is too tight, I don't know what's happened."

Dan rolled his eyes out of Sharon's view. This had happened many times before. Sharon had been a yo-yo dieter for years. She rotated in a circle of size six, eight, ten and back to six again in about three-year cycles. He had figured years ago it was how she justified doing so much shopping. Her frequent excuse was "Nothing fits!"

There was a bigger concern than simply the budget and Sharon's obvious frustration that was coming to the surface. Dan had noticed that she seemed more and more focused on quick fixes and diet aids.

In the past four years they had acquired a stationary bike, stairstepper, and many other weights and gadgets. When she had gotten bored with these after two or three weeks, she had convinced Dan that a gym membership was the answer. Unfortunately, Sharon found the people at the gym were too serious. They tried to put her on a program of aerobics and weight training, but she just wasn't having fun.

In addition, Sharon had filled their cupboards with every vitamin and pill imaginable, each label declaring some new "fat-burning formula." Fat-free frozen treats overflowed in the freezer and low-fat, no-fat sweets were everywhere. With all this low-fat eating, exercise equipment, and gym memberships, why was Sharon having such difficulty? More importantly, why had she lost her normally energetic and vivacious spirit?

As a Popular Sanguine Sharon had always been full of life and optimism. Dan had watched her sacrifice nutrition for taste and common sense for results. She seemed much more concerned with how she looked than how she felt.

His concerns increased considerably over the next several months. Almost miraculously, Sharon seemed to be melting off her most recent weight gain and was back in her favorite size six dress within ten weeks. At first, she seemed to be her old energetic self, full of life and happiness. But the more she lost, the more irritable and forgetful she became. It reached its peak one Wednesday, when their eight-year-old son, Josh, called Dan at the office sobbing, "Dad, I've been standing outside school for an hour in the rain. I think Mom forgot to pick me up!"

Dan confronted Sharon with his concerns and she flew off the handle, claiming her forgetfulness was due to lack of sleep. "What are you taking anyway, Sharon? This can't be good for you!"

"Dan, my doctor prescribed it, it's totally safe. It's the latest, most effective medication. He's monitoring me closely. I'm just fine. And I look better than I did at twenty!"

"Actually, the last few weeks, you look too thin," he retorted. "What doctor in his right mind would continue giving diet pills to someone who doesn't need to lose weight?"

"That's it, Dan!" Sharon hollered back. "You just don't want me to look this good, do you?"

The fight escalated and Sharon's irritability increased. It became harder to deny the symptoms of nervousness and forgetfulness over the next few weeks. She slept through her alarm three days in a row and left Josh waiting thirty minutes another afternoon before admitting it was time to put away the pills. Sadly, the weight began to come back, more quickly than before. Five months later and almost back in her size ten jeans, she saw the advertisement in her local paper and knew she had to go . . .

Time to Make It Happen

The ad that captured the attention of these four personalities read:

Personality Power and Lifestyle Change Workshop!
Have **FUN** losing fat!
Get **CONTROL** of your life!
Find **PEACE** with your body!
The **PERFECT** plan for you!

When the night for that first workshop came, I watched as the room filled with all sizes, shapes, and ages of people. I could see the looks of anxiety and anticipation on their faces. I was certain many wondered if they were wasting their time looking for another answer to the same old question, *"How can I possibly change my habits and body for good?"* Janet and her husband found a seat next to Frank and Susan and exchanged smiles. Karen had convinced her friend Elise to come along. Sharon and Dan sneaked into the room just as I stepped forward to speak.

"Good evening! My name is Danna and I used to be a compulsive-eating couch potato weighing about twenty-five pounds more than I do tonight. Is there anyone here who would like to change at least one little thing about their body or habits?" Hands went up all over, and the room was filled with snickers and laughs. "So, I guess we have something in common," I continued.

"In a group this size, there will be many who want to lose weight, increase fitness, or improve energy levels. Let's face it, our body is our vehicle for life. If it doesn't look or run well, life cannot be lived to its fullest. I'm sure most of you have owned more than one car in your life. Unfortunately, this body is the only one you'll ever have this side of heaven. You can't trade it in. You wouldn't be here tonight if you had fully figured out how to maintain a healthy, high-energy body. So, what do you think the problem is? Why is it so hard to change habits? I propose to you that much of the problem in living healthfully lies in your approach.

"Each of you is at this lecture because you saw an advertisement in the local paper. What was it that drew you here? First, you had a need to make a change in your lifestyle or habits for one reason or another. Second, a word or phrase probably caught your attention. Do the words *fun, perfect, control,* or *peace* speak to any of you?" I could see finger pokes, elbow jabs, and eyebrows raise around the room.

"These words describe a primary motivator peculiar to each personality type." After a brief overview of the four personalities, I explained how focusing on our unique personalities could dramatically impact our ability to make effective lifestyle changes.

Every person was given the Personality Profile to determine their primary personality. Then the group was divided into four smaller "Personality" segments. Each was coached to develop their own customized lifestyle plan based on their goals and personality type.

Everyone was encouraged to support one another in their differences. I told them, "An understanding of your unique personalities will help you better accept why your wife, husband, or friend can't do things just like you do. Accept and celebrate the differences, and we all can reach our goals with a whole lot less heartache and frustration!"

"Now remember, we have to first base all lifestyle change on some fundamental truths about the human body," I cautioned them. "You have to base your plan on a healthy long-term approach. Ask yourself: 'Can I live with this behavior for the rest of my life? Would it be healthful, practical, or even possible?' If the answer is no, don't add it to your plan! If you are unsure about what healthy eating and exercising look like, get educated BEFORE designing your plan. Then use *The Power of Your Personality Lifestyle Guide* to help you create an action plan that works for you!"

Peaceful Phlegmatic Janet was relieved to know she didn't have to go on another restrictive diet to lose her excess weight. She understood that she would always do better with a simple "one-step-at-a-time" approach. She also recognized the need for a partner or personal trainer other than Jim who could keep her accountable to those day-by-day baby steps that would move her toward her goal. Jim also gained some insights and made a promise to himself and Janet not to try to make her do things his way. That alone gave her tremendous comfort.

Powerful Choleric Frank had been a little impatient with the introductions and leery of the new "diet and exercise plan" he was sure would be prescribed for him before the evening was over. However, even he had to admit he was relieved and very pleased that he would be encouraged to develop and implement his own plan. He hadn't missed the gentle stare from his wife when I reminded the Powerful Cholerics not to jump into their new lifestyle changes with too much vigor. He knew from his professional experience that that had been his undoing. This time he would recognize that some of his energy and determination would need to be channeled slowly into this new way of living more healthfully.

Perfect Melancholy Karen had already begun a list of things she would do this week to find the best workout equipment or gyms in the area. She had even created a "healthy" shopping list before she was stopped by a special caution to all the Perfect Melancholy personalities. I warned, "You Perfect Melancholies may take all this so seriously that you spend more time planning and researching your new lifestyle than actually doing it. Everything doesn't have to be perfect before you start. Enjoy the journey of developing your new habits and fine-tune it as you go. However, you will enjoy and get great satisfaction from keeping accurate charts of your activities and progress. Go for it!"

Popular Sanguine Sharon was so excited she couldn't wait to get started. She began enthusiastically sharing her new ideas and plan with her husband, Dan, and caught herself in midsentence. "Hmm," she pondered out loud, "here I go again taking off on a new program without measuring the cost. I think the first thing I'll do is get an accountability partner and take one step at a time." She was encouraged that she could make healthy changes by taking small, consistent steps. She understood that she didn't have to compromise her long-term health or budget in the process.

When the whole group reconvened, I was thrilled to see a sense of hope and encouragement on many of the faces in the room as I wrapped up our first meeting. "Ladies and gentlemen, I want to conclude this evening with one simple thought. No matter what your goals, your plan, or your personality, remember this: *God delights in each good step we take. And small steps taken consistently can add up in a big way over time!*"

24 Shopping

What Kind of Shopper Are You?

VENNA BISHOP

Venna Bishop's passion for being a "Flying Angel" in the Glory of Christmas and Easter pageants at the Crystal Cathedral launched her career as the "Angel Lady Rep" in the wholesale gift industry and prompted her speaking career. She established a market niche for her business, ANGELIC POSSIBILITIES, and is nationally recognized for her knowledge of angels. Venna was interviewed by Robert H. Schuller and also featured on an ABC-TV Special. Clients worldwide value her assessment of buyers and shoppers in stores, malls, and trade shows.

I know that I will never see
A day as great as a shopping spree,
And I wonder if there could ever be
Someone who shops just like me?
Flitting daily to and fro,
Finding bargains as I go,
Knowing if I get depressed
The sight of a store
Will renew my zest!

Now Rita Return
Is nothing like me
As she clips her coupons
To get things free.
She plods through stores
And avoids deep sorrow,
Knowing the purchase today
Can return tomorrow!

285

Now Practical Patty
Has no time to waste.
She must buy things quickly
And without much taste.
She avoids the crowds,
Takes a list to the store,
And while I'm still looking,
She's out the door!

My friend Ursula stays uninvolved
Only goes along for the ride.
Can't buy anything for herself,
Too hard to decide.
She sits and watches,
Hands neatly in her lap,
Then after all this effort,
She goes home to take a nap!

Forgetful Fran's a lot like me.
We have fun together.
We shop every single day
In fair or stormy weather.
We entertain other shoppers,
Put everyone at ease.
But when we wander to the car,
We find we've lost the keys!

So read ahead
And you will see
What kind of shopper
you may be!

Rita Return—the Perfect Melancholy Shopper

My friend Rita is an avid list maker with a variety of daily planners. She has numerous shopping lists categorized for each occasion, and even a list of possible items to be put on a list someday. Attention is given to every detail, a trait typical of a Perfect Melancholy shopper. Rita will start shopping months ahead in order to find the perfect item. We recently went shopping for a blouse for her daughter's birthday. The blouse needed to be striped or polka-dotted to go with her blazers. Rita had collected coupons, studied the newspaper advertisements, and looked over the record of purchases she had made for her daugh-

Shopping with the Personalities

Popular Sanguine *Forgetful Fran*	Powerful Choleric *Practical Patty*
• shops anytime—spend thrift • wanders in and out of every store • impulsive buyer—charms salesperson • delights in sales and bargain bins • finds coupons but forgets to use them • loves crowds—enjoys taking friends • likes choices—easily swayed • risk taker—tries new things • no fun returning things *Fun-loving Buyer*	• controls shopping time—savy about money • decides ahead on specific stores • opinioned buyer—intimidates salesperson • selective about sales and discounts • scans specific coupons and sorts on site • avoids crowds—prefers to shop alone • likes choices—makes own selection • judicious about trying new things • can manipulate returning things *Decisive Buyer*
Peaceful Phlegmatic *Uninvolved Ursula*	Perfect Melancholy *Rita Return*
• delays shopping time—overspends budget • prefers small stores and makes repetitive visits • procrastinating buyer—puzzles salesperson • likes bargains if easy to find • brings wrong or outdated coupons • stays home to avoid crowds—sends someone else • wants few choices—needs encouragement • likes routine—avoids trying new things • too much work to return *Laid-back Buyer*	• shedules shopping time—budget-oriented • makes lists of stores and cross references items • critical, nit-picking buyer—ignores salesperson • seeks bargains and best value for lowest price • organizes, categorizes, and uses coupons • battles crowds alone as a last resort for best buy • needs space and time to evaluate choices • cautious about new things—assesses each detail • practical and systematic about returns *Bottom-line Buyer*

ter over the past five years—she even had a column to check off whether or not she had ever seen her daughter wearing each item!

When I go shopping with Rita, I must be willing to follow her organized plan and not get sidetracked by the Hootenanny Band playing in the commons area or a "blue light" special. She will solicit my opinion on each piece of clothing, thoroughly examining the construction and checking to see if the plaids, stripes, or dots match. If she considers the item to be a good investment and has my approval, she will buy it. This purchase will be so exhausting, however, it will terminate our shopping adventure for the day, as she retreats to the quietness of her home.

As for me, I am a Popular Sanguine and could have shopped all day, so I politely say good-bye and head out to another shopping center, wondering how Rita could always be so tired.

It is not uncommon for Rita to call me a week later and tell me she took her daughter's blouse back to the store. I do believe one of Rita's biggest thrills is taking things back and getting credit for her shopping excursions. While she was returning the blouse, she found an absolutely beautiful green jacket for herself that she bought without even trying it on. It was more expensive than she had anticipated, so after having it at home for a few days, she decided it was a bit large. She drove back to the store and exchanged it for a smaller size. It didn't come as any surprise to me, after she'd gone to all this trouble, that she even returned the second jacket. She no longer liked the color. Only Rita can fully understand the thrill of having her returns reflect a positive balance on her credit card account.

One evening Jane and I met Rita at a restaurant for dinner. Whenever the three of us get together, one of us is sure to ask Rita, "Well, what purchases have you returned recently?" This time she immediately started to laugh and quickly extended us an invitation to stop by her house on the way home. She wanted us to give our opinion on some shoes she bought. You would have thought we were at a shoe store as she displayed and modeled seven different pairs of shoes. As we watched her try on and model the shoes, she informed us that five pairs came from three different catalog companies and the two other pairs were purchased at the shopping center. Just trying to keep the different pairs separated as to what came out of which box was a challenge, much less remembering which pair came from each location. Obviously, they could not be mixed up; she might want to return them. All of the shoes were sandals or flats and mostly summer colors. Two pairs were identical in style and size, but one pair was white and the other tan. While we "oohed" over some of her finds, Rita was commenting on the imperfections in fit or design and, at the same time, applauding the prices. Added to this entertaining fashion array were a couple of suit jackets, a blouse, and an evening ensemble. While a few of the items did not receive unanimous approval, the consensus was that she had made some great purchases and would be keeping them.

Two weeks later, when the three of us went to see a movie, Rita beamed when she told us she had returned six pairs of the shoes and all the clothes. She was quite proud of her decision and the fact that her credit card bill had a zero balance.

I do believe Rita's greatest joy and fulfillment comes from returning the catalog items. A friend simply takes the items to Rita's former spouse's office, UPS picks up all the packages, and Rita's returns are sent back at her former spouse's expense! Rita takes a sadistic joy in this procedure.

Personally, I loathe taking things back, either because the packaging and mailing are too much work, or I always forget the package itself when I go back to that store. The day I was debating whether or not to buy a Mickey Mouse pen for my son's girlfriend, Rita was most encouraging. She even went so far as to offer to return it for me if I changed my mind about keeping it. Her offer was tempting, but I decided to wait. It was just as well; his girlfriend already had one.

While traveling on business in another state, I bought a skirt with angels floating on puffy clouds. When I tried it on at home, I decided all those clouds made my hips look big, so I called the store and asked if I could send it back. It was the first time in ten years I tried to send something back. Unfortunately for me, I had paid cash, and returns were against their store policy. I immediately called Rita, assuming she would sympathize with my frustration and have some helpful suggestions. Instead, her response was more like a gentle reprimand for even considering buying anything without checking out the return policy first. After all, credit cards were invented for just these kinds of situations.

Practical Patty—the Powerful Choleric Shopper

The Powerful Cholerics are very practical when it comes to buying gifts, no matter what the occasion. On our twenty-fifth wedding anniversary I expected a romantic gift. Our marriage was having its challenges, and I thought the significance of the event would help put it in perspective. Imagine how I felt when I opened the package and it was—of all things—an electric can opener! My very practical spouse had watched me struggle with a can of tomato sauce a few days prior, so he selected something he thought I really needed and could use. Think of the irony of this situation and how this simple gift could be interpreted to convey a negative message. Since I understood his Powerful personality, I was able to smile and thank him for being so observant.

Shopping with a Powerful Choleric can be an overwhelming experience, beginning with the initial car ride to the shopping mall. This is especially true for me when the driver is a Powerful Choleric male such as my friend Joe. He, as well as all other Powerful Cholerics, likes to drive. It puts the Powerful Choleric in the control position. At an intersection, the driver of the car in front of us better be ready to go when the light turns green, or they will hear a blast from Joe's horn. As a Popular Sanguine, I am really uncomfortable when this happens. I immediately begin giving reasons to justify the slow driver. Joe dismisses my comments as frivolous chatter. In the midst of all the traffic and frustration, he makes a wrong turn and continues to drive round and round muttering to himself rather than stopping and asking for directions. However, if the person riding along with Joe is a Peaceful Phlegmatic instead, Joe's behavior is completely unnoticed. The Phlegmatic will be calmly gazing out the window, quite content to be just sitting and riding to the mall.

My Powerful Choleric friend Patty is always in control and is an organized, confident, and decisive shopper. When we go shopping together, she takes charge of me, and we only stop at the stores she has preselected. None of this wandering in and out of every store looking at whatever might catch my fancy. In my opinion, she really misses out on lots of bargains and often ruins my fun.

Patty quickly selects each item based on how it will fit into her entire wardrobe, household, or whatever the situation dictates. One day on our way home from a shopping excursion, I needed to make a quick stop at the grocery store, so Patty accompanied me. When I selected the largest box of cereal and put it into my grocery cart, Patty grabbed the cereal box out of my cart and flipped it back on the shelf. I was shocked and immediately went into my "best buy" chatter. She merely shrugged her shoulders and replied, "The large box is too tall for your cupboard." She then proceeded to select a smaller-sized box, dropped it into my cart, and continued pushing my cart down the aisle. It did not occur to her to ask whether or not I liked her choice. She knew she was right!

Delegating gift buying is not a problem for a Powerful Choleric boss. If this individual is a male, he wouldn't hesitate asking the secretary to buy his spouse a gift. After all, business is more important than shopping. He has no time to waste. Better yet, why not give cash?

Patty prefers shopping alone and avoids crowds. She will do routine grocery shopping at 10:00 at night or in the wee hours of the morning. You will never find her at the mall on the day after Thanksgiving, the busiest shopping day of the year. The Perfect Melancholy will avoid that day also and will consider it as a possibility if they believe it is the *only* day they can get the *best buy* on the *perfect* item for their needs. The Popular Sanguine personality will be basking among the crowds of people, finding bargains galore, and looking at the event as a gigantic party. Meanwhile, the Peaceful Phlegmatic may never even get started in time to take advantage of any of the sales on that particular weekend—plus, with those crowds, shopping is just too much like work.

Once I dated a fellow with Powerful Choleric traits who enjoyed meeting for breakfast. Whenever I ordered eggs, I would ask to have them poached and specify not to have them runny. For me, it was a real treat to have someone else prepare poached eggs. On my birthday my observant date gave me two Royal Worcester porcelain cylinders about two and a half inches high with hand-painted flowers and stainless tops. I didn't have the vaguest idea what they were or what to do with them, so I just smiled. He quickly moved into action and told me how useful these were for me. He was quite proud to tell me about his shopping endeavors and his ability to explore every major department store until he found this particular gift. Meanwhile, I put my fingers through the hooks on top and dangled them like Christmas ornaments. To his chagrin, I still did not know what to do with them. "They are egg coddlers for poaching eggs," was his rather sharp reply. He continued in a rather sophisticated tone of voice to tell me, "This particular pair was made in England." He was quite pleased with his purchase and the fact that now I could poach my own eggs at home. Oh joy! I always considered it a treat to go to a restaurant and have a chef poach my eggs. Just for the record, we stopped dating a few months later, and I've not made any coddled eggs since then!

Uninvolved Ursula—the Peaceful Phlegmatic Shopper

Ursula is a classic when it comes to shopping. She can always find a chair, stool, or ledge to sit on or lean against in any store. As I stepped out of a dressing room, my Phlegmatic friend was crouched contentedly on a bench under a large philodendron and was gazing at all the people passing by.

I enjoy going shopping with Ursula. She helps me dig through sale bins and doesn't mind if I want to try on clothes. She will even go into the dressing room with me, and she seems to have a nose for finding the only little stall with a chair.

It is not uncommon for me to take six items into a dressing room. Ursula may take two things but only try on one of them. Yet she will sit and watch me try on all six items, and she will even exchange sizes and colors for me, as long as she doesn't have to get undressed again.

She listens so intently to my babbling about each garment and accessory that she has me convinced I can justify my intended purchases. Who else would encourage me to buy a light blue purse with clouds on it to match my speaking brochures? Do you think anyone in my audience will ever make the connection?

It is easier for me to change accessories than it is for Ursula. She has this conservative green print pant outfit and wears the same beads and earrings every time we shop. She refers to it as her spring shopping outfit. She has one for each season so she won't have to think about what to wear. I spotted a fabulous scarf the other day that I tried to encourage her to buy. "It would give your green outfit a fall look," I exclaimed. Ursula merely nodded and said, "Seems like a lot of trouble to me." The thought of a seasonal change was definitely not appealing for her, yet I get bored if I have to wear the same thing twice in the same month.

Equally overwhelming to Ursula is the thought of shopping in large stores that have racks and racks of things up and down the aisle all crowded together. Department stores with their different sections are not Ursula's hangouts. She prefers, instead, the smaller stores without much clutter. She likes it when she can walk into a store and the owner says, "Hi, Ursula, I am glad you stopped. I have something I think you will like." If someone else does the work, it saves her energy.

Shopping for a new appliance or a piece of furniture is a major undertaking for Ursula. Her husband, Ted, kept telling her she needed to get two new matching chairs for the living room. Her old chairs had outlived their usefulness, with stuffing peeking out and throws of conflicting patterns and colors tossed over the worn spots. However, this situation remained unchanged for another six months, until Powerful Choleric Ted took charge and insisted they go shopping. Finding a chair to fit short Ursula and tall Ted proved to be too big a challenge. They concluded that they needed two different chairs, one for her and one for him. This doubled the burden. The choice of fabrics and colors was so overwhelming that Ursula had to go home and think about it for a few more months. A purchase became imminent when they decided to host a party. With Ted in charge, a decision was made and two chairs were selected, delivered, and placed in the same exact location in the living room where the other had been for years. Not wanting to part with the old, worn yet comfortable chairs, she pushed them aside and lined them up like the front row in a theater. On the day of the party, Ted dragged them out to the garage, where they are still sitting. Peaceful Phlegmatics tend to be resistant to change, while Popular Sanguines want something different every day and love to have any excuse to go shopping!

If this had been my house, I would have used the situation to rearrange my furniture. Nothing stays in one place for very long because I enjoy decorating and changing things seasonally. The fall is particularly exciting with all the holidays. At Christmas I have lights and decorations in every room of the house including the patio and garage. Everything stays lit until after Epiphany! Then I can immediately put up things for Valentine's Day, followed by St. Patrick's Day. It doesn't make any difference that I am not Irish, because decorating for St. Patrick's Day just gives me another excuse to shop.

Ursula and I enjoy making things for each other. Both of us have been known to forget an occasion or to recycle gifts. Two years ago Ursula wrapped a needlepoint angel kit for my birthday. I was excited! Angels are my passion. I couldn't believe it when she said, "I want it back." She had meant to do the work on it but hadn't quite gotten around to it. Months went by, followed by another birthday, and the next Christmas it finally reappeared. This beautiful angel was finished, framed, and ready to hang. I would not have had the patience, nor would I have sat still long enough, to finish it. However, my Peaceful Phlegmatic friend likes making homemade gifts and does not mind spending the time as long as it can be done in a sitting position whenever she feels like it.

Forgetful Fran—the Popular Sanguine Shopper

No one has more energy or enthusiasm for shopping than my Popular Sanguine friend Fran. If her family is asked to wait in the car a minute while she runs into the grocery store, they sigh and ask, "Mom, is this stop going to be measured in real minutes or mom-shopping minutes?"

When we shop together we bounce from one store to another without thinking about eating. Fran's glasses only come into focus on sale signs, and I do believe her optometrist gets a kickback on all her purchases. Digging through sale merchandise evolves into a party, which gains momentum as we move into the dressing room and begin modeling our selections. Before long other shoppers, hearing our laughter, come out of their dressing rooms and join in the fun of the moment, often as a Perfect Melancholy salesperson looks on in astonishment.

We don't mind who sees us undressed and we love it when our new friends evaluate our choices.

Fran and I have been friends for years, and we have shopped together hundreds of times. We have difficulty remembering anything connected with numbers like sizes, telephone numbers, and zip codes. Our philosophy is if you can look it up why waste the brain space trying to remember it? Fran has a passion for cows, so she buys things with a cow motif. She assumes I share her interest, since I was raised on a farm and milked cows. She was ecstatic when she found a cutesy cow sweater on sale and gave it to me three months before my birthday. She thought if she put it away, she might forget where she put it—something that has happened more often than she cares to admit. However, there was a more serious problem with the sweater. It was huge! In fact, it probably would have fit the former Chicago Bears football player who was so large that they called him "The Refrigerator"! Because she bought it off an "all sales final" table, it couldn't be returned, an act that neither of us would bother to do anyway. Where was Rita when I needed her? I considered giving it away, but instead it became a great Halloween costume for the twins next door.

Shopping as a Business

All of us have heard about shopaholics who are usually Popular Sanguine personalities. We so easily become addicted to shopping and fall in love with our possessions. Imagine the fun I had turning my enthusiasm for shopping into a business career as a manufacturer's representative in the wholesale gift industry focusing only on angel product lines. It all began when I was performing as a "Flying Angel" in the Glory of Christmas and Easter pageants at the Crystal Cathedral in Southern California. Soaring ninety feet in the air above audiences was my passion, and after two years of commuting eight hundred miles round-trip for rehearsals and performances as a volunteer, I had to find a way to ease the commute and keep a job. While attending the Los Angeles Gift Show, I got the idea to create a business selling angels wholesale to retail stores while I was commuting. This was in 1988, before angels were as popular as they are today. I became known internationally as the "Angel Lady Rep" and turned shopping on a daily basis into a successful business venture that evolved into a career speaking about marketing, sales, and customer service.

As a part of my business endeavors, I attend and exhibit at trade shows. At the Christian Booksellers Convention in Anaheim, I was eager to get an early start on the opening morning. They were expecting eighty thousand people. I parked my car in a lot near the Anaheim Convention Center, opened the trunk, and took out my luggage cart and bag. I was off for a day of trade-show shopping. Nine hours later, I returned to my car. My feet were aching and my cart was loaded with pamphlets and show samples. I was rummaging through my large Popular Sanguine purse, when my friends from CLASS (Christian Leaders, Authors, & Speakers Seminar) came walking by lugging their bags. "I must start carrying a smaller purse," I commented. "I have too much stuff in here and can't find my keys." Marita Littauer casually remarked, "Maybe you better check what is hanging from the trunk of your car." I looked down and there were my keys! They were suspended all day from a four-inch key ring in the trunk of my car. My car was parked in a busy lot near the Anaheim Convention Center and only a half mile from Disneyland. The license plate holder on my car reads, "Angels Are Watching Over Me!" The angels certainly must have been present on this day to watch over this forgetful friend. Not only was my car still around, but all my manufacturers' product samples were still in my trunk. Popular Sanguines are like kittens, they seem to have nine lives!

With all the focus on health and fitness, mall walking has become a business. This is a perfect job for a Popular Sanguine who loves to talk and shop. We can identify all the stores having sales or offering discounts to walkers. Imagine the fun it would be gathering people and making a party of walking the malls while promoting stores and getting exercise simultaneously!

Shopping is undertaken by every personality at some time or another. In order to survive, we—

> Sublime Melancholies
> Harmonious Phlegmatics
> Outgoing Sanguines
> Practical Cholerics
> —all **SHOP!**

The difference is in our approach to shopping, as you can see from the differences in my shopping friends. Which one are you: Rita Return, Uninvolved Ursula, Forgetful Fran, or Practical Patty?

Friends

The Care and Feeding
of All Kinds of Personalities

PAM STEPHENS

Pam Stephens has been speaking since 1980, when she began teach-
ing Bible studies in her own church in Lake Arrowhead, California,
where she also is the director of Women's Ministries. She is a popular
speaker for women's retreats and conferences, speaking on many sub-
jects, including friendships. Pam has been part of Florence Littauer's
CLASS teaching staff since 1984. She participated in the research and
contributed stories for two of Florence's previous books, Dare to Dream
and Wake Up, Women. *She also has a featured chapter in* Bounce
Back *(Christian Publications, Inc., 1997) compiled by Diana James.*

o you have a favorite *I Love Lucy* episode? Perhaps
it is the one about Lucy and Ethel getting a job at
the chocolate factory, trying to wrap the chocolates
in tissue paper as they roll by, stuffing them into their mouths, and
pocketing the ones that can't be wrapped quickly enough. Or maybe
it's the one where Ethel helps Lucy wallpaper her bedroom, and Lucy
papers Ethel right into the closet! One of my favorites is the one where
Lucy and Ethel are putting on a talent show for the women's club.
Their act for the show is a duet singing a song called "Friendship."
As they arrive for the dress rehearsal, they are stunned to see that they

have chosen the same dress! As most women will tell you, this can be the test of any friendship! While it is a song about friendship, it is not a "twin sister act." Each of them agrees to take their dress back to the shop the next day. Once home, however, each one realizes that since the other is taking her dress back, it would be foolish to give up such a great find! The night of the talent show comes, and now the two friends are furious at each other for having kept their original purchase. As they seethe and glare at one another, they sing their song, "Friendship, friendship, just a perfect blendship. When old acquaintances are long forgot, ours will still be hot!" But as they sing each line, they are pulling off sashes and attached flowers on their friend's treasured frock.

Fortunately for them, Ethel and Lucy never stayed angry for long. By the end of each television show, they had resolved their differences and could laugh about their distinctive personalities. However, not all of us have been able to joke and snicker about the troubled situations we have found ourselves in, or about the idiosyncrasies of another person, all in the time frame of a sitcom. Perhaps thirty minutes is an unrealistic time frame in which we can solve anything of major significance, but we all love to wish it were so.

Lucy and Ethel had a longtime friendship, but just as in any friendship, it wasn't without its difficulties. Have you ever had troubles with your friendships? Had any difficult people in your garden? Ever wondered why you choose the friends you do? Have you considered going it alone because your "gardening" experience hasn't produced the crop you thought you planted? Perhaps you don't have the "green thumb" you would like to have, and you seem to be in the "hothouse" more than you would care to be. What have you been feeding your seedlings? Do you have weeds, sucker shoots, blight, or pests eating at your productivity? Does your garden need the pruning shears? Why is it that each of us has had some horrendous friendship encounters that we'd like to forget? Like the old nursery rhyme says, "Mary, Mary, quite contrary, how does your garden grow?" Is yours overrun, spindly, barely blooming? Take heart, there is hope! We can begin to understand some of these fears and questions as we take a look at our garden of friendship through the personalities!

Most of us have at one time or another tried to plant a garden. Provided we have done it correctly, we have had to first make a plan as to what kind of garden we wanted. Whether we are planting flowers, vegetables, or a variety of both, we must first have a plan. How much room do I have in the backyard? How much time will it take to cultivate? What must I do to prepare my soil? What kind of tools will I need to take care of my garden? Will the care of my garden mean that I must feed it with certain kinds of nutrients that I need to invest in? Just what will the cost be to have the type of garden and the quality of garden that I am looking for?

Preparing the Soil

Once we have thought about the above questions pertaining to our garden, we must then begin to prepare the soil. We turn the sod over and pull out any unwanted rocks or weeds. We make sure the soil is rich with the right nutrients for planting. If we need to add sand or peat moss, we do that before we begin sowing seeds or adding plants.

Just as you would do that for your garden, we must consider the "soil of our heart" before we begin sowing the seeds of friendship. If there are any old "rocks" or "weeds" or any other "junk" from previous relationships that would prevent the kind of growth we are looking for, it is best to get rid of them. How do we do that? It is best if we consult with the Master Gardener. He Himself has said, "I am the vine, you are the branches; he who abides in Me, and I in him, he bears much fruit; for apart from Me you can do nothing" (John 15:5 NASB).

Unlike the sometimes heavy manual labor it takes to clean out a plot for planting, this is certainly much easier. Simply pray to our Lord Jesus that He will come and clean out all the old "junk, weeds, and rocks" of hurt feelings, unmet expectations, and preconceived ideas of what a garden of friendship should be. The wonderful thing is, He is faithful to do just that. Ask Him to put a layer of healing balm over those places from the past and condition your heart to accept what He has for you in the way of friendships. Ask Him to give you understanding as to what you need in those desired relationships. Pray also that He will protect you in advance against any "unhealthy sucker shoots, blight, or pests" that could cause damage to your new crop. Thank Him in advance for what He will do in the soil of your heart and in that of your new friendships.

Selecting the Seed

What kind of plants, flowers, or vegetables do you want to grow? The kinds of seeds we choose determine what we will produce. Just

Personality Garden of Friendships

Popular Sanguine

Plant:
in full sun, spotlights if possible

Care:
will thrive with continuous approval and attention

Feeding:
fertilize with tons of affection and personal compliments

Watch Out For:
wild-paced, rapid growth, can become busy and overdone

Powerful Choleric

Plant:
in the center of your garden where she can direct the others

Care:
will demand loyalty and wants it her way now!

Feeding:
fertilize with appropriate credit for job well done and for her dedication

Watch Out For:
can crowd out others in the garden, thorns can be lethal, will take over garden if not pruned

Peaceful Phlegmatic

Plant:
in partial sun/shade with lots of peace and away from chaos

Care:
will grow best when shown her value and worth in your garden

Feeding:
fertilize with encouragement to stretch beyond her fears

Watch Out For:
indecision as to whether to bloom where she is planted, may lack self-esteem, tends to lie dormant if not moved to hothouse

Perfect Melancholy

Plant:
in full shade, away from the busyness of the garden, be sure to give her plenty of quiet and space

Care:
will grow best when given lots of support and sensitivity, and others meet her standards

Feeding:
fertilize with perfection, silence, and understanding

Watch Out For:
can become too withdrawn and depressed when others don't comply with her requirements, growth can be stunted by lack of energy

as it says in Galatians 6:7, we reap what we sow. Have you noticed that God's Word is full of gardening terms? Isn't it amazing that no matter what seed packet or bulb you choose, that is what comes up? How do those daisies know not to be sweet peas? Or those bluebells know not to be nasturtiums? God has ordained that each seed will reproduce after its own kind. Just as each seed knows what to be, we all have been created with a specific personality. Each friend will be just as God created them to be.

Popular Sanguine

If you were planting this little seed, it might have jumped right out of your hand into the little home you dug for it, laughing and saying, "I can hardly wait to see what a fun time we are going to have together!" If it were a flower, it might be a sunflower: bright, big, and beautiful with its head turned up facing the sun, just inviting all to notice it! Or it might be a forget-me-not wanting to be remembered always for the fun and excitement it can bring into a friendship.

However you choose to see them, Popular Sanguines can be great friends. They never know a stranger and make friends easily, loving people and charming them with their sparkling, vivacious personality. They respond immediately to compliments and attention of any kind. This friend thrives on spontaneity and will drop almost everything to participate in whatever sounds like a good time.

Are you looking for someone to go shopping with, or do you need company at the last minute? They are your ready traveling companion! Just give them time to apply a spot of lipstick or grab their purse. If you need to be refreshed and given a shot of adrenaline in the arm, call a Popular Sanguine friend. Just the energy that comes over the phone wires is often enough to keep you running for a few more hours!

There is never a dull moment when a Popular Sanguine is around. Prudy, a Popular Sanguine friend who had moved away some years ago, dropped by as I was writing this chapter and reminded me that more than once we had to stop and pray that she would find her keys to the car! If it is rather slow and boring, you can count on them to "spice it up" by causing a commotion or by entertaining others with the extraordinary ad-lib stories of their adventures. If there is an "I'm sorry" to be said, they will be the first to say it, even if they really don't know what they are apologizing for. They hate for anyone to dislike or disapprove of them and will go to almost any length for acceptance—a need that often can get a Popular Sanguine into deep trouble.

Don't be surprised, however, if they become forgetful about the appointments they make with you. Popular Sanguines are more than human and have weaknesses, just as all the personalities do (even our own). Popular Sanguines can be forgetful of their commitments, leaving some to be disappointed with their seeming lack of responsibility. Their weaknesses are just as evident as their strengths because they are so vocal and such up-front people! They never tire of telling tales and can keep you in stitches with their horror stories of traumas and exciting happenings. Sometimes we can tire of these stories if we have heard them over and over, although often they have surprise endings. The Popular Sanguines do tend to repeat colorful events or jokes if there is even one new person to hear them in the group, often interrupting others to tell about something that just popped into their minds.

Popular Sanguines also dislike being alone and will make untiring efforts to woo others into accompanying them on their errands and escapades. "Can you beat this?" and one-upmanship contests can become exasperating to those around Popular Sanguines, especially when you would like your Popular Sanguine friend to be excited about *your* adventure. They really need to feel they are center stage when others are close by to enjoy their stories. Don't be disappointed either when your Popular Sanguine friends seem to be plotting their answers to your last statement. They often will not be listening to you totally, especially if what you are saying sounds predictable or the least bit boring. If you do not speak up quickly enough when someone asks you a question, Popular Sanguines will fill in the blanks for you, even if they fill them incorrectly.

While they are Johnny-on-the-spot with an apology for a perceived wrong, they will also take the defensive with many excuses as to the "whys" and "hows" that caused them to let you down. If you ask a Popular Sanguine to do a favor for you, be sure to make it fun and give them lots of credit and acknowledgment for completing it.

Perfect Melancholy

Planting this little seed, are you? Unlike the Popular Sanguine Sunflower, this seedling is more a bluebell with its head pointing in a downward direction. This bluebell isn't jumping out of your hand into the ground, exclaiming that she can hardly wait to see what fun you will have; she is analyzing the condition of the soil and whether or not you've prepared it to her specifications. Don't even begin to think that it will be a perfect fit. Even if you had done it all right, she would find even a minuscule degree of incorrectness about your attitude with which you dropped her into the hole. Perfect Melancholies tend to be introspective, perfectionistic, and self-conscious.

Unfortunately, they see perfectionism as a gift and desire to pass it on to those around them, trying to make friends fit into their patterns. These Perfect Melancholy friends tend to stay in the background, not quickly forming deep friendships, but cautiously searching for one or two hearts to become attached to. Once located, this Little Bluebell Perfect Melancholy will be a loyal and devoted confidant. She will listen diligently, not just to the words you are speaking, but to the inflection of your voice, and will mentally make note of how you sigh through each word. Perfect Melancholies are great at solving problems and have a truly deep concern and empathy for you—so much so, that they find it hard to let go of the emotions shared with you, once you have gone home. They quickly "tear up" when they recall your telling of the stories of your day. One Perfect Melancholy friend was deeply dismayed one day when she telephoned me several days after our latest get-together. She was crying as she recounted the feelings she had about the situation I was going through. However, I had trouble remembering what she was talking about. While the situation had been devastating to me at the time, I had quickly put it out of mind. Perfect Melancholies will sit down and write you a note, which can rapidly turn into a letter or a chapter, with terrific amplification of how she would go about eliminating your concerns.

Just as with the Popular Sanguine, the Perfect Melancholy definitely has weaknesses too. Because they tend to stay in the background, Perfect Melancholies love to vicariously live life through their friends. They are insecure socially because they never quite measure up to their own standards and would rather be alone with a good book or project. Perfect Melancholy friends can demand perfection by continually moving the "goal line" five yards farther ahead. Just when you think you've done something that will please them, they remind you how it could be just a tad better next time, if only you would . . .

In contrast to a Popular Sanguine who will control others with charm, words, and smiles, the Perfect Melancholy will attempt to control others by moodiness, or the threat of it. They are suspicious by nature, feeling that you are bringing them gifts with an underlying motivation that will put them at a deficit to be discovered shortly. Don't take it personally when a Perfect Melancholy gets angry and hurt if you disagree with them in regard to philosophies or opinions, even though they will take it personally. To disagree with them equates in their minds to outright rejection, not just a difference of thought. They can be withdrawn and remote when you want to draw them in closer; they may even hold back their affection and become antagonistic or vengeful.

Little Bluebell Perfect Melancholy can sulk and be unforgiving if you have come against her in some way. They are often so full of contradictions, they are hard to understand for the novice gardener. Consulting the Master Gardener often, reading the "Gardening Book" continually, and praying for wisdom will certainly be an advantage when planting this precious seed.

Powerful Choleric

While the Popular Sanguine could be a sunflower, and the Perfect Melancholy a bluebell, the Powerful Choleric has to be a rose. Roses are magnificent, fragrant, and a leader among flowers. We all have picked up a rose too haphazardly and come away with a bloody finger from the prickly thorns that accompany this gorgeous climbing bloomer!

Rather than jumping up and down with excitement over the prospect of fun like the Popular Sanguine, or looking for perfection in all aspects of life like the Perfect Melancholy, the Powerful Choleric Rose will be directing you as you place them in the ground: "A little more to the left. . . . What colors are around me? Put me down, now!"

Powerful Cholerics are born leaders and tend to take charge in any relationship. They not only will direct the conversation, but will let you know it's time to move on to another subject—and then they'll choose the subject. They will lead and expect you to follow or get out of their way! The amazing and unnerving thing is that Powerful Choleric Roses are usually right, which makes those of us around them fearful when it is us they are questioning.

Yet Powerful Choleric Roses will work very, very hard to make things right. They can run anything and often take over where angels fear to tread. Just give them a slight hesitation, and they jump right in and make a decision. Don't know where you will have lunch? Need to get an opinion on which sofa to buy? Never fear! The Powerful Cholerics rarely are left without a certitude on any issue. You will not even need to ask; they will volunteer. They have an incredible, uncanny knack for the obvious solution and step in to carry it out with nary a thought about how it may be perceived by others.

Powerful Choleric friends will see how we could be better people and encourage us to go back and get that education finished or lose a few pounds. They will even come up with a plan so that we can accomplish it with stupendous results. Gloria, a Peaceful Phlegmatic, shared with Donna, a Powerful Choleric, her desire to finish getting her degree but told Donna all the obstacles that stood in her way. At their next meeting, Donna came with Gloria's educational plan all mapped out for her and was deeply offended when Gloria procrastinated making a decision.

Powerful Cholerics will tend to use people for what they can do for them, instead of using things. They can dominate and decide for others continuously until their friends are sick of being bullied into decisions they never intended to make. Then those friends begin to avoid the thorny Powerful Choleric Rose because it hurts too much to be around her.

Powerful Cholerics also dismay their buddies when they become possessive and manipulate ways to have friends all to themselves. They can also be so independent that they really come to believe they don't truly need anyone, not even that dear sweet friend who has patiently put up with them all these years. In fact, they are so independent, they often forget to consult with the Master Gardener and take matters or the garden into their own hands. Before you know it, there can be mass mutiny in the garden! Saying "I'm sorry" is extremely difficult for Powerful Choleric Roses, and when they do say it, it is always with an added inference that, "If you were offended by something I said or did, I am sorry that your perception was so inaccurate." While Powerful Choleric Rose is usually right, it may make her very unpopular!

Peaceful Phlegmatic

This little seedling may seem not to care what you do with her in the garden. Because a Peaceful Phlegmatic fits into any situation, she won't direct you, like the Powerful Choleric, where to plant her. No, this darling daisy will be pleasant and enjoyable from any direction! This Peaceful Phlegmatic Daisy is easy to get along with because she dislikes conflict so much. In fact, she will go to another garden if chaos and dissension break out! Peaceful Phlegmatics are extremely inoffensive and are careful not to express opinions and feelings that may upset those around them. This can also be perceived by the other flower friends in the garden as being wishy-washy. Taken to an extreme, Phlegmatic Daisies do compromise in areas where they shouldn't to avoid hassles. Carolyn, a Peaceful Phlegmatic, was afraid of offending Betsy, a Popular Sanguine friend who had been dabbling with horoscopes. Carolyn would rather keep Betsy's friendship than cause a rift by challenging her belief system. Peaceful Phlegmatics need to be aware of this weakness and speak up at the appropriate times.

But we need these little daisies in every garden because they are great mediators. As friends they can "explain" to Popular Sanguine Sunflower why Powerful Choleric Rose is trying to get her to act more responsibly, by saying that she thinks so highly of Little Sanguine Sunflower that she doesn't want others to get the wrong impression. To Powerful Choleric Rose she says that Popular Sanguine Sunflower didn't mean to appear irresponsible, she just simply had so much going on, she completely forgot her committee meeting.

Because Peaceful Phlegmatic Daisy is so compassionate and pleasant, she has scads of friends. They love to have her around because she listens so well, and that dry, one-liner sense of humor sneaks up on them and sends them into hysterical laughter. Peaceful Phlegmatic Daisy loves to go to the mall with Popular Sanguine Sunflower, but when she gets tired of running back and forth looking for the right dress, she will be found sitting on a bench people-watching. This is a favorite pastime!

While Peaceful Phlegmatic Daisy's weaknesses aren't as obvious as Popular Sanguine Sunflower's or Powerful Choleric Rose's, still there are a few. Daisy can be indifferent to the plans others have made tremendous efforts to impress her with. Because becoming overinvolved sounds too much like work, Peaceful Phlegmatic Daisy stays on the fringes and calculates just how much effort and energy it will take to participate in any event.

Change may as well be a four-letter word to Miss Daisy! Just when she was getting used to this garden, now you are moving her into another spot where there is not enough light or people to watch! Once the change is made, however, she does adapt well.

It is so difficult for her to make a decision, and there are so many other friends like Powerful Choleric Rose who are eager to make them for her, she puts it off, hoping that if she procrastinates long enough, someone will step in and make the decision for her. Her lack of enthusiasm about new ideas may cause those close to her to think she is against them, but she knows it takes effort and energy to exert excitement over something that may never happen anyway. She will wait and watch before making a decision on her own! When a daisy finally makes up her mind, however, look out! That stubborn will of iron has snapped closed and may not be penetrated again. Because she doesn't like conflict or confrontation, when Peaceful Phlegmatic Daisy gets angry, it tends to come out as sarcasm or teasing. She hides her true feelings under this cloak.

Watering the Garden

Now that we have prepared the soil of our hearts and selected the seeds for our gardens, the next step is watering them. Water provides the refreshment that the roots will need to go down deep into the soil. Likewise, to water our friendships will mean that we will provide the necessary nurturing to allow the roots to be established. When our root system is good, we can withstand the winds of adversity, which blow in any relationship. A solid foundation provides the stability and strength we need for the long haul. Water also provides the young, barely visible shoots with just the drink they need in order to not burn up under the hot sun.

Just as our seedlings need water to prevent burnout, we must refresh our friendships with a cool drink from time to time. When we apply the water of time spent together in our gardens of friendship, we soon begin to see which "flower" tends to grow faster. But just because a friendship grows quickly doesn't mean it will be lasting growth. Similar to our backyard gardens, some friendships grow only to burn out over time. Sometimes it's overexposure to one another, and soon either we forget to come back and add water, or we grow weary of the repetitiveness or neediness involved in caring for it. Jesus traveled with twelve men for three and a half years while He was here on earth. There were three, however, whom He seemed closer to than the others: Peter, James, and John. Obviously, in our lives we cannot adequately maintain too many friendships that are deep relationships. There just aren't enough hours in the day.

Most of us have friends at three different levels of intimacy. The A level is an acquaintance, someone you know or work with, with whom you share briefly at any given time. At this level we share facts, not feelings. The B level of intimacy would be brotherly or sisterly persons with whom we share activities or produce projects at work. They may be good neighbors you can count on, but with this level we always hold back feelings or opinions that may be judged as unacceptable to that person. There are boundaries and limits for our sharing. The next level is the C level. At this level is the close companion with whom we share our hearts; this friend is our sounding board. We share not only facts and feelings, but our hopes, fears, dreams, and disappointments.

This C-level friend is what Anne of Green Gables described as a "kindred spirit." Do you remember reading those books? Anne said she had been looking for her all her life . . . a kindred spirit. That kind of friend is one who accepts you at your worst, listens to you always. They keep what is worthy of you, throwing the rest away because they love you. These are the flowers of friendship that last, that return, that multiply in sweetness.

Feeding the Garden

Just as we must fertilize our backyard gardens, we must also feed our friendships. We must nurture them if they are to bloom. What are you tossing around on your friends? Does it feed them or does it kill them? Does it encourage? Is it positive? Or would you say it falls on them more like criticism and negativity? Remember that what we sow, we shall reap. My daughter, who is now a grown woman of twenty-seven years, said once, "You know, Mom, roses are beautiful and so are friends, but sometimes they can be thorns in our sides." How true that is! Who was it who said, "I never promised you a rose garden"? Friends take lots of water, feeding, and care. But the end result is well worth the time!

Different friends as well as different plants, need their own unique brand of care. While one flourishes with verbal acknowledgment, the other likes to see you act on the love you have for them. Another wants to be remembered with notes, cards, and little gifts. Still another seems happy just to be with you. As long as we remember to give our friends what they need in their own personalities, instead of what our personalities would like to give them, we will be on the right response track.

Weeding and Debugging the Garden

Have you ever noticed how fast the weeds seem to pop up in your garden? Why is that? How can they grow so fast and the good stuff come along so slowly? It can be the same, unfortunately, in our friendships.

The weeds of bitterness and strife must be pulled out as soon as you see them! Be careful to pull them out by their roots, or they will return as quickly as they left. What about bugs and pests? Have you seen any of those in your garden? The bugs of envy, jealousy, or competitiveness can kill overnight! They spread from one beautiful flower to another, wiping out each one, and they are no respecter of persons. The contagion can spread sometimes before the Tender of the Garden can spray forgiveness over each one.

Pruning the Garden

It has been said that pruning isn't punishment, but purposeful planning. It says in the Book of John that God cuts off every branch that doesn't bear fruit so that it will be clean and bear more fruit (John 15:2). How do you know when to prune your garden? Is it overrun by leggy vines? Are there stocks at cross-purposes to one another? Has it gotten misshapen? Can you see ugly diseases eating away at the beauty? Then it's time to get out the shears!

How do we know if our friendships are unhealthy? Some of those same pruning principles above can apply. Ask yourself these questions: "Is this person weakening my faith?" "Are they keeping me from growing?" "Do they bring out the best in me or the worst?" "Am I depending on them more than I should? More than I depend on the Master Gardener?" "Are they possessive of my friendship?" "Do they manipulate to arrange my time?" "Do we argue more than we should?"

Diane and Sue were great friends. Their husbands worked together and this situation brought Diane and Sue together very naturally. They were very different from one another; actually they were opposites in personality. Diane was Powerful Choleric and Sue was Popular Sanguine. Diane challenged Sue to take on leadership roles; and Sue brought fun and light into Diane's busy life. Diane and Sue were able to join their husbands on a business trip to a very busy metropolis for several days. They were all very excited about this opportunity and were looking forward to it for months.

The two men were already gone when Diane drove to Sue's home to pick her up for the airport. Sue began bringing out her luggage; first a garment bag, then a suitcase, and finally a carry-on bag. Diane took one look at the pile and quipped, "The first thing you learn when traveling, Sue, is not to bring more than you yourself can carry." Sue was not sure if Diane was joking or if she was serious, but she laughed it off and got into the car.

They had a great time while they were in the city, but when it came time for the women to fly home, the men gave each of them a briefcase to carry back. Diane and Sue were dropped off at the airport for the return trip home. Sue looked around for a skycap to carry the bags into the airport and get them to their final destination. There were none to be found. Diane just looked at Sue, smiled, and said, "Don't bring more than you yourself can carry. It's about time you learned this lesson." With that, Diane picked up her only bag and slung it over her shoulder. In the other hand she lifted the briefcase her husband had given her and started to walk into the airport. Sue shouted out, "Aren't you going to help me?" Diane threw a glance over her shoulder and said, "NO!"

Sue did the best she could. She slipped the garment bag over her shoulder, along with the carry-on bag, picked up the suitcase, and with her foot, slid the briefcase along a step at a time. When Sue finally reached the counter to sign in for her flight, there was Diane sitting across the terminal. Once checked in, Sue took a seat next to Diane. Diane got up and walked across the aisle and bought a newspaper. When she returned, she took a seat across the aisle from Sue. "Is there something wrong, Diane?" Sue asked. Diane didn't answer her. When Sue finally got Diane to talk, Diane stated that if she could take a different plane home she would.

What happened? Why had Diane insulted, ignored, and rebuked Sue? Was this really necessary? From Sue's point of view, Diane had no reason to be so belligerent. After all, what had she done, except bring too many pieces of luggage?

Sue was devastated for weeks, until she realized what had been at the bottom of this disastrous event. Many months later, when Sue finally ventured to ask Diane about the incident, she found out that it wasn't the excess luggage that had upset Diane, it was the excess baggage Diane was carrying around inside her that had caused the outburst directed at Sue. Diane's husband's company was about to go under and Diane's marriage was in trouble. You see, sometimes in our friendships we unload on whomever is closest to us instead of the person with whom we are really angry.

Instead of telling Sue that she was upset for other reasons, she let loose all her frustrations, anxieties, and fears onto a dear friend. Their relationship was never again the same. Diane had allowed bugs, blight, and weeds to choke out a beautiful friendship. Diane couldn't say she was sorry or take responsibility for the blowup, so she just blew off their friendship.

With a "spray" of forgiveness on this attack of bugs, this friendship could have been saved and could have produced a bountiful harvest. Instead it was stomped out. We all have had similar experiences with one friend or another. Take heart! It doesn't have to happen. We can prevent the invasion of insects and disease from ruining our gardens!

Sometimes pruning can be a very painful process. Remember, we need to be aware that even friendships that begin with a very positive sowing experience can become overgrown and leggy, just as some of our vines do. When our morning glories branch out and cover the trellis, they are doing what they were purposed to do. But if our morning glories cling to our rose bushes, they can smother the very growth that the Master Gardener intended and hide the beauty of one another. We must be sure that our garden is well manicured, and we also need to be alert that our friendships aren't overly dependent on the wrong things.

Becky and Linda's friendship blossomed after just a short time. They were in leadership at Bible study together and realized that they had much in common. The two of them were "kindred spirits," seeming to know instinctively what the other was thinking. Before long, however, it became evident to many around them that this relationship had taken on unhealthy dimensions. Becky was sharing deep information that probably should have been reserved for her husband and God with Linda. At first Linda was flattered that Becky trusted her so intensely with these things, but more and more their gatherings seem to be more like counseling sessions. Becky's dependence on Linda began to smother their friendship. Linda's husband became concerned about the amount of time Becky was taking away from their family, yet Linda felt obliged to be available for Becky's phone calls and lunch dates.

One conversation with a mutual friend, however, signaled trouble to Linda. This acquaintance told Linda that she really wanted to visit with her during Linda's recovery from an illness, but Becky had discouraged it. Becky elaborated that Linda really didn't want to be called on and was going through a difficult time, requesting she not have visitors. This was a complete surprise to Linda. Not only was the story not true, but a visit would have been exactly what Linda needed—encouragement from her friends. It was at this point that Linda realized she needed to prune away some unhealthy branches that were at cross-purposes to one another. Upon discussing this incident and the concerns of her husband with Becky, Linda told her that she felt the need to cut back some on the amount of time they were spending together in order to become more available to the others who needed her. Becky didn't understand this and was incredibly hurt that Linda would do it. Becky was an "all or nothing" personality who had difficulty accepting any changes in her deep friendships. Linda didn't want to end their relationship, but she sought to make it healthier and challenged Becky to spend some time in prayer about it. Becky saw this as the closing of a door and felt shut out of Linda's life.

Perhaps you are or have been involved in an unhealthy friendship too. It is never the fault of only one person that a bond has become ill. Both friends have contributed to the neediness of the other. This is why we must be so careful to consult with the Master Gardener over our garden of friendships. He has told us, "If any of you lacks wisdom, let him ask of God, who gives to all men generously and without reproach, and it will be given to him" (James 1:5 NASB). Ask Him about your friend, talk to Him about your friend to see what He would have you do. I like the quote by Robert Trench that says, "None but God can satisfy the longings of an immortal soul; that as the heart was made for Him, so He can only fill it."

Many of us would love to have that kindred spirit in our garden of friendship, and we can, but we must be watchful that we don't miss out on all the exquisite varieties of flowers around us. Each one brings a different view of life and another hue of magnificent color to our garden of friends bouquet.

Harvesting the Garden

Doesn't it bring you joy to see your garden in full bloom? All the time, energy, and waiting have finally come to fruition! Reaping the harvest in our garden of friendships certainly delivers that same elation. When I think back over the years that I have invested in my garden, there were some failures that were disappointing at the time, but these same failures helped me to grow up and appreciate the successes!

A few of my friendships are newer blooms that have budded and begun to open, promising a future delight. But others are old dear friends like Sally, who has known me since my late teens. We married about the same time and spent many weekends watching husbands play softball (and every other sport) while keeping our children from running onto the field. We shared our trials as young moms and wives, bouncing ideas off one another. I prayed for Sally to meet Jesus, and rejoiced as she made her decision. Even today, though we don't see one another enough, when we do it is as if we have never been apart!

Other friends like Barbara and Kelly have encouraged and challenged me to greater heights both personally and professionally, for which I am deeply appreciative. I remember our speakers group in which we all practiced our newest topics for retreats. The many critiques, laughter to the point of tears, and lunches we shared then and now are a perennial source of joy to me.

I couldn't overlook my mentor, Florence Littauer, who saw a spark within me and ignited my enthusiasm for writing and speaking. Her constant prodding and watering of my spirit has so enriched my life! As we travel together with CLASS, we look forward to the "next chapter" in our friendship. There is never a dull moment with Florence! She has taught me what it means to be gracious with strength, and she exudes class in every way.

What about you? How has your garden grown? Have you let it become so overgrown that the beauty is no longer evident? Or have you let it die out because you failed to give it the care it needed? It is never too late to begin planting again! Isn't that hopeful? Plow over the sod, throw out the rocks and garbage, enrich the nutrients of the soil, and begin again. If you are faithful, you will reap a bountiful harvest!

Don't allow your garden to go unattended. It may take work, you may have to get your hands dirty in the weeding or get out the pruning shears, but if you devote the time now, you will not regret it in the future.

Watching *I Love Lucy*, we all knew Lucy and Ethel really loved one another. Even when Lucy tried Ethel's patience and ours, theirs was a friendship planted with heart. They went through the wars together, the parades of life together, and came out a shining tribute to what friendship is all about: commitment. "Mary, Mary, how does your garden grow?"

Home and Hospitality

Martha Stewart, Martha Washington, or Just Plain Martha

SUSAN PONVILLE

With warmth and humor, Susan Ponville speaks frequently to women's groups about gracious living. At her seminars, Susan shares a treasury of ideas for savoring each day by adding simple but distinctive touches that transform the ordinary into the extraordinary.

Are you a Martha? (And I don't mean "Stewart"!) I love the story in Luke 10 about Powerful Choleric Martha and Peaceful Phlegmatic Mary. As Jesus was on a journey to Jerusalem with His disciples, He stopped along the way at the home of Martha and Mary. Martha, anxious about the meal she was preparing for Jesus, buzzed around the kitchen like a bee. (Sound familiar, anyone?) All the while, Mary focused her attention on Jesus, listening to Him as she sat at His feet. Can't you just see Martha banging those pots while she shot dirty looks at Mary, who paid her absolutely no attention? Then, in classic sibling rivalry form, Martha just had to bring this unfair situation to Jesus' attention.

"Jesus, can't You see Mary has left me to do all the work?" Hoping He'd take her side, she continued, "Doesn't this seem unfair to You?"

Jesus gently and lovingly spoke her name, "Martha, Martha. Mary has discovered the one important thing and I won't take this from her."

Maybe because I am a "Martha" when it comes to entertaining, I think she gets a bum rap in many translations of this story. Martha, like Mary, thought in her heart she was doing the right thing, working hard to serve Jesus through her version of hospitality. Mary's gift of hospitality was the undivided attention and caring she gave to her guest, Jesus.

So many times we are so preoccupied with Martha-type hospitality that we have no time for Mary-type hospitality. How can we show love, concern, and caring for our guests when we're off in the kitchen with our heads in the oven? (Not literally, of course!)

Entertaining other Christians creates a wonderful fellowship and strengthens our bond. Extending hospitality to nonbelievers by welcoming them into our home demonstrates a kind of caring they may have never experienced. Hospitality "gives" when the rest of the world "takes."

The word and the subject of hospitality are mentioned throughout the New Testament. Just to name a few, see, for example, Luke 14:13; Romans 12:13; Hebrews 13:2; and 1 Peter 4:9.

In the Greek language in which the New Testament was originally written, the word *hospitality* is literally translated as "the love of strangers." When a non-Christian spends time in the home of a Christian, they see the difference Christ makes in our lives and in the lives of our family. Your home is a God-given resource that can be used to touch people in a very special way!

So why do so many people wince at the thought of opening their home to others? More often than not, it is a self-consciousness about the appearance of their home. We may feel our decor is inadequate, or maybe we feel our home just isn't organized or clean enough to pass inspection.

The ways the different personalities will approach home decorating and hospitality are as different as the ways of Martha and Mary.

At Home with the Popular Sanguine

Recently Bonnie, a fellow Certified Personality Trainer and a fellow Popular Sanguine, was a guest in my home while in town for a speaking engagement. Upon seeing my home for the first time, as she entered the living room she exclaimed, "Oh! Look at this room. It's so . . . Sanguine!" Yes, that was a compliment—at least from one Popular Sanguine to another, it was!

Home, Hospitality . . . Help!

Popular Sanguine	Powerful Choleric
• loves to shop • never is completely finished decorating her home because all this is just too much fun to stop! • home is set up for entertaining • door is always open to friends and family at a minute's notice • can go to the store and pick an exact color match for fabric or accessories without use of a color swatch	• home is very efficient and functional • the study or work area has a very prominent place in the home • very often you'll find an elaborate exercise area in the home • sees the overall picture rather than small details • feels loss of control when house is out of order
Peaceful Phlegmatic	**Perfect Melancholy**
• comfort is more important than appearance • tends to always have unfinished decorating projects lying around • decor often reflects the tastes of a family member with a stronger, expensive personality • TV holds a prominent place in the home—often one in every room	• a place for everything and everything in its place • lots of gadgets for organizing • home accessories tend to be the very best available • can't relax if the house is out of order • loves symmetry in the home's decor

Just as the Popular Sanguine is easy to spot due to their clothing choices, they are easily recognized by the decor of their home. In the home of a Popular Sanguine, there are always touches of whimsy. You'll find bold colors (to a Popular Sanguine, the term *neutral* applies only to the gear we use while waiting for a car to leave that good parking spot at the mall). Because the Popular Sanguine has such a great memory for color, she can pick up items at the local home decor boutique without any color swatches, and you can bet it will be a perfect match to what's already in place at her home.

Since the Popular Sanguine loves to shop, she constantly is aware of the latest trends in home fashions. A Popular Sanguine is never completely finished decorating her home—the process is just too much fun to ever be finished!

A few years back, when all those infomercials began advertising the grids used to make beautiful valances in minutes without any sewing (no doubt invented by a Peaceful Phlegmatic with bare windows), I thought it looked like a fun thing to try, so I ordered a set, which came with an instructional video. When my kit arrived in the mail, I ran upstairs to the television to begin my "Window Wonder" adventure, lugging twelve yards of fabric. With the perky lady on the videotape giving me step-by-step instructions, I spread my goods out before me and chose the look I would create. My daughters, Terri and

Jamie, looked on in a state of confused curiosity, wondering what Mommy could possibly make from plastic chicken wire and twelve yards of fabric. The lady on the video kept cheerfully instructing me to "pull and pouf . . . pull and pouf." The lady's overzealous voice began to get on my nerves as she got a couple of "pulls and poufs" ahead of me. I grabbed the remote to pause her in the middle of a pouf so I could catch up. All was going well when I hit a snag. No matter how hard I pulled, the fabric absolutely refused to go through the hole in the grid. I repositioned, tugged, and pulled over and over, but it wouldn't budge. Frustrated, I thought I'd scan the tape for any troubleshooting advice, but when I reached for the remote control, it was nowhere to be found. You guessed it! The remote was lodged in the section of fabric I was trying so hard to pull and pouf! Now, whenever guests compliment me on my lovely window valance, in true Popular Sanguine form, my daughter Jamie can hardly wait to tell them about Mommy and the remote control!

In the home of a Popular Sanguine, the plants are either silk or dead. It's just so hard to remember to water them! My oldest daughter, Terri, a Perfect Melancholy, takes all the once beautiful houseplants I've half killed up to her room to revive them. She doesn't allow me to go near them, and before long, they're healthy and thriving once again.

The Popular Sanguine is so much on the go with the fun adventures in life, she tends to have little time to keep her home in order. She is forever having to hunt for lost items because things are thrown down in a hurry with no accompanying thought as to where they can be found the next time they are needed.

Popular Sanguine Dora thought she had the perfect quick fix for her messy living room the day her Amway distributor neighbor called to tell her she'd be by in a few minutes to demonstrate a new product in which she felt Dora would be interested. Dora quickly grabbed armloads of the various strewn objects, threw them in the bathtub, and pulled the shower curtain closed just as the doorbell rang. Much to Dora's dismay, the new product her neighbor wanted to demonstrate was *bathtub cleaner!*

Popular Sanguines, being such social people, are naturals at entertaining socially in their homes. Their hospitality is genuine yet disorganized. It's best for a Sanguine to have her parties catered if she can afford to, or to have everything prepared well in advance of the guests arriving, because she'd much rather be regaling guests with her stories than filling hors d'oeuvre trays. All in all, the Popular Sanguine enjoys her own parties more than most!

Home and Hospitality Helps for the Popular Sanguine

1. Learn to use balance and proportion when using bold colors and prints so as not to overwhelm.
2. Don't feel you must constantly change your entire decor to keep up with the latest home fashion trends. Learn to simply add a few new accessories here and there to maintain an updated look.
3. Shop for fun containers, crates, folders, and bins to make organizing your home fun, colorful, and convenient.
4. Keep your house in order by disciplining yourself to neaten up things a few minutes in the morning before you leave for the day, and a few minutes in the evening before going to bed.
5. When entertaining, plan ahead and have everything ready before the guests arrive so you can join the fun without your guests going hungry! The key here is to get organized and keep it simple.

At Home with the Powerful Choleric

The main objective of the Powerful Choleric is to have a functional home that runs efficiently. The aesthetics of the home are secondary. Powerful Cholerics tend not to pay attention to details because instead they focus on the overall picture.

In our first home, the wall that housed the entertainment center was painted an accent color. The surrounding walls remained white. Once while my Powerful Choleric husband, D. J., and I were shopping, I called his attention to a pair of drapes. I went on and on about how well the color of these drapes would match the accent wall. (Remember, I'm a Popular Sanguine—no color swatch needed!) My husband stared at me blankly and asked, "What accent wall? All our walls are the same color, white." This accent wall was the same wall he faced nightly while watching television, yet he had never noticed it was painted a different color. But if asked, he could have probably drawn the house's floor plan to scale. (Just don't ask him what color the walls are!)

An organized study or workplace in the home is very important to a Powerful Choleric. If the dining room is the only place to fit a desk and computer, then that's where you'll find it—in lieu of a dining-room table. The same goes with exercise equipment. It is much more important to the Powerful Choleric that this is readily available than that it fits with the decor.

The Powerful Choleric's home is decorated in a classic, functional style. You'll find no frills or "froufrou" looks here.

The Powerful Choleric's home is usually very orderly because living in messy, unkempt surroundings makes the Powerful Choleric feel a sense of loss of control. Or as my husband puts it, "A messy house makes me nervous!"

Powerful Cholerics generally don't enjoy an abundance of social entertaining. However, business-related entertaining does have its appeal because of the networking opportunities. At social gatherings, the Powerful Choleric is not amused by party games and idle chatter. This seems to them a great waste of precious time.

Popular Sanguine Elyse loved to entertain in her home, much to her Powerful Choleric husband, Lee's, dismay. One evening in particular, while entertaining guests in their home, Elyse found her husband orchestrating the evening much like a parent prompting and guiding children at a birthday party. He was all but telling the guests where to stand and what to say. Realizing Lee needed to be busy and feel in control, Elyse, rather than giving up on entertaining all together, devised a plan. She decided the next time she and Lee had guests over for the evening, she would ask him to be in charge of various things throughout the evening. At the next event, Lee felt good that his input was needed. He happily took charge in the areas in which his expertise was needed, such as music selection, roast carving, and adjourning all to the parlor for coffee.

Home and Hospitality Helps for the Powerful Choleric

1. Work to create a balance between career and home.
2. Try not to let "functional" overpower "hominess." Soften the home office area with cozy items such as family pictures and fresh flowers.
3. Take pride in your proficiency at quick, practical organization. Then relax! Don't make it a twenty-four-hour-a-day job.
4. If you don't enjoy entertaining socially in your home, don't feel pressured to do so on a regular basis. Just be careful not to overlook or avoid opportunities of hospitality that could serve as a time of Christian fellowship.

At Home with the Perfect Melancholy

The Perfect Melancholy strives for a perfect home. When guests drop by unexpectedly, they'll find the Perfect Melancholy's home spotless. (Because if it's not, Perfect Melancholy just won't answer the door!)

Perfect Melancholies have a wonderfully artsy and creative side, which is reflected throughout the home's decor in accessories and fine fabrics. You'll also find symmetry in the Melancholy's home (matching end tables with matching lamps, for example).

The Perfect Melancholy must be careful not to become a slave to the home in their quest for perfection, though. A minister visiting in the home of one of his Perfect Melancholy colleagues decided to secretly conduct a little test for his own amusement. Aware of his colleague's obsessive tidiness, the minister, in the midst of conversation, very nonchalantly reached over and ever so slightly moved a decorative trinket on the coffee table askew. He was curious how long it would take his friend to correct the out-of-place item. Without missing a beat, the Perfect Melancholy had the item back in its proper place before the minister could count to ten!

Perfect Melancholies are the "cobweb finders" of the world. In their own home, a room that would look completely neat and lovely to another personality type would be filled with flaws in the Perfect Melancholy's eyes. "Good enough" just never is.

My friend Pam was wallpapering the bathroom of her Perfect Melancholy mother's apartment. Although the entire wallpapering job was close to perfection, she took extra care to do a neat job on one particular seam when she realized it had ended up in direct view of the toilet!

Perfect Melancholies are very hospitable because they are so sensitive to the needs of others. It is important to the Melancholy that the guests enjoy themselves. Perfect Melancholies will often overwork themselves when hosting an event because they wrap themselves up in days of preparation, then tend to the needs of the guests, and finally tidy up behind messy guests. (A few crumbs on the carpet can be a serious matter for the Perfect Melancholy hostess.) The Perfect Melancholy will often work for days in advance of hosting an event.

My Perfect Melancholy sister, June, and her husband, David, had been married only about eighteen months when she wanted to do something really special for his upcoming birthday. She decided to throw a birthday dinner party for which she would prepare Crepes Florentine, a fancy recipe from the *New York Times International Cookbook*. There were many steps in the preparation of the crepes, so each day for a week, she completed a step in order to be ready to assemble them on Friday, the night of the birthday dinner party.

That Friday afternoon, after picking up their black Labrador, Tosha, from a long stay at the vet's, she finished the Crepes Florentine down to the baking. She pushed the crepes as far back on the counter as they would go. Ordinarily, June would have put the dog outside, but because Tosha was so happy to be back home, she was allowed to stay inside while June drove to pick up David at the bus stop. When they got back home, she discovered a single black hair left in the dish where the crepes had been! Company was due in thirty minutes, and Tosha, the dog, had eaten every bite! David made an emergency run to the market and came back with steaks to grill. June says she thinks the guys were secretly glad about the crepes' disappearance, as they enjoyed their "manly" meal of steaks.

Years later, June learned the hard way, once again, not to get depressed when all that Perfect Melancholy advance preparation is done for naught. She, David, and their son, Josh, were camping their way across Canada. Before leaving for this extended vacation, she had ever so carefully prepared many meals ahead of time that could be quickly put together and enjoyed by the campfire each night. Much to June's dismay, one night very early into the vacation a bear helped himself to the entire large ice chest of delicious meals!

Home and Hospitality Helps for the Perfect Melancholy

1. Relax your standards. Don't become a slave to the vision of a perfect home. Allow yourself a brief tidying-up time each morning and each evening and don't let the lived-in look bother you in between!
2. You've worked hard to create a beautiful home; schedule time regularly for yourself to just relax and enjoy your surroundings.
3. When friends are visiting in your home, realize time with you is much more important to them than how orderly the house is. Remember, your guests are not demanding or expecting perfection.

At Home with the Peaceful Phlegmatic

The homes of the Peaceful Phlegmatics will reflect their desire for peaceful surroundings through soft colors and comfortable furnishings. When a Peaceful Phlegmatic is furnishing a home, the comfort of a piece of furniture is much more important to them than style or appearance.

The Peaceful Phlegmatic strives for a low-maintenance setting and is not bothered in the least if an unexpected guest drops in on a mess in the living room (the mess that they, of course, planned to clean up tomorrow).

Since the Peaceful Phlegmatic often escapes and finds relaxation through watching TV, you are very likely to see a TV as the focal point in more than one room in the home. Peaceful Phlegmatics never seem to be finished decorating the home (if they've even begun) because this just isn't one of life's necessities. The home often remains unfinished or "in process."

When Perfect Melancholy Frances wanted to spruce up the family room, her Peaceful Phlegmatic husband, Dwight, refused to have his old, tattered but comfortable recliner replaced with a newer model. "After all," he explained, "it took years for me to get this chair broken in just right!" Once Frances had finished redecorating the rest of the room, Dwight's old chair stuck out worse than ever. Then Frances had a brilliant idea: a slipcover! Now Frances had a totally refurbished room that looked great, and Dwight still had the comfort of his favorite recliner underneath the removable slipcover.

A Peaceful Phlegmatic's favorite type of event to host at home is a potluck dinner where all the guests contribute a dish. Company tends to feel very welcome and at ease in the home of a Peaceful Phlegmatic because of the host's easygoing nature.

Peaceful Phlegmatics tend to serve their guests tried-and-true dishes that they've prepared often. To try out new recipes would mean making lists and shopping for groceries not already found in the pantry—all just too much trouble!

Peaceful Phlegmatic Tina made delicious-looking desserts. But you never knew how they were going to taste, because if Tina did not have an ingredient, rather than bother with going to the market, she substituted ingredients. However, her substitutions were white powder for white powder, regardless of the taste or purpose—if the recipe called for baking powder and she was out of it, she might use cornstarch. Sometimes this approach created new delights, but more often than not, the results were dismal.

The Homemakers Club to which Tina belonged decided to have each member make the same dessert recipe for an upcoming function.

The ladies in charge said, "Tina, here is the recipe, and *no substitutions!*" On the day of the function, Tina told the other club members, "You'll be so proud of me. If I didn't have an ingredient, I just left it out!"

Home and Hospitality Helps for the Peaceful Phlegmatic

1. If there is a certain decorating project you wish to undertake, set the goal of a completion date. If you meet your deadline, reward yourself with an uninterrupted day of rest and relaxation.
2. Since tackling all the household maintenance chores in one day can be tiring and overwhelming, divide up the duties so that a small chore gets done each day. For example: laundry on Monday, dusting on Tuesday, vacuuming on Wednesday, bathrooms on Thursday.
3. When planning to entertain in your home, don't wait until the last minute to prepare. Make a simple schedule of advance preparations for yourself and stick to it. This will allow for entertaining with ease.

Our home should be an oasis, a safe haven to us and to our families. Our homes and all the possessions within are gifts from God to be used with care and shared with thanksgiving. So take great joy in the "nesting" rituals like decorating, cooking, and cleaning that transform your house into a home. And open its doors in Christian hospitality!

Epilogue

Now that I have read this book
And given life a second look,
I see that different isn't wrong.
I've learned just how to get along
With teachers, pastors, and all I see,
Even those who aren't like me.

I don't so easily get mad
At others who I thought were bad.
Now I smile and nod my head,
Enjoying differences instead.

Oh, how pleasant the world can be
Now that I have been set free,
Not needing images of me
But letting other people be.
My attitude has surely turned
With all these things that I have learned.

Enjoy the Sanguine's sense of humor,
Acknowledging truth may be a rumor.
Be grateful for Phlegmatic ways
As they bring peace to all our days.
Admire the Melancholy mind,
With manners that are so refined.
Praise Cholerics for what they've done,
Working from morn to setting sun.

Yes, my life is much more fun
Now that I like everyone!

Appendix A

Your Personality Profile

On the following page you'll find our Personality Profile. In each of the following rows of four words across, place an X in front of the word (or words) that most often applies to you. Continue through all forty lines. If you are not sure which word "most applies," ask a spouse or a friend, or think of what your answer would have been when you were a child. Use the word definitions in Appendix B for the most accurate results.

Once you've completed the profile, transfer all your Xs to the corresponding words on the Personality Scoring Sheet, and add up your totals. For example, if you checked Animated on the profile, check it on the scoring sheet. (Note: The words are in a different order on the profile and the scoring sheet.)

Once you've transferred your answers to the scoring sheet, added up your total number of answers in each of the four columns, and added your totals from both the strengths and weaknesses sections, you'll know your dominant personality type. You'll also know what combination you are. If, for example, your score is 35 in Powerful Choleric strengths and weaknesses, there's really little question. You're almost all Powerful Choleric. But if your score is, for example, 16 in Powerful Choleric, 14 in Perfect Melancholy, and 5 in each of the others, you're a Powerful Choleric with a strong Perfect Melancholy. You'll also, of course, know your least dominant type.

Personality Profile

Place an X in front of the word (or words) on each line that most often applies to you.

Strengths

1 ___ Adventurous	___ Adaptable	___ Animated	___ Analytical
2 ___ Persistent	___ Playful	___ Persuasive	___ Peaceful
3 ___ Submissive	___ Self-sacrificing	___ Sociable	___ Strong-willed
4 ___ Considerate	___ Controlled	___ Competitive	___ Convincing
5 ___ Refreshing	___ Respectful	___ Reserved	___ Resourceful
6 ___ Satisfied	___ Sensitive	___ Self-reliant	___ Spirited
7 ___ Planner	___ Patient	___ Positive	___ Promoter
8 ___ Sure	___ Spontaneous	___ Scheduled	___ Shy
9 ___ Orderly	___ Obliging	___ Outspoken	___ Optimistic
10 ___ Friendly	___ Faithful	___ Funny	___ Forceful
11 ___ Daring	___ Delightful	___ Diplomatic	___ Detailed
12 ___ Cheerful	___ Consistent	___ Cultured	___ Confident
13 ___ Idealistic	___ Independent	___ Inoffensive	___ Inspiring
14 ___ Demonstrative	___ Decisive	___ Dry humor	___ Deep
15 ___ Mediator	___ Musical	___ Mover	___ Mixes easily
16 ___ Thoughtful	___ Tenacious	___ Talker	___ Tolerant
17 ___ Listener	___ Loyal	___ Leader	___ Lively
18 ___ Contented	___ Chief	___ Chartmaker	___ Cute
19 ___ Perfectionist	___ Pleasant	___ Productive	___ Popular
20 ___ Bouncy	___ Bold	___ Behaved	___ Balanced

Weaknesses

21 ___ Blank	___ Bashful	___ Brassy	___ Bossy
22 ___ Undisciplined	___ Unsympathetic	___ Unenthusiastic	___ Unforgiving
23 ___ Reticent	___ Resentful	___ Resistant	___ Repetitious
24 ___ Fussy	___ Fearful	___ Forgetful	___ Frank
25 ___ Impatient	___ Insecure	___ Indecisive	___ Interrupts
26 ___ Unpopular	___ Uninvolved	___ Unpredictable	___ Unaffectionate
27 ___ Headstrong	___ Haphazard	___ Hard to please	___ Hesitant
28 ___ Plain	___ Pessimistic	___ Proud	___ Permissive
29 ___ Angered easily	___ Aimless	___ Argumentative	___ Alienated
30 ___ Naive	___ Negative attitude	___ Nervy	___ Nonchalant
31 ___ Worrier	___ Withdrawn	___ Workaholic	___ Wants credit
32 ___ Too sensitive	___ Tactless	___ Timid	___ Talkative
33 ___ Doubtful	___ Disorganized	___ Domineering	___ Depressed
34 ___ Inconsistent	___ Introvert	___ Intolerant	___ Indifferent
35 ___ Messy	___ Moody	___ Mumbles	___ Manipulative
36 ___ Slow	___ Stubborn	___ Show-off	___ Skeptical
37 ___ Loner	___ Lord over others	___ Lazy	___ Loud
38 ___ Sluggish	___ Suspicious	___ Short-tempered	___ Scatterbrained
39 ___ Revengeful	___ Restless	___ Reluctant	___ Rash
40 ___ Compromising	___ Critical	___ Crafty	___ Changeable

Now transfer your Xs to the scoring sheet on the following page.

Personality Scoring Sheet

Strengths

	Popular Sanguine	Powerful Choleric	Perfect Melancholy	Peaceful Phlegmatic
1	___ Animated	___ Adventurous	___ Analytical	___ Adaptable
2	___ Playful	___ Persuasive	___ Persistent	___ Peaceful
3	___ Sociable	___ Strong-willed	___ Self-sacrificing	___ Submissive
4	___ Convincing	___ Competitive	___ Considerate	___ Controlled
5	___ Refreshing	___ Resourceful	___ Respectful	___ Reserved
6	___ Spirited	___ Self-reliant	___ Sensitive	___ Satisfied
7	___ Promoter	___ Positive	___ Planner	___ Patient
8	___ Spontaneous	___ Sure	___ Scheduled	___ Shy
9	___ Optimistic	___ Outspoken	___ Orderly	___ Obliging
10	___ Funny	___ Forceful	___ Faithful	___ Friendly
11	___ Delightful	___ Daring	___ Detailed	___ Diplomatic
12	___ Cheerful	___ Confident	___ Cultured	___ Consistent
13	___ Inspiring	___ Independent	___ Idealistic	___ Inoffensive
14	___ Demonstrative	___ Decisive	___ Deep	___ Dry humor
15	___ Mixes easily	___ Mover	___ Musical	___ Mediator
16	___ Talker	___ Tenacious	___ Thoughtful	___ Tolerant
17	___ Lively	___ Leader	___ Loyal	___ Listener
18	___ Cute	___ Chief	___ Chartmaker	___ Contented
19	___ Popular	___ Productive	___ Perfectionist	___ Pleasant
20	___ Bouncy	___ Bold	___ Behaved	___ Balanced

Total—Strengths

___   ___   ___   ___

Weaknesses

	Popular Sanguine	Powerful Choleric	Perfect Melancholy	Peaceful Phlegmatic
21	___ Brassy	___ Bossy	___ Bashful	___ Blank
22	___ Undisciplined	___ Unsympathetic	___ Unforgiving	___ Unenthusiastic
23	___ Repetitious	___ Resistant	___ Resentful	___ Reticent
24	___ Forgetful	___ Frank	___ Fussy	___ Fearful
25	___ Interrupts	___ Impatient	___ Insecure	___ Indecisive
26	___ Unpredictable	___ Unaffectionate	___ Unpopular	___ Uninvolved
27	___ Haphazard	___ Headstrong	___ Hard to please	___ Hesitant
28	___ Permissive	___ Proud	___ Pessimistic	___ Plain
29	___ Angered easily	___ Argumentative	___ Alienated	___ Aimless
30	___ Naive	___ Nervy	___ Negative attitude	___ Nonchalant
31	___ Wants credit	___ Workaholic	___ Withdrawn	___ Worrier
32	___ Talkative	___ Tactless	___ Too sensitive	___ Timid
33	___ Disorganized	___ Domineering	___ Depressed	___ Doubtful
34	___ Inconsistent	___ Intolerant	___ Introvert	___ Indifferent
35	___ Messy	___ Manipulative	___ Moody	___ Mumbles
36	___ Show-off	___ Stubborn	___ Skeptical	___ Slow
37	___ Loud	___ Lord over others	___ Loner	___ Lazy
38	___ Scatterbrained	___ Short-tempered	___ Suspicious	___ Sluggish
39	___ Restless	___ Rash	___ Revengeful	___ Reluctant
40	___ Changeable	___ Crafty	___ Critical	___ Compromising

Total—Weaknesses

___   ___   ___   ___

Combined Totals

___   ___   ___   ___

The Personality Profile, created by Fred Littauer, is from *After Every Wedding Comes a Marriage* by Florence Littauer. Copyright © 1981, Harvest House Publishers. Used by permission. Not to be duplicated. Additional copies may be ordered by calling 1-800-433-6633.

Appendix B

Personality Test Word Definitions

1

Adventurous. Takes on new and daring enterprises with a determination to master them.

Adaptable. Easily fits and is comfortable in any situation.

Animated. Full of life, lively use of hand, arm, and facial gestures.

Analytical. Likes to examine the parts for their logical and proper relationships.

2

Persistent. Sees one project through to its completion before starting another.

Playful. Full of fun and good humor.

Persuasive. Convinces through logic and fact rather than charm or power.

Peaceful. Seems undisturbed and tranquil and retreats from any form of strife.

3

Submissive. Easily accepts any other's point of view or desire with little need to assert their own opinion.

Self-sacrificing. Willingly gives up their own personal being for the sake of, or to meet the needs of others.

Sociable. Sees being with others as an opportunity to be cute and entertaining rather than as a challenge or business opportunity.

Strong-willed. Determined to have one's own way.

4

Considerate. Having regard for the needs and feelings of others.

Controlled. Has emotional feelings but rarely displays them.

Competitive. Turns every situation, happening, or game into a contest and always plays to win!

Convincing. Can win you over to anything through the sheer charm of their personality.

5

Refreshing. Renews and stimulates or makes others feel good.

Respectful. Treats others with deference, honor, and esteem.

Reserved. Self-restrained in expression of emotion or enthusiasm.

Resourceful. Able to act quickly and effectively in virtually all situations.

6

Satisfied. Easily accepts any circumstance or situation.

Sensitive. Intensively cares about others and about what happens.

Self-reliant. Can fully rely on their own capabilities, judgment, and resources.

Spirited. Full of life and excitement.

7

Planner. Prefers to work out a detailed arrangement beforehand, for the accomplishment of project or goal, and prefers involvement with the planning stages and the finished product rather than the carrying out of the task.

Patient. Unmoved by delay, remains calm and tolerant.

Positive. Knows it will turn out right if they are in charge.

Promoter. Urges or compels others to go along, join, or invest through the charm of their own personality.

8

Sure. Confident, rarely hesitates or wavers.

Spontaneous. Prefers all of life to be impulsive, unpremeditated activity, not restricted by plans.

Scheduled. Makes, and lives, according to a daily plan, dislikes their plan to be interrupted.

Shy. Quiet, doesn't easily instigate a conversation.

9

Orderly. Having a methodical, systematic arrangement of things.

Obliging. Accommodating, quick to do it another's way.

Outspoken. Speaks frankly and without reserve.

Optimistic. Sunny disposition who convinces self and others that everything will turn out all right.

10

Friendly. Responds rather than initiates, seldom starts a conversation.

Faithful. Consistently reliable, steadfast, loyal, and devoted sometimes beyond reason.

Funny. Sparkling sense of humor that can make virtually any story into a hilarious event.

Forceful. A commanding personality against whom others would hesitate to take a stand.

11

Daring. Willing to take risks; fearless, bold.

Delightful. Upbeat and fun to be with.

Diplomatic. Deals with people tactfully, sensitively, and patiently.

Detailed. Does everything in proper order with a clear memory of all the things that happen.

12

Cheerful. Consistently in good spirits and promoting happiness in others.

Consistent. Stays emotionally on an even keel, responding as one might expect.

Cultured. Interests involve both intellectual and artistic pursuits, such as theater, symphony, ballet.

Confident. Self-assured and certain of own ability and success.

13

Idealistic. Visualizes things in their perfect form, and has a need to measure up to that standard.

Independent. Self-sufficient, self-supporting, self-confident, and seems to have little need of help.

Inoffensive. Never says or causes anything unpleasant or objectionable.

Inspiring. Encourages others to work, join, or be involved, and makes the whole thing fun.

14

Demonstrative. Openly expresses emotion, especially affection, and doesn't hesitate to touch others while speaking to them.

Decisive. Quick, conclusive, judgment-making ability.

Dry humor. Exhibits "dry wit," usually one-liners that can be sarcastic in nature.

Deep. Intense and often introspective with a distaste for surface conversation and pursuits.

15

Mediator. Consistently finds him- or herself in the role of reconciling differences in order to avoid conflict.

Musical. Participates in or has a deep appreciation for music, is committed to music as an art form, rather than the fun of performance.

Mover. Driven by a need to be productive, is a leader whom others follow, finds it difficult to sit still.

Mixes easily. Loves a party and can't wait to meet everyone in the room, never meets a stranger.

16

Thoughtful. Considerate, remembers special occasions and is quick to make a kind gesture.

Tenacious. Holds on firmly, stubbornly, and won't let go until the goal is accomplished.

Talker. Constantly talking, generally telling funny stories and entertaining everyone around, feeling the need to fill the silence in order to make others comfortable.

Tolerant. Easily accepts the thoughts and ways of others without the need to disagree with or change them.

17

Listener. Always seems willing to hear what you have to say.

Loyal. Faithful to a person, ideal, or job, sometimes beyond reason.

Leader. A natural born director who is driven to be in charge, and often finds it difficult to believe that anyone else can do the job as well.

Lively. Full of life, vigorous, energetic.

18

Contented. Easily satisfied with what they have rarely envious.

Chief. Commands leadership and expects people to follow.

Chartmaker. Organizes life, tasks, and problem solving by making lists, forms, or graphs.

Cute. Precious, adorable, center of attention.

19

Perfectionist. Places high standards on self, and often on others, desiring that everything be in proper order at all times.

Pleasant. Easygoing, easy to be around, easy to talk with.

Productive. Must constantly be working or achieving, often finds it very difficult to rest.

Popular. Life of the party and therefore much desired as a party guest.

20

Bouncy. A bubbly, lively personality, full of energy.

Bold. Fearless, daring, forward, unafraid of risk.

Behaved. Consistently desires to conduct self within the realm of what he feels is proper.

Balanced. Stable, middle of the road personality, not subject to sharp highs or lows.

WEAKNESSES

21

Blank. Shows little facial expression or emotion.

Bashful. Shrinks from getting attention, resulting from self-consciousness.

Brassy. Showy, flashy, comes on strong, too loud.

Bossy. Commanding, domineering, sometimes overbearing in adult relationships.

22

Undisciplined. Lack of order permeates most every area of their life.

Unsympathetic. Finds it difficult to relate to the problems or hurts of others.

Unenthusiastic. Tends to not get excited, often feeling it won't work anyway.

Unforgiving. Has difficulty forgiving or forgetting a hurt or injustice done to them, apt to hold onto a grudge.

23

Reticent. Unwilling or struggles against getting involved, especially when complex.

Resentful. Often holds ill feelings as a result of real or imagined offenses.

Resistant. Strives, works against, or hesitates to accept any other way but their own.

Repetitious. Retells stories and incidents to entertain you without realizing they have already told the story several times before, is constantly needing something to say.

24

Fussy. Insistent over petty matters or details, calling for a great attention to trivial details.

Fearful. Often experiences feelings of deep concern, apprehension, or anxiety.

Forgetful. Lack of memory which is usually tied to a lack of discipline and not bothering to mentally record things that aren't fun.

Frank. Straightforward, outspoken, doesn't mind telling you exactly what they think.

25

Impatient. Finds it difficult to endure irritation or wait for others.

Insecure. Apprehensive or lacks confidence.

Indecisive. Finds it difficult to make any decision at all. (Not the personality that labors long over each decision in order to make the perfect one.)

Interrupts. More of a talker than a listener, who starts speaking without even realizing someone else is already speaking.

26

Unpopular. Intensity and demand for perfection can push others away.

Uninvolved. Has no desire to listen or become interested in clubs, groups, activities, or other people's lives.

Unpredictable. May be ecstatic one moment and down the next, or willing to help but then disappears, or promises to come but forgets to show up.

Unaffectionate. Finds it difficult to verbally or physically demonstrate tenderness openly.

27

Headstrong. Insists on having his own way.

Haphazard. Has no consistent way of doing things.

Hard to please. Standards are set so high that it is difficult to ever satisfy them.

Hesitant. Slow to get moving and hard to get involved.

28

Plain. A middle-of-the-road personality without highs or lows and showing little, if any, emotion.

Pessimistic. While hoping for the best, generally sees the down side of a situation first.

Proud. Has great self-esteem and sees self as always right and the best person for the job.

Permissive. Allows others (including children) to do as they please in order to keep from being disliked.

29

Angered easily. Has a childlike flash-in-the-pan temper that expresses itself in tantrum style and is over and forgotten almost instantly.

Aimless. Not a goal-setter with little desire to be one.

Argumentative. Incites arguments generally because they are right no matter what the situation may be.

Alienated. Easily feels estranged from others, often because of insecurity or fear that others don't really enjoy their company.

30

Naive. Simple and child-like perspective, lacking sophistication or comprehension of what the deeper levels of life are really about.

Negative attitude. Attitude is seldom positive and is often able to see only the down or dark side of each situation.

Nervy. Full of confidence, fortitude, and sheer guts, often in a negative sense.

Nonchalant. Easygoing, unconcerned, indifferent.

31

Worrier. Consistently feels uncertain, troubled, or anxious.

Withdrawn. Pulls back and needs a great deal of alone or isolation time.

Workaholic. An aggressive goal-setter who must be constantly productive and feels very guilty when resting, is not driven by a need for perfection or completion but by a need for accomplishment and reward.

Wants credit. Thrives on the credit or approval of others. As an entertainer this person feeds on the applause, laughter, and/or acceptance of an audience.

32

Too sensitive. Overly introspective and easily offended when misunderstood.

Tactless. Sometimes expresses themself in a somewhat offensive and inconsiderate way.

Timid. Shrinks from difficult situations.

Talkative. An entertaining, compulsive talker who finds it difficult to listen.

33

Doubtful. Characterized by uncertainty and lack of confidence that it will ever work out.

Disorganized. Lack of ability to ever get life in order.

Domineering. Compulsively takes control of situations and/or people, usually telling others what to do.

Depressed. Feels down much of the time.

34

Inconsistent. Erratic, contradictory, with actions and emotions not based on logic.

Introvert. Thoughts and interest are directed inward, lives within themselves.

Intolerant. Appears unable to withstand or accept another's attitudes, point of view, or way of doing things.

Indifferent. Most things don't matter one way or the other.

35

Messy. Living in a state of disorder, unable to find things.

Moody. Doesn't get very high emotionally, but easily slips into low lows, often when feeling unappreciated.

Mumbles. Will talk quietly under the breath when pushed, doesn't bother to speak clearly.

Manipulative. Influences or manages shrewdly or deviously for their own advantage, *will* get their way somehow.

36

Slow. Doesn't often act or think quickly, too much of a bother.

Stubborn. Determined to exert their own will, not easily persuaded, obstinate.

Show-off. Needs to be the center of attention, wants to be watched.

Skeptical. Disbelieving, questioning the motive behind the words.

37

Loner. Requires a lot of private time and tends to avoid other people.

Lord over. Doesn't hesitate to let you know that they are right or is in control.

Lazy. Evaluates work or activity in terms of how much energy it will take.

Loud. Laugh or voice can be heard above others in the room.

38

Sluggish. Slow to get started, needs push to be motivated.

Suspicious. Tends to suspect or distrust others or ideas.

Short-tempered. Has a demanding impatience-based anger and a short fuse. Anger is expressed when others are not moving fast enough or have not completed what they have been asked to do.

Scatterbrained. Lacks the power of concentration or attention, flighty.

39

Revengeful. Knowingly or otherwise holds a grudge and punishes the offender, often by subtly withholding friendship or affection.

Restless. Likes constant new activity because it isn't fun to do the same things all the time.

Reluctant. Unwilling or struggles against getting involved.

Rash. May act hastily, without thinking things through, generally because of impatience.

40

Compromising. Will often relax their position, even when right, in order to avoid conflict.

Critical. Constantly evaluating and making judgments, frequently thinking or expressing negative reactions.

Crafty. Shrewd, one who can always find a way to get to the desired end.

Changeable. A child-like, short attention span that needs a lot of change and variety to keep from getting bored.

Appendix C

An Overview of the Personalities

Popular Sanguines
"Let's do it the fun way"

Desire:	have fun
Emotional needs:	attention, affection, approval, acceptance
Key strengths:	ability to talk about anything at any time at any place, bubbling personality, optimism, sense of humor, storytelling ability, enjoyment of people
Key weaknesses:	disorganized, can't remember details or names, exaggerates, not serious about anything, trusts others to do the work, too gullible and naive
Get depressed when:	life is no fun and no one seems to love them
Are afraid of:	being unpopular or bored, having to live by the clock, having to keep a record of money spent
Like people who:	listen and laugh, praise and approve
Dislike people who:	criticize, don't respond to their humor, don't think they are cute
Are valuable in work for:	colorful creativity, optimism, light touch, cheering up others, entertaining
Could improve if they:	got organized, didn't talk so much, learned to tell time
As leaders they:	excite, persuade, and inspire others; exude charm and entertain; are forgetful and poor on follow-through

Tend to marry:	Perfect Melancholies who are sensitive and serious, but whom they quickly tire of having to cheer up and by whom they soon tire of being made to feel inadequate or stupid
Reaction to stress:	leave the scene, go shopping, find a fun group, create excuses, blame others
Recognized by their:	constant talking, loud volume, bright eyes

Powerful Cholerics
"Let's do it my way"

Desire:	have control
Emotional needs:	sense of obedience, appreciation for accomplishments, credit for ability
Key strengths:	ability to take charge of anything instantly and to make quick, correct judgments
Key weaknesses:	too bossy, domineering, autocratic, insensitive, impatient, unwilling to delegate or give credit to others
Get depressed when:	life is out of control and people won't do things their way
Are afraid of:	losing control of anything (e.g., losing a job, not being promoted, becoming seriously ill, having a rebellious child or unsupportive mate)
Like people who:	are supportive and submissive, see things their way, cooperate quickly, let them take credit
Dislike people who:	are lazy and not interested in working constantly, buck their authority, become independent, aren't loyal
Are valuable in work because they:	can accomplish more than anyone else in a shorter time, are usually right
Could improve if they:	allowed others to make decisions, delegated authority, became more patient, didn't expect everyone to produce as they do
As leaders they have:	a natural feel for being in charge, a quick sense of what will work, a sincere belief in their ability to achieve, a potential to overwhelm less aggressive people
Tend to marry:	Peaceful Phlegmatics who will quietly obey and not buck their authority, but who never accomplish enough or get excited over their projects
Reaction to stress:	tighten control, work harder, exercise more, get rid of the offender
Recognized by their:	fast-moving approach, quick grab for control, self-confidence, restless and overpowering attitude

Perfect Melancholies
"Let's do it the right way"

Desire:	have it right
Emotional needs:	sense of stability, space, silence, sensitivity, support
Key strengths:	ability to organize and set long-range goals, have high standards and ideals, analyze deeply
Key weaknesses:	easily depressed, too much time on preparation, too focused on details, remembers negatives, suspicious of others
Get depressed when:	life is out of order, standards aren't met, and no one seems to care
Are afraid of:	no one understanding how they really feel, making a mistake, having to compromise standards
Like people who:	are serious, intellectual, deep, and will carry on a sensible conversation
Dislike people who:	are lightweights, forgetful, late, disorganized, superficial, prevaricating, and unpredictable
Are valuable in work for:	sense of detail, love of analysis, follow-through, high standards of performance, compassion for the hurting
Could improve if they:	didn't take life quite so seriously, didn't insist others be perfectionists
As leaders they:	organize well, are sensitive to people's feelings, have deep creativity, want quality performance
Tend to marry:	Popular Sanguines for their outgoing personality and social skills, but whom they soon attempt to quiet and get on a schedule
Reaction to stress:	withdraw, get lost in a book, become depressed, give up, recount the problems
Recognized by their:	serious and sensitive nature, well-mannered approach, self-deprecating comments, meticulous and well-groomed looks

Peaceful Phlegmatic
"Let's do it the easy way"

Desire:	avoid conflict, keep peace
Emotional needs:	sense of respect, feeling of worth, understanding, emotional support
Key strengths:	balance, even disposition, dry sense of humor, pleasing personality

Key weaknesses:	lack of decisiveness, enthusiasm, and energy; a hidden will of iron
Get depressed when:	life is full of conflict, they have to face a personal confrontation, no one wants to help, the buck stops with them
Are afraid of:	having to deal with a major personal problem, being left holding the bag, making major changes
Like people who:	will make decisions for them, will recognize their strengths, will not ignore them, will give them respect
Dislike people who:	are too pushy, too loud, and expect too much of them
Are valuable in work because they:	mediate between contentious people, objectively solve problems
Could improve if they:	set goals and became self-motivated, were willing to do more and move faster than expected, could face their own problems as well as they handle those of others
As leaders they:	keep calm, cool, and collected; don't make impulsive decisions; are well-liked and inoffensive; won't cause trouble; don't often come up with brilliant new ideas
Tend to marry:	Powerful Cholerics who are strong and decisive, but by whom they soon tire of being pushed around and looked down upon
Reaction to stress:	hide from it, watch TV, eat, tune out life
Recognized by their:	calm approach, relaxed posture (sitting or leaning when possible)

Appendix D

Recommended Resources

Personality Plus

With about 1,000,000 copies in print in twelve languages, this is Florence Littauer's most popular book. Her first book on the Personalities, *Personality Plus* will give you an excellent understanding of the four basic Personalities. Filled with Florence's humorous examples, this book thoroughly covers the strengths and weaknesses of each Personality and will help you gain new understanding of what makes people the way they are. The Personality Profile test included in the book will help you identify your own personality type. This book is an excellent resource for group study.

Personality Plus Tape Set

The famous four-tape series by Florence is still available in this convenient set. These hilarious tapes are packaged with the book and two personality profiles. A two-tape condensed version is also available.

Personality Plus Video Series

For years Florence Littauer's fans have been waiting for this video series. The three-tape set features five hours of live teaching by Florence, Fred, and Marita Littauer divided into six lessons that apply the Personalities to nearly every aspect of life. Sessions include *Understanding Yourself, Meeting Your Mate's Emotional Needs, Raising Balanced Children, Having a Positive Effect on Your Grandchildren,* and *Getting Along with Difficult People.*

Your Personality Tree

The sequel to *Personality Plus,* this best-selling book begins by reviewing the basics but quickly moves on to deeper areas of the Personalities such as understanding basic desires and emotional needs, identifying things that depress and tempt each Personality, and uncovering the concept of personality masking. Based on Florence's study of her own family tree, this book will help you chart your own Personality Tree and uncover the roots of your personality. Helpful features include word definitions for the Personality Profile test and a chart comparing other personality programs with Florence's approach.

Personality Puzzle: Piecing Together the Personalities in Your Workplace

Whether you work in an office, a school, a hospital, or even at home, you probably work and come into contact with people who don't see things your way. In *Personality Puzzle* Florence and Marita Littauer combine their expertise and years of teaching on the Personalities to give you a practical guide for understanding the people around you in the workplace. "The Visible Piece of the Puzzle" will teach you how to identify the personality style of others simply by observation; "The Various Pieces" will help you understand each personality type's natural gifts and abilities; and "The Valuable Pieces" will show you how to meet the emotional needs of those with whom you work. Whether you are an employer, employee, client, or coworker, this book will help you piece together the personalities in your workplace!

Personality Puzzle (audio)

The entertaining and educational tape features Marita Littauer teaching you to understand the people with whom you live and work. You'll not only learn to identify each personality type using the visual pieces of the puzzle, but you'll also gain insight into their various strengths and weaknesses and be able to relate to them effectively.

Freeing Your Mind from Memories That Bind

The next step in personality study, *Freeing Your Mind* offers in-depth help and healing for the personality disorders you uncovered in *Personality Tree.* If you struggle with painful personality traits due to emotional, physical, or sexual abuse, let Fred and Florence Littauer help you identify the source of your pain and lead your through healing in Christ.

Personality Profiles

This popular personality test included in each book is also available by itself. The *Updated Profile* includes the test, scoring sheet, strengths and weaknesses, word definitions, and instructions for evaluation. The *Marketplace Profile* contains the same pieces, but the evaluation instructions specifically target interpretation for business and team building.

Personality Testing Software

Attractively packaged, this 3.5 inch disk contains everything you need to instantly identify your personality type on screen or in printed form and is great for church, business, or home use. Windows 3.1 and Windows 95 compatible.

To order any of these resources or to receive a free book and tape catalog, please call 800/433-6633.

• Are you fascinated by the new understanding the Personalities have given you?
• Have you been wanting to teach this life-changing material to others?
• Or, are you already teaching but feel you'd like additional training?

Now you have the opportunity to become a Certified Trainer of the popular Personality concepts found in *Getting Along with Almost Anybody, Personality Plus, Personality Tree,* and *Personality Puzzle.* Two Personality Training Workshops are held each year, one in the East and one in the West.

Please call 800/433-6633 to request a complete brochure or visit the CLASS web site at **www.classervices.com** for the current schedule.